THE COO MBA

Your Blueprint to Operational Excellence

by

Robert N. Jacobs

All rights reserved
Copyright © Robert N. Jacobs, 2025
The right of Robert N. Jacobs to be identified as the author of this
work has been asserted in accordance with Section 78
of the Copyright, Designs and Patents Act 1988
The book cover is copyright to Robert N. Jacobs
This book is published by
Growth Seeker Publishing Ltd.

This book is sold subject to the conditions that it shall not, by way of trade or otherwise, be lent, resold, hired out or otherwise circulated without the author's or publisher's prior consent in any form of binding or cover other than that in which it is published and without a similar condition including this condition being imposed on the subsequent purchaser.
This book is a work of fiction. Any resemblance to
people or events, past or present, is purely coincidental.
ISBN: 9798319405432

Foreword

As a COO with 30 years of experience in operations, primarily in the manufacturing sector, I've witnessed firsthand the challenges and rewards of striving for operational excellence. Organisations rise and thrive when they fine-tune their operations to run like well-oiled machines. But I've also seen how inefficiencies, miscommunication, and lack of strategy can erode profits, lower morale, and create bottlenecks that slow progress.

This book, The COO's MBA: The COO's Blueprint to Operational Excellence, is a vital resource for COOs, whether you're a seasoned veteran or a newly appointed leader. It's designed to help you sharpen your operational strategy and deliver top-tier performance, acknowledging the ever-evolving nature of the COO's role and the increasing complexity of operations management. This book provides a structured, actionable guide to navigate the multifaceted responsibilities unique to the COO.

The Purpose of This Blueprint

In recent decades, the manufacturing landscape has significantly transformed from simple process optimisation to cutting-edge technologies like automation, AI, and predictive analytics. This book embraces these shifts and anticipates future trends for which every COO should be prepared, ensuring its relevance in the ever-evolving manufacturing sector.

The COO's MBA is a comprehensive guide to achieving operational excellence, packed with actionable insights, real-world case studies, and adaptable frameworks. It's not just theoretical knowledge; it's a practical resource that can be tailored to any manufacturing operation, making it a must-read for anyone looking to enhance their organisation's operations.

Who Is This Blueprint For?

This book is written for current and aspiring COOs and leaders responsible for delivering operational results. It's for those who understand that the COO role is no longer just about managing day-to-day operations but strategically leading the company towards its long-term goals. Whether you're taking your first steps into this role or have been a COO for years, the insights and tools provided here will help you sharpen your leadership skills and refine your operational strategies.

This book is also for those who want to foster a culture of excellence within their organisations. You'll learn how to implement systems and processes that lead to continuous improvement and create an environment where every employee is engaged in improving the company. The lessons apply to manufacturing and any industry where operational excellence is the backbone of success.

What You Will Get From This Blueprint

One of the greatest advantages of this book is that it cuts through the need for expensive MBAs and lengthy academic courses. Many COOs, including myself, have spent years studying in formal settings, investing time and money. While these experiences are valuable, they are not the only way to achieve excellence. The COO's MBA provides a fast track to operational mastery, equipping you with the essential tools, strategies, and insights to elevate your operations function and company to unparalleled excellence.

This blueprint will give you everything you need to excel as a COO without the burden of spending years in a traditional MBA programme. The practical, real-world knowledge contained in these pages ensures that you can immediately apply what you learn, saving you time and enabling you to drive tangible improvements in your organisation.

I've distilled decades of experience into these pages, sharing lessons learned and strategies proven to deliver results. For the modern COO, success requires more than just operational oversight; it demands strategic vision, technological savvy, and the ability to lead through change. With The COO's MBA, you'll be well-equipped to advance your organisation and career.

Robert Jacobs
Curious By Design

Table of Contents

Chapter 1
Laying The Foundation For Operational Excellence 1

   1.1 - Understanding Operational Excellence 1

   1.2 - The Coo's Strategic Vision 3

   1.3 - Building a Strong Leadership Foundation 4

   1.4 - Developing an Operational Strategy 6

   1.5 - Understanding the Manufacturing Landscape 9

   1.6 - Creating a Culture of Excellence 11

   1.7 - Establishing Clear KPIs 13

   1.8 - Effective Communication Strategies 16

   1.9 - Risk Management 18

   1.10 - Setting Up for Success 21

Chapter 2
Mastering Operational Efficiency 24

   2.1 - The Efficiency Imperative 24

   2.2 - Lean Manufacturing Principles 26

   2.3 - Process Optimisation 29

   2.4 - Automation and Technology 31

   2.5 - Supply Chain Management 34

   2.6 - Inventory Management 36

   2.7 - Quality Management Systems 39

   2.8 - Performance Metrics 42

   2.9 - Case Study: Efficiency Success Stories 45

   2.10 - Overcoming Efficiency Challenges 48

Chapter 3
Financial Acumen for COOs 51

3.1 - Understanding Key Financial Metrics 51

3.2 - Budgeting and Forecasting 54

3.3 - Cost Control Strategies 57

3.4 - Investment Decisions 60

3.5 - Financial Reporting 62

3.6 - Cost-Benefit Analysis 66

3.7 - Profitability Improvement 68

3.8 - Cash Flow Management 72

3.9 - Financial Risk Management 75

3.10 - Case Study: Financial Turnarounds and Success Stories 78

Chapter 4
Leading and Developing High-Performance Teams 82

4.1 - Building High-Performance Teams 82

4.2 - Leadership Styles 85

4.3 - Talent Acquisition and Retention 88

4.4 - Training and Development 91

4.5 - Performance Management 93

4.6 - Motivating Your Team 96

4.7 - Conflict Resolution 99

4.8 - Creating a Collaborative Culture 102

4.9 - Succession Planning 105

4.10 - Case Study: Success Stories of Outstanding Leadership 108

Chapter 5
Enhancing Customer Focus 113

5.1 - Understanding Customer Needs 113

5.2 - Customer Experience Management 115

    5.3 - Feedback Mechanisms 118

    5.4 - Building Strong Customer Relationships 121

    5.5 - Quality Assurance 123

    5.6 - Customer Service Excellence 126

    5.7 - Managing Customer Expectations 129

    5.8 - Case Study: Customer-Centric Success Stories 133

    5.9 - Handling Customer Complaints 135

    5.10 - Creating a Customer-Centric Culture 138

Chapter 6
Driving Innovation and Embracing Change 142

    6.1 - The Role of Innovation in Manufacturing 142

    6.2 - Fostering a Culture of Innovation 145

    6.3 - Change Management 147

    6.4 - Implementing New Technologies 150

    6.5 - Innovation Strategies 153

    6.6 - Benchmarking and Best Practices 157

    6.7 - Managing Disruptions 160

    6.8 - Case Study: Successful Innovations in Manufacturing 163

    6.9 - Balancing Risk and Innovation 165

    6.10 - Future Trends 169

Chapter 7
Building a Resilient Organisation 173

    7.1 - Understanding Organisational Resilience 173

    7.2 - Risk Assessment and Management 175

    7.3 - Crisis Management Planning 178

    7.4 - Business Continuity Planning 181

    7.5 - Adaptability and Flexibility 183

7.6 - Employee Resilience 186

7.7 - Maintaining Operational Stability 189

7.8 - Case Study: Resilient Organisations Navigating Crises
.... 193

7.9 - Recovery and Learning 195

7.10 - Building a Resilient Culture 198

Chapter 8
Strategic Partnerships and Collaboration 202

8.1 - The Importance of Strategic Partnerships 202

8.2 - Identifying Key Partners 204

8.3 - Building Strong Partnerships 207

8.4 - Collaborative Strategies 210

8.5 - Negotiation Skills 213

8.6 - Managing Partnerships 217

8.7 - Case Study: Successful Partnerships 219

8.8 - Leveraging Partnerships for Growth 223

8.9 - Addressing Partnership Challenges 225

8.10 - The Future of Strategic Partnerships 229

Chapter 9
Technology and Digital Transformation 233

9.1 - The Role of Technology in Manufacturing 233

9.2 - Digital Transformation Strategies 236

9.3 - Data Analytics and Insights 240

9.4 - Cybersecurity 243

9.5 - smart manufacturing 246

9.6 - IoT and Connectivity 249

9.7 - Case Study: Successful Digital Transformations 253

9.8 - Managing Technological Change 255
9.9 - Balancing Technology and Human Factors 259
9.10 - Future Technological Trends 261

Chapter 10

Measuring and Sustaining Excellence **266**

10.1 - Defining Operational Excellence 266
10.2 - Developing a Measurement Framework 268
10.3 - Continuous Improvement 271
10.4 - Benchmarking and Performance Reviews 274
10.5 - Recognising and Rewarding Success 276
10.6 - Sustainability and Corporate Responsibility 280
10.7 - Case Study: Sustained Operational Success 283
10.8 - Overcoming Plateaus 287
10.9 - Evolving with the Industry 289
10.10 - Creating a Legacy of Excellence 292

Conclusion **296**

"The true art of operations lies in perfecting the unseen and solving the unnoticed."
Robert N. Jacobs

Chapter 1

Laying The Foundation For Operational Excellence

> "Operations never sleep, and neither should your pursuit of excellence."
>
> **Robert N. Jacobs**

Operational excellence is the cornerstone of success in manufacturing, serving as the engine that drives efficiency, quality, and long-term competitiveness. This chapter explores the essential principles and frameworks that lay the groundwork for achieving operational excellence. From understanding its core definitions to aligning strategic goals with operational execution, this chapter provides a comprehensive guide to building a strong leadership foundation, fostering a culture of continuous improvement, and developing an operational strategy that adapts to the ever-evolving manufacturing landscape. The insights shared here form the basis for COOs to begin their journey toward sustainable and impactful operational success.

1.1 - Understanding Operational Excellence

Operational excellence is often mistaken for a vague aspiration. Still, a concrete and systematic approach drives a company to achieve and sustain superior performance across all operations. Operational excellence is about maximising value for the business and its customers through streamlined processes, continuous improvement, and a focus on efficiency and quality. The seamless alignment of people, processes, and technology creates a robust and resilient organisation capable of outperforming competitors.

One of the core principles of operational excellence is customer-centricity. The success of any operational strategy begins and ends with the customer. COOs must constantly ask themselves how their operations impact customer satisfaction. Are products being delivered on time and within budget? Is the quality up to standard? When every operation decision is viewed through the lens of customer value, inefficiencies quickly become apparent, and improvements can be prioritised. Another fundamental principle is continuous improvement. Operational excellence is not a destination; it's an ongoing journey. The Japanese philosophy of Kaizen, meaning "change for the better," has long been a hallmark of this principle. This concept encourages every employee, from the factory floor to top management, to look for incremental improvements in processes, systems, and workflows. A company fostering a continuous improvement culture is better equipped to respond to market changes, technological advances, and customer demands.

Lean manufacturing and Six Sigma are two methodologies often associated with operational excellence. While Lean focuses on eliminating waste, Six Sigma reduces process variability to ensure high-quality output. Combining these two approaches creates a powerful framework for enhancing operational efficiency and effectiveness. But it's essential to remember that these are not silver bullets; they are tools tailored to each organisation's unique needs and challenges.

In my experience, operational excellence has been a guiding force in turnaround situations and high-growth phases. One instance involved a company experiencing severe bottlenecks in its production line, leading to missed deadlines and poor customer feedback. By implementing Lean practices, we identified and eliminated unnecessary steps in the production process, reducing cycle time by 40%. This improved customer satisfaction and created additional capacity for new orders, driving revenue growth.

Finally, empowering employees is a vital aspect of operational excellence. Employees are often the first to notice inefficiencies, yet these opportunities go unnoticed without a culture that encourages them to voice their insights and take ownership of improvements. A COO must foster an environment where employees feel empowered to contribute to operational improvements through formal continuous improvement programmes or informal problem-solving initiatives.

In summary, operational excellence is the systematic pursuit of superior performance, achieved through customer-centricity, continuous improvement, and strategic use of Lean and Six Sigma methodologies. It requires a commitment to empowering people at all levels to seek and implement improvements. For any aspiring COO, understanding these core principles is the first step toward building an operational strategy that drives sustainable growth and success.

1.2 - The Coo's Strategic Vision

The COO's strategic vision is the roadmap that bridges the gap between high-level business objectives and the day-to-day operations that drive them. To be effective, a COO must align operational goals with the company's broader strategy, ensuring that every action taken within the operational function contributes to the company's long-term vision and mission. This alignment is critical for achieving organisational success and maintaining a cohesive, motivated team that understands its purpose.

The starting point for any COO is a deep understanding of the company's overall strategy. This requires close collaboration with the CEO and other key executives to clarify what the business aims to achieve in the short and long term. Whether the goal is to expand market share, enter new markets, or improve profitability, the COO's task is to translate these strategic objectives into operational plans that are actionable, measurable, and attainable.

One of the key challenges COOs face is balancing efficiency with flexibility. While operational excellence requires streamlined, efficient processes, the business environment constantly changes, particularly manufacturing. Supply chain disruptions, technological advances, and evolving customer demands require COOs to build flexibility into their operational strategies. This might mean investing in agile manufacturing systems or creating contingency plans, allowing quick pivots in response to market shifts.

From my own experience, I recall a time when I led the operational overhaul of a company facing declining profitability due to rising raw material costs. The company's strategic goal was maintaining market share while navigating these cost increases. My operational vision involved finding efficiencies across the supply chain, renegotiating supplier contracts, and implementing automation where possible. By aligning our operational goals with the strategic imperative to control costs without sacrificing quality, we preserved profitability and enhanced our competitive positioning in the market.

A critical component of the COO's strategic vision is ensuring that operational metrics align with business goals. Too often, companies fall into the trap of focusing on metrics that, while important, may not directly contribute to strategic objectives. For example, a factory may focus on increasing production speed, but if that increase comes at the expense of product quality or customer satisfaction, it undermines its broader goals. Therefore, the COO must ensure that the KPIs used to measure operational performance are directly linked to the company's strategic priorities.

Communication is another key aspect of aligning operational goals with company strategy. The COO must clearly articulate the operational strategy to all levels of the organisation, ensuring that employees understand how their work contributes to the company's larger vision. This requires clear, consistent messaging and ongoing feedback loops where employees can provide insights from the ground up.

The COO's strategic vision directly links the company's overarching goals and the operational processes that support them. It requires a balance between efficiency and flexibility, a focus on the right metrics, and clear communication to ensure that everyone in the organisation is moving in the same direction. By aligning operational goals with the company's strategy, COOs ensure that their operations run smoothly and contribute to the business's long-term success.

1.3 - Building a Strong Leadership Foundation

Leadership in the COO role is about more than just managing operations, inspiring a team, fostering a culture of excellence, and driving organisational change. The modern COO must possess a unique blend of leadership qualities that enable them to navigate complex challenges, make critical decisions, and lead their teams toward sustained success. Strong leadership in this role is not just a nice-to-have; it is a fundamental prerequisite for achieving operational excellence.

One of the most critical leadership qualities for a COO is emotional intelligence. While technical skills and operational knowledge are essential, a COO must also be able to connect with people on an emotional level. This means understanding employees' motivations, concerns, and aspirations at all levels of the organisation. A COO with high emotional intelligence can build trust, inspire loyalty, and foster an environment where employees feel valued and engaged.

Another essential quality is strategic thinking. The COO must always focus on the bigger picture, ensuring daily operational decisions align with the company's long-term strategy. This requires anticipating future challenges, identifying emerging trends, and making decisions that position the company for long-term success. A strategic thinker can balance the immediate needs of the business with the foresight required to navigate the complexities of a rapidly changing industry.

Decisiveness is another vital leadership trait for a COO. In the high-pressure manufacturing environment, where production schedules are tight and downtime can be costly, COOs are often called upon to make quick, high-stakes decisions. Whether investing in new technology, making staffing changes, or responding to supply chain disruptions, a COO must be confident in making the right decision quickly and effectively.

I recall an instance early in my career when a major piece of production equipment failed unexpectedly, threatening to halt the entire operation for days. Faced with this crisis, I quickly waited for the original supplier to provide replacement parts (which would have taken a week) or invested in a more expensive local supplier who could get us back online within 48 hours. While the latter option was more costly in the short term, it was the right decision for the business as it minimised production losses and allowed us to meet critical delivery deadlines.

A COO must also exhibit resilience. Leading an operational function is fraught with challenges, from production delays to supply chain disruptions, staff issues, and budget constraints. Resilience means staying calm under pressure, maintaining focus during crises, and returning quickly from setbacks. Resilient leaders can lead their teams through difficult times without losing sight of their goals or allowing the quality of operations to slip.

Finally, collaborative leadership is key to success in the COO role. The COO works at the intersection of multiple functions, from finance to human resources to product development. To succeed, the COO must be able to collaborate effectively with leaders across the organisation, breaking down silos and ensuring that all departments are working toward a common goal. Collaborative leadership also extends to building strong relationships with external stakeholders, suppliers, customers, and regulatory bodies.

In conclusion, a strong leadership foundation for a COO is built on emotional intelligence, strategic thinking, decisiveness, resilience, and collaboration. These qualities enable the COO to lead effectively and inspire and empower their teams to achieve operational excellence. For aspiring COOs, developing these leadership traits is essential to driving success in the ever-changing, complex world of manufacturing operations.

1.4 - Developing an Operational Strategy

Developing a robust operational strategy is one of the most critical tasks a COO must undertake. This strategy is the blueprint for how the operational function will contribute to the company's overall objectives, ensuring that production, supply chain, and quality control processes align with broader business goals. The operational strategy is not static; it is a living framework that evolves as the market, technology, and organisational needs change. Creating this strategy requires the application of proven frameworks and tools alongside a deep understanding of the company's unique operational challenges and opportunities.

Conducting a thorough operational audit is the first step in developing an operational strategy. This involves assessing the current state of the business, including the efficiency of production processes, supply chain logistics, cost structures, and workforce capabilities. A common tool used in this stage is a SWOT analysis (Strengths, Weaknesses, Opportunities, Threats), which helps the COO identify internal and external factors that could impact the operational function. This audit provides a baseline to build, ensuring that the strategy addresses the company's most pressing operational challenges.

Once the audit is complete, the next step is to define key operational objectives. These objectives should be specific, measurable, attainable, relevant, and time-bound (SMART), providing clear direction and accountability. For example, an objective could be to reduce production costs by 10% over the next year by implementing Lean manufacturing techniques. Another might be to improve on-time delivery performance by 15% by optimising supply chain processes.

COOs can leverage various strategic frameworks to bring these objectives to life. One widely used approach is the Hoshin Kanri methodology, which provides a structured process for aligning operational goals with the company's strategic vision. Hoshin Kanri involves setting long-term objectives and breaking them into smaller, actionable steps, ensuring that every department and team works towards the same overarching goals. This methodology also emphasises regular reviews and adjustments, making it a flexible and adaptive tool for operational strategy development.

Another valuable framework is the Balanced Scorecard. It helps COOs translate their strategic objectives into performance metrics across four key areas: financial performance, customer satisfaction, internal processes, and learning and growth. Using the Balanced Scorecard, COOs can ensure that their operational strategy is not overly focused on one area (e.g., cost reduction) at the expense of others (e.g., product quality or employee development). This holistic approach helps maintain balance and ensures sustainable growth.

In my career, I've successfully applied both Hoshin Kanri and the Balanced Scorecard. In one instance, I led a manufacturing company through a rapid expansion phase, which required doubling production capacity within two years. Using Hoshin Kanri, we developed a detailed roadmap that aligned our capacity-building efforts with the company's growth targets. This included investing in new machinery, optimising our supply chain, and hiring additional staff. The Balanced Scorecard ensured we didn't lose sight of other critical metrics, such as maintaining product quality and employee engagement, even as we scaled.

Technology also plays a crucial role in modern operational strategy. Integrating Industry 4.0 technologies, such as automation, data analytics, and the Internet of Things (IoT), can significantly enhance operational efficiency and decision-making. As part of the operational strategy, COOs should evaluate how these technologies can be implemented to optimise processes, reduce downtime, and enhance predictive maintenance capabilities. For example, data analytics can provide real-time insights into production bottlenecks, enabling quicker interventions and improved productivity.

Finally, successful operational strategies require a focus on agility. In today's rapidly changing business environment, operational strategies must be flexible enough to adapt to unforeseen challenges, such as supply chain disruptions, new regulatory requirements, or shifts in customer demand. Scenario planning is a valuable tool for building agility into your strategy. By anticipating potential risks and developing contingency plans, COOs can ensure that their operations are resilient and capable of responding to changing market conditions without losing momentum.

In conclusion, developing an operational strategy involves a comprehensive assessment of the current state of operations, setting clear and measurable objectives, and applying strategic frameworks such as Hoshin Kanri and the Balanced Scorecard. By incorporating advanced technologies and ensuring agility, COOs can create a dynamic, adaptable strategy that aligns operational processes with the company's long-term goals. For any COO looking to achieve operational excellence, mastering the art of strategic planning is essential to building a high-performing organisation.

1.5 - Understanding the Manufacturing Landscape

The manufacturing industry constantly evolves, shaped by new technologies, market forces, and shifting consumer expectations. For COOs, understanding the current landscape of the manufacturing sector is critical for developing strategies that are effective today and future-proof. The industry's trends and challenges are numerous, ranging from the rise of automation to increasing pressure for sustainable practices. Navigating these complexities requires COOs to stay informed, agile, and prepared to adapt their operations in response to emerging trends.

The industry's rapid digital transformation is one of the most significant manufacturing trends. Industry 4.0, encompassing automation, data analytics, artificial intelligence, and the Internet of Things (IoT), is reshaping how products are designed, manufactured, and delivered. Smart factories, where machines communicate with each other and optimise production in real-time, are becoming increasingly common. For COOs, this presents both an opportunity and a challenge. While digital technologies can vastly improve operational efficiency and product quality, implementing these systems requires significant investment, workforce training, and a shift in organisational culture.

Another major trend is the push toward sustainability. Manufacturing is one of the largest contributors to global carbon emissions, and as regulatory requirements and consumer expectations evolve, COOs are under increasing pressure to reduce their environmental impact. This includes everything from minimising waste and energy consumption in production processes to responsibly sourcing materials. Sustainable manufacturing practices help companies comply with regulations and enhance brand reputation and customer loyalty. However, transitioning to more sustainable practices can be costly and complex, requiring COOs to balance environmental goals with financial considerations.

Global supply chain disruptions have also emerged as a key challenge in recent years, exacerbated by events such as the COVID-19 pandemic and geopolitical tensions. These disruptions have highlighted the vulnerabilities in traditional supply chain models, leading many manufacturers to reconsider their reliance on global suppliers. COOs now focus on building more resilient supply chains, emphasising diversification, localisation, and strategic partnerships. This shift requires careful planning and the ability to react swiftly to changing market conditions while ensuring supply chain disruptions do not derail production.

Labour shortages and the growing skills gap in manufacturing are additional challenges that COOs must address. As older generations of workers retire and fewer young people pursue manufacturing careers, many companies struggle to find skilled workers to fill critical roles. This shortage is particularly acute in areas requiring technical expertise, such as operating advanced machinery or managing digital systems. To combat this, COOs must invest in workforce development, including upskilling current employees and creating attractive career paths for new talent. This often involves collaborating with educational institutions and industry organisations to ensure that the next generation of workers has the skills necessary for modern manufacturing.

Another trend shaping the manufacturing landscape is the increasing demand for customisation and flexibility. Consumers today expect personalised products that meet their specific needs and preferences, and manufacturers must be able to deliver customised solutions at scale. This has led to the rise of flexible manufacturing systems, where production lines are reconfigurable and capable of handling various products with minimal downtime. Implementing such systems can be challenging, particularly for manufacturers traditionally relying on high-volume, standardised production. COOs must create flexible operations that quickly adapt to shifting consumer demands without sacrificing efficiency.

In my experience, one of the most significant challenges we faced was adapting to the growing demand for customisation. In the past, our production lines were optimised for mass production, which allowed for high efficiency but limited our ability to meet unique customer requirements. Investing in flexible manufacturing technologies and reconfiguring our production processes increased our ability to offer custom solutions without sacrificing speed or quality. This not only improved customer satisfaction but also opened new revenue streams.

In conclusion, the manufacturing landscape is evolving rapidly, driven by digital transformation, sustainability, supply chain resilience, and the demand for customisation. For COOs, understanding these trends and challenges is critical to developing strategies that ensure their operations' long-term success and competitiveness. By staying informed and agile, COOs can lead their organisations through this complex environment and position them for sustained growth.

1.6 - Creating a Culture of Excellence

Building a culture of operational excellence is one of the most vital yet challenging tasks for a COO. While operational tools like Lean, Six Sigma, and automation technologies are essential, they are insufficient if the organisational culture does not support continuous improvement. A culture of excellence ensures that every individual in the company, from the factory floor to the executive boardroom, is focused on improving processes, reducing inefficiencies, and delivering the highest quality products. The most successful manufacturing businesses are those where operational excellence is not just a goal but a deeply ingrained mindset.

Creating such a culture begins with leadership. As COO, your role is to set the tone for the organisation. You must demonstrate a commitment to excellence in everything you do, making it clear that continuous improvement is not just an initiative but a core value. This involves being highly visible, actively engaging with employees at all levels, and showing that their contributions to improvement efforts are valued and recognised. When employees see that leadership is dedicated to excellence, they are more likely to adopt the same mindset.

An important element in fostering a culture of excellence is empowering employees to take ownership of their work. Too often, organisations fall into the trap of imposing top-down mandates for process improvement. While leadership is key in setting strategic direction, real operational excellence happens when frontline employees are empowered to identify inefficiencies, suggest improvements, and implement changes. Creating an environment where employees feel safe to experiment, make suggestions, and even fail without fear of punishment is crucial. This is where Lean's principle of respect for people comes into play; employees must be viewed as partners in the improvement process, not just executors of top-down decisions.

Cross-functional collaboration is another cornerstone of a culture of excellence. Silos between departments often hinder improvement efforts, as they lead to fragmented processes and a lack of shared ownership over outcomes. A COO must work to break down these silos, encouraging collaboration across departments. For example, production teams should regularly interact with supply chain, quality assurance, and even customer service teams to better understand how their actions impact the overall business. In my experience, fostering cross-functional teams focused on solving specific operational challenges leads to better solutions and builds a sense of shared accountability across the organisation.

One of the most powerful tools for embedding a culture of continuous improvement is the Kaizen approach. Kaizen encourages employees to focus on small, incremental improvements that collectively lead to significant gains over time. This approach is highly effective because it empowers individuals at all levels to contribute to the organisation's success. In one company where I implemented a Kaizen programme, we saw a dramatic improvement in efficiency within six months, with employees identifying bottlenecks and suggesting changes that leadership had not considered. These small wins collectively led to a 15% increase in productivity and a notable boost in employee morale.

Recognition and rewards also play a critical role in sustaining a culture of excellence. Employees must feel that their efforts to improve processes and performance are appreciated. This doesn't always mean financial rewards, public recognition, opportunities for career advancement, and even something as simple as a thank-you note can tremendously impact employee motivation. I recall when we instituted a "Continuous Improvement Champion" programme, where employees who contributed significantly to operational improvements were recognised company-wide. This encouraged more participation and reinforced the idea that continuous improvement was integral to our success.

Lastly, transparency is vital in creating a culture of excellence. Employees must see how their efforts contribute to the company's goals. Regular communication of key performance indicators (KPIs), updates on improvement initiatives, and sharing success stories can help employees understand the tangible impact of their work. In one of my previous roles, we implemented a system where every department's KPIs were displayed in common areas alongside progress reports on ongoing improvement projects. This visibility helped maintain momentum and created a shared responsibility for achieving operational goals.

In conclusion, creating a culture of excellence requires leadership commitment, employee empowerment, cross-functional collaboration, and consistent recognition of contributions. By fostering an environment where continuous improvement is part of the organisational DNA, COOs can drive sustainable operational success. This culture improves performance metrics and enhances employee engagement, innovation, and long-term competitiveness.

1.7 - Establishing Clear KPIs

Key Performance Indicators (KPIs) are the backbone of operational excellence. They provide the metrics by which a COO can gauge the success of various initiatives, track progress, and identify areas for improvement. Without clear and well-defined KPIs, operational efforts risk becoming disjointed, unfocused, and ultimately ineffective. Establishing the right KPIs is more than just measuring outputs; it's about aligning these metrics with the company's broader strategic goals and ensuring everyone understands their importance.

The first step in setting up KPIs is to ensure they align with the company's strategic objectives. For example, if the company aims to reduce costs and improve profitability, KPIs might focus on production efficiency, waste reduction, and supply chain optimisation. On the other hand, if the company focuses on growth and market expansion, KPIs might include metrics related to production scalability, on-time delivery, and customer satisfaction. As COO, it is your responsibility to bridge the gap between high-level business strategy and operational execution, and KPIs are the tools that enable this alignment.

One of the most important qualities of effective KPIs must be SMART, Specific, Measurable, Achievable, Relevant, and Time-bound. This framework ensures that KPIs are actionable and provide clear targets for improvement. For instance, a vague KPI like "improve production efficiency" lacks direction and clarity. A SMART KPI, on the other hand, might be "increase production line efficiency by 10% over the next six months by reducing machine downtime." This gives the team a clear goal and timeframe to achieve it, making it easier to track progress and measure success.

In manufacturing, KPIs typically fall into several categories: financial, operational, quality, and customer-focused metrics. Financial KPIs might include cost per unit, return on assets (ROA), or gross margin. Operational KPIs often focus on production cycle time, equipment effectiveness (OEE), and machine utilisation rates. Quality KPIs could include defect rates, scrap rates, and first-pass yield. Finally, customer-focused KPIs might measure on-time delivery, customer satisfaction scores, or order lead time. A COO must ensure these KPIs are tracked, regularly reviewed, and acted upon.

In my own experience, I've seen how the right KPIs can drive dramatic improvements. In one particular instance, a company I worked for struggled with inconsistent product quality, leading to high rates of customer returns. We could track and measure defects at each production stage by introducing a KPI focused on first-pass yield. This led to identifying specific bottlenecks, which we addressed through process re-engineering and additional staff training. Within six months, we reduced defect rates by 30%, which directly impacted customer satisfaction and reduced rework costs.

It's also essential that KPIs are *communicated clearly* throughout the organisation. Employees should understand how their daily actions contribute to the company's key performance indicators. One effective approach is publicly displaying KPIs in common areas, ensuring that progress is visible and celebrated. Regular meetings to review KPI performance can help keep teams focused on their targets and allow for course corrections when necessary. In one manufacturing plant I managed, we held weekly "KPI huddles" on the shop floor, reviewing performance metrics, discussing challenges, and celebrating wins. This fostered a sense of ownership and accountability across all workforce levels.

Data integrity is another critical aspect of KPI management. COOs must ensure that the data used to measure KPIs is accurate, timely, and reliable. Poor data quality can lead to misguided decisions and undermine trust in the KPI system. Investing in proper data collection systems, whether through manual reporting processes or automated systems like Enterprise Resource Planning (ERP) software, is essential to ensuring that KPI tracking is accurate and actionable.

Finally, KPIs should not remain static. As the company evolves, so too should its performance indicators. Regularly reviewing and updating KPIs to reflect changing business priorities or new operational challenges is crucial for maintaining relevance. For example, during a period of rapid growth, a manufacturing company might shift its focus from cost reduction to production scalability, requiring a corresponding adjustment in KPIs. The COO must stay attuned to these shifts and ensure the organisation's metrics evolve accordingly.

In conclusion, establishing clear KPIs is fundamental to driving operational excellence. By aligning these indicators with the company's strategic goals, ensuring they are SMART, and fostering a culture of transparency and accountability around their achievement, COOs can create a powerful mechanism for continuous improvement. The right KPIs provide insight into current performance and guide the organisation toward its future goals.

1.8 - Effective Communication Strategies

Effective communication is a COO's most important yet often overlooked aspect. A COO must bridge the gap between the operational function and other parts of the organisation, ensuring that strategies, objectives, and expectations are clearly understood at every level. In a manufacturing business, where the smooth operation of production lines, supply chains, and logistics depends on clear, timely communication, even small missteps can result in costly delays or inefficiencies. Therefore, mastering the art of communication is essential for driving operational excellence.

The first aspect of effective communication is clarity. Whether communicating with the board of directors, senior management, or the production floor, the COO must be able to convey complex information in a way that is easily understood by the audience. This means avoiding jargon, being concise, and focusing on the key messages that must be delivered. For example, when discussing operational performance with executives, the COO should distil detailed reports into the most critical KPIs, highlighting trends and offering actionable insights. In contrast, when communicating with production teams, the focus should be on specific tasks, goals, and immediate actions they can take to improve performance.

In my own experience, I've found that one of the most effective ways to ensure clarity is to use visual aids like dashboards, process flow diagrams, or Gantt charts. These tools make it easier for different stakeholders to grasp the current state of operations and understand where improvements or changes are necessary. For instance, when leading a multi-department project to integrate a new ERP system, I used a Gantt chart to track progress visually and clearly show task dependencies. This kept everyone aligned and prevented bottlenecks, as team members could see how their work impacted the timeline.

Consistency is another key component of effective communication. The COO must ensure that the messaging around operational goals and expectations remains consistent across the organisation. This involves aligning communication with the company's strategic objectives and regularly reinforcing these messages. In a manufacturing environment, where teams are often focused on their specific tasks, it's easy for the broader operational strategy to get lost in the daily grind. The COO must regularly communicate how these individual tasks contribute to the larger goals, keeping everyone aligned and motivated. Consistency also builds trust; employees and stakeholders are more likely to buy into the vision when they hear the same messages over time.

Two-way communication is equally critical. Effective communication is not just about delivering messages; it's about fostering dialogue and listening to feedback. The COO must create channels where employees feel comfortable voicing concerns, suggesting improvements, and sharing insights. In many cases, frontline workers have the most detailed knowledge of operational inefficiencies, but without a culture that encourages upward communication, these insights may never reach the decision-makers. Regular check-ins, town halls, and open-door policies effectively encourage this dialogue. In one organisation, we implemented monthly "listening sessions" where employees could bring up any operations-related issues or ideas. This initiative led to several key process improvements that significantly reduced downtime and improved employee morale.

Another powerful technique is storytelling. While data and metrics are crucial for operational decision-making, they can sometimes fail to inspire action. Storytelling helps bridge that gap by connecting the numbers to real-world outcomes. For example, instead of simply reporting that on-time delivery has improved by 10%, the COO might share a story about how a specific customer received their product ahead of schedule and the positive feedback. This makes the data more relatable and gives teams a sense of the tangible impact of their work.

Additionally, cross-cultural communication can be challenging in manufacturing, where operations often span multiple locations or countries. The COO must be sensitive to cultural differences in communication styles, work expectations, and decision-making processes. In a global manufacturing company I worked with, I noticed that our European teams preferred more collaborative decision-making processes. In contrast, our North American teams were more comfortable with direct, top-down directives. We improved engagement by adapting communication styles to fit each team's cultural context and ensured smoother operations across regions.

Leveraging technology can also greatly enhance communication. Tools like Slack, Microsoft Teams, or other enterprise communication platforms allow real-time updates, instant feedback, and more dynamic collaboration across departments. Implementing such platforms can streamline communication, reduce email clutter, and promptly address urgent operational issues. In one of my previous roles, we introduced a digital platform where all operational updates, performance dashboards, and project statuses were shared in real-time. This drastically reduced miscommunication and improved response times to operational challenges.

Lastly, emotional intelligence plays a critical role in communication. As COO, understanding your team's emotional and psychological landscape can help you tailor messages that motivate, reassure, or inspire action. Communication with empathy is crucial during organisational change, such as introducing new technologies or restructuring. Employees may feel uncertain or resistant to change, and it's the COO's job to address these concerns to alleviate anxiety and build confidence. When I led the automation of several manual processes in a factory, I held meetings where employees could express their concerns about job security. By being transparent about the long-term benefits of automation and ensuring there were retraining programmes for impacted workers, we could foster a smoother transition with minimal resistance.

In conclusion, effective communication is essential for a COO to lead operational excellence. Whether it's about ensuring clarity and consistency, fostering dialogue, or using storytelling and technology, communication strategies must be tailored to the audience and situation. By focusing on these elements, COOs can create a more aligned, engaged, and motivated workforce that is well-equipped to achieve the company's operational goals.

1.9 - Risk Management

Risk management is a critical component of any COO's operational strategy. In the fast-paced and often unpredictable manufacturing world, risks can arise from numerous sources, including supply chain disruptions, equipment failures, regulatory changes, and market fluctuations. The COO's job is to identify these potential risks and develop robust mitigation strategies that ensure the continuity of operations and protect the organisation's profitability.

The first step in risk management is to conduct a comprehensive risk assessment. This involves identifying potential risks across all areas of operations, from production and supply chain to human resources and compliance. A helpful tool in this process is the Risk Matrix, which allows you to evaluate risks based on their likelihood and impact. By categorising risks in this way, COOs can prioritise the most critical threats and allocate resources to mitigate them. For instance, a supply chain risk that could cause a two-week delay in production might be prioritised over a minor equipment malfunction that can be repaired in a day.

In my experience, one of the most significant risks manufacturing businesses face is supply chain disruption. Global events, such as the COVID-19 pandemic, highlighted how vulnerable supply chains can be to external shocks. As COO, it's essential to have a deep understanding of your supply chain, including the sources of raw materials, the reliability of suppliers, and any geopolitical or environmental factors that could impact availability. One effective strategy is diversifying suppliers, ensuring the company is not overly reliant on a single source for critical components. Additionally, establishing relationships with local suppliers can provide a backup option in the event of international supply chain disruptions.

Preventive maintenance is another key risk mitigation strategy, particularly in manufacturing, where equipment failure can lead to significant downtime and lost revenue. By implementing a predictive maintenance programme, COOs can use data analytics and IoT technologies to monitor equipment performance in real-time, identifying potential failures before they occur. In one plant I managed, we introduced sensors on critical machinery that provided early warnings of wear and tear. This allowed us to schedule maintenance during planned downtime rather than responding to unexpected breakdowns, which reduced unplanned downtime by 30% over a year.

Regulatory and compliance risks are also a major concern in the manufacturing sector. Environmental regulations, labour laws, and safety standards constantly evolve, and failure to comply can result in hefty fines, legal action, or reputational damage. COOs must stay informed of regulatory changes and ensure their operations are fully compliant. This may involve conducting regular audits, implementing safety protocols, and training employees on new regulations. In one case, I worked with a company that faced increased environmental regulations regarding waste disposal. By investing in more efficient waste management systems and training employees on sustainable practices, we achieved compliance and reduced waste-related costs by 20%.

Another significant area of risk is market volatility. Changes in demand, raw material costs, or competitor actions can all impact operational performance. COOs must conduct thorough market analysis and scenario planning to mitigate this risk. The operational team can develop contingency plans, allowing quick adaptation by anticipating potential market shifts. For example, if raw material costs are expected to rise, the COO might explore alternative suppliers, negotiate long-term contracts, or adjust inventory levels to buffer against price fluctuations. In my career, I've used scenario planning to prepare for sudden demand surges, ensuring we had the production capacity and supply chain flexibility to scale up without compromising quality or lead times.

Cybersecurity is an emerging risk that has gained increasing attention as manufacturing becomes more digitally integrated. With the rise of automation, IoT, and cloud-based systems, manufacturing operations are more vulnerable to cyberattacks. A data breach or ransomware attack can disrupt operations, compromise sensitive information, and damage customer trust. As COO, working closely with the IT department to implement robust cybersecurity measures, including firewalls, encryption, employee training on cybersecurity best practices, and regular system audits, is crucial.

Risk transfer mechanisms like insurance can also be important in risk management. While insurance doesn't prevent risks from occurring, it provides a financial safety net in the event of a significant loss. COOs should work with finance and legal teams to ensure the organisation has appropriate coverage for operational risks, including property damage, business interruption, liability, and cybersecurity.

Finally, crisis management planning is essential for dealing with risks that do materialise. A well-thought-out crisis management plan allows the organisation to respond quickly and effectively, minimising the impact on operations. This plan should outline clear roles, responsibilities, communication protocols, and recovery strategies. In one of my previous roles, we developed a crisis management plan that proved invaluable when a natural disaster disrupted one of our key suppliers. We could pivot quickly because we had a clear plan, sourcing alternative suppliers and keeping production running with minimal delays.

In conclusion, risk management is a dynamic and ongoing process that requires the COO to be proactive, strategic, and vigilant. By conducting thorough risk assessments, implementing preventive measures, and developing robust crisis management plans, COOs can protect their operations from unforeseen events and ensure business continuity. Effective risk management safeguards the company's assets and builds resilience, enabling the organisation to thrive despite challenges.

1.10 - Setting Up for Success

Stepping into the role of COO is a significant milestone in any leader's career, but it also comes with immense responsibility and pressure. The first 100 days in the COO role are crucial for setting the tone, building credibility, and establishing a foundation for long-term success. Whether you are moving into this role for the first time or transitioning from another senior leadership position, a well-structured plan will ensure a smooth and effective transition.

The priority for any new COO should be to *understand the current state of the business*. This involves thoroughly assessing the operational function, including production processes, supply chain management, financial performance, and workforce capabilities. In my experience, the best way to get a clear picture is to engage directly with teams across all levels of the organisation. Spend time on the shop floor, meet with department heads, and review key performance data. This will provide valuable insights into the operation's strengths, weaknesses, and potential bottlenecks.

Building relationships with the *executive team* is another critical step. As COO, you will work closely with the CEO, CFO, and other key leaders, so aligning your vision with the company's strategic goals is essential. Early on, schedule one-on-one meetings with each executive to understand their priorities, expectations, and concerns. This helps build rapport and ensures that the operational strategy you develop supports the broader business objectives. In one company I joined as COO, the CEO had a clear vision for expanding into new markets while the CFO was focused on cost containment. Balancing these priorities required clear communication and a strategy addressing growth and efficiency.

Establishing *early wins* is another way to build credibility quickly. These don't have to be large-scale projects but small, impactful changes demonstrating your ability to drive improvement. For example, you might identify a quick fix to reduce production bottlenecks or streamline a supply chain process. In my first 100 days as COO at a previous company, I identified an opportunity to automate a manual inventory tracking process, which led to a 15% reduction in stock discrepancies within the first quarter. This small but significant improvement built trust with the team and showed that I was committed to delivering results.

Another essential element of a successful transition is *team building*. The operational function relies heavily on the team's expertise, motivation, and collaboration, so ensuring that you have the right people in the right roles is crucial. This doesn't mean making immediate staffing changes but rather assessing the strengths and weaknesses of your leadership team. Sometimes, you may need to provide additional training or mentorship to help team members grow into their roles. In others, it may become clear that new talent is needed to bring fresh perspectives and capabilities to the organisation.

One common mistake new COOs make is implementing too many changes too quickly. While it's important to set a clear direction, it's equally important to take the time to fully understand the organisation's culture and processes before making sweeping changes. Change management is a delicate process; moving too fast can result in employee resistance or unintended operational disruptions. Instead, focus on building a strong foundation through thoughtful, incremental improvements that align with the company's long-term goals.

Communication during the transition is paramount. Be transparent about your plans, objectives, and vision for the future. This helps alleviate any concerns or uncertainty among the workforce, particularly if they are accustomed to a different leadership style. Regular updates, town halls, and open forums can help build trust and ensure employees are aligned with the operational strategy. In one organisation I worked with, I held bi-weekly all-hands meetings during my first three months as COO. I updated my findings, outlined upcoming initiatives, and addressed employee questions. This level of transparency helped build trust and fostered a collaborative environment.

Lastly, it's important to take a *long-term view*. While the first 100 days are critical for establishing momentum, the true test of a COO's effectiveness is sustaining and scaling operational improvements over time. Develop a roadmap that outlines short-term and long-term priorities, ensuring you have a clear plan for the next 6-12 months. This roadmap should be flexible enough to adapt to changing circumstances but detailed enough to provide clear direction for the team.

In conclusion, the initial transition into the COO role is a period of intense learning, relationship building, and strategic planning. By focusing on understanding the current state of the business, aligning with the executive team, establishing early wins, and building a strong operational team, COOs can set themselves up for long-term success. With the right approach, the first 100 days can lay the foundation for operational excellence and position the organisation for sustained growth and success.

Chapter 2

Mastering Operational Efficiency

> "For COOs, every challenge is just another process waiting to be optimised."
>
> Robert N. Jacobs

In today's highly competitive business environment, operational efficiency is a desirable trait and an essential driver of success. For Chief Operating Officers (COOs), the ability to streamline processes, reduce waste, and optimise resources is pivotal in maintaining profitability and delivering value to customers.

This chapter delves into the multifaceted nature of operational efficiency, particularly within the manufacturing sector. From enhancing workflow and adopting Lean principles to leveraging technology and fostering continuous improvement, mastering operational efficiency requires a strategic approach. This chapter will explore key methodologies, tools, and real-world applications that COOs can employ to lead their organisations towards sustainable operational excellence.

2.1 - The Efficiency Imperative

Operational efficiency in manufacturing is not just a competitive advantage but a fundamental necessity for business survival. Efficiency directly impacts profitability, product quality, customer satisfaction, and business agility. In a highly competitive market, where margins are often tight and customers demand rapid delivery of high-quality products, inefficient processes can quickly erode a company's bottom line. For a COO, mastering efficiency is about driving operational excellence while reducing waste, improving speed, and optimising resources.

Efficiency in manufacturing extends beyond merely producing more units at a lower cost. It's about ensuring that every step in the production process adds value, that resources, whether labour, materials, or time, are used optimally, and that the business can adapt quickly to changing market demands. In this context, efficiency is as much about flexibility and responsiveness as it is about cost control. It requires a comprehensive approach, where everything from production techniques to supply chain logistics is continuously evaluated and refined. One of the core reasons efficiency is vital is its direct link to profitability. When operations run smoothly, with minimal downtime and reduced waste, the cost per unit decreases, improving profit margins. I recall an example early in my career where a company I worked for had high production costs due to excessive machine downtime. By implementing preventive maintenance programmes and optimising production schedules, we significantly reduced unplanned downtime and saw a 12% reduction in production costs within the first six months. These cost savings often mean staying competitive or losing ground to more efficient rivals.

Efficiency also plays a key role in *customer satisfaction*. In a world where customers expect fast delivery and customisation, operational efficiency allows companies to meet these demands without sacrificing quality or incurring additional costs. A streamlined manufacturing process ensures that products are delivered on time, orders are accurate, and any issues that arise can be quickly addressed. This builds customer trust and loyalty, which is critical for long-term success.

In addition to profitability and customer satisfaction, efficiency enhances a company's ability to innovate. When a manufacturing operation runs efficiently, with well-optimised processes and clear metrics, it frees up time and money resources that can be reinvested in research and development, new product lines, or strategic initiatives. This creates a continuous improvement cycle, where efficiency gains fuel innovation, and innovation drives further efficiency.

Efficiency in manufacturing also supports sustainability efforts, which are increasingly important in today's business environment. Reducing waste, optimising energy usage, and minimising resource consumption are good for the environment and reduce costs. Numerous examples of companies embracing sustainability as part of their efficiency strategy, resulting in operational and reputational benefits. In one instance, a company I worked with reduced material waste by 25% through more efficient production planning, improving profitability and positioning the company as a leader in environmentally responsible manufacturing.

However, achieving and maintaining efficiency requires constant vigilance. The manufacturing environment is dynamic, with new technologies, market demands, and regulatory requirements always on the horizon. COOs must be prepared to continuously assess and refine processes, invest in new technologies, and engage employees at all levels to achieve operational efficiency. For instance, in one company, we implemented a system where employees were encouraged to submit ideas for process improvements. Over two years, these suggestions resulted in several small but impactful changes that collectively boosted overall efficiency by 8%.

In conclusion, operational efficiency is the lifeblood of a successful manufacturing business. It drives profitability, enhances customer satisfaction, supports innovation, and contributes to sustainability. For COOs, mastering efficiency is about fostering a culture of continuous improvement, leveraging data and technology, and ensuring that every aspect of the operation is aligned with the company's broader strategic goals. It is a continuous journey essential for long-term success in competitive manufacturing.

2.2 - Lean Manufacturing Principles

Lean manufacturing is a powerful methodology that minimises waste while maximising value. Lean has become a widely adopted approach from the Toyota Production System across the manufacturing industry, helping businesses streamline operations, reduce costs, and improve quality. The core principle of Lean is to focus on value from the customer's perspective and to eliminate anything in the production process that does not directly contribute to delivering that value.

Waste elimination is at the heart of Lean manufacturing, known in Japanese as Muda. Waste in this context refers to anything that does not add value to the customer, such as excess inventory, overproduction, waiting times, unnecessary movement, defects, and inefficient processes. By systematically identifying and eliminating these wastes, manufacturers can reduce costs, increase efficiency, and deliver higher-quality products faster.

One of the key tools in Lean is Value Stream Mapping (VSM). This involves creating a detailed flowchart that maps out every step in the production process, from raw materials to finished goods, to identify where waste occurs. By visualising the entire process, VSM allows COOs and their teams to see where bottlenecks, delays, and inefficiencies exist and provides a framework for streamlining operations. In one project I led, we used value stream mapping to identify an inefficient handoff between production and quality control, which added unnecessary delays to the process. By redesigning the workflow and implementing more direct communication channels, we reduced lead time by 15%.

Another critical Lean tool is 5S, which stands for Sort, Set in order, Shine, Standardise, and Sustain. This workplace organisation method helps optimise the factory floor for efficiency and safety. The 5S methodology promotes a clean and organised workspace where tools and materials are stored in designated places. This allows workers to spend less time searching for what they need and more time adding value. I've seen dramatic improvements in efficiency and morale simply by implementing 5S in production areas where clutter and disorganisation were hindering productivity.

Kaizen, or continuous improvement, is a foundational element of Lean. Kaizen encourages all employees, from top management to line workers, to contribute to improving processes. Small, incremental changes lead to significant efficiency gains when implemented consistently. I remember a particularly successful Kaizen event at a company struggling with high defect rates. By involving employees from various departments and encouraging them to identify small changes, we implemented process improvements that reduced defects by 20% within three months.

One of Lean's most well-known tools is Just-in-Time (JIT) production. JIT aims to reduce inventory costs by producing goods only as they are needed rather than holding large quantities of inventory. This approach requires precise coordination with suppliers and a well-organised production schedule to ensure that materials arrive just in time for production. When implemented successfully, JIT reduces waste, frees up working capital, and improves cash flow. However, implementing it can be challenging, especially in volatile supply chains. In my experience, companies that succeed with JIT have robust supplier relationships and effective contingency plans in place.

Another key Lean concept is Poka-Yoke or mistake-proofing. This technique involves designing processes to prevent errors before they happen. Whether through physical devices or automated systems, Poka-Yoke ensures that defects are caught and corrected early in the process, reducing the likelihood of costly rework or product recalls. I've seen this approach applied in various settings, from simple fixtures that prevent parts from being assembled incorrectly to sophisticated sensors that detect anomalies during production.

Finally, Lean manufacturing emphasises the importance of respect for people. Lean recognises that employees are the most valuable asset of any organisation and that their knowledge, creativity, and engagement are essential to achieving operational excellence. Empowering employees to participate in continuous improvement efforts, providing them with the tools and training they need to succeed, and fostering a culture of respect and collaboration are all central to the Lean philosophy.

In conclusion, lean manufacturing is a holistic approach that provides powerful tools and techniques for improving operational efficiency. By focusing on waste elimination, process improvement, and respect for people, Lean enables manufacturing companies to reduce costs, improve quality, and respond more quickly to customer needs. For COOs, mastering Lean principles is essential for driving long-term success and creating a culture of continuous improvement.

2.3 - Process Optimisation

Process optimisation is the art and science of improving how work gets done. In manufacturing, this involves identifying inefficiencies, bottlenecks, and redundancies in production processes and implementing solutions that enhance speed, reduce costs, and improve quality. Effective process optimisation boosts operational efficiency and helps a company become more flexible, agile, and responsive to changing market demands.

One of the most common techniques for process optimisation is workflow analysis. This involves mapping out the steps in a process to identify inefficiencies and opportunities for improvement. Flowcharts and process maps help COOs visualise how work moves through the system, where delays or bottlenecks occur, and where resources may be underutilised. In one company I worked with, we used workflow analysis to tackle a production process that took longer than expected. By breaking down each step and identifying the root cause of delays, we could reallocate resources more effectively, reducing the overall production time by 20%.

Bottleneck analysis is another critical technique for process optimisation. Bottlenecks are points in the production process where work gets backed up, slowing down the entire operation. These can occur due to machine downtime, inefficient workstations, or resource constraints. By identifying bottlenecks and addressing them, whether through better scheduling, equipment upgrades, or process redesigns, COOs can unlock significant gains in efficiency. In one factory, I noticed a particular machine causing frequent slowdowns due to outdated software. By investing in a software upgrade, we increased throughput by 15% without adding additional labour or machinery.

Standardisation is another essential process optimisation technique. Inconsistent processes lead to variability in quality, inefficiencies, and higher costs. By standardising processes, companies can ensure that every product is made using the same best practices, reducing errors and increasing efficiency. Standard operating procedures (SOPs) and work instructions are key tools for standardisation. I've seen dramatic efficiency improvements when companies standardise processes across multiple shifts, ensuring that every team follows the same guidelines, regardless of who is on duty.

Another valuable approach to process optimisation is the use of automation. Manufacturers can reduce labour costs and increase speed and accuracy by automating repetitive tasks. From robotic assembly lines to automated quality inspections, technology can dramatically improve the efficiency of operations. However, automation is not a one-size-fits-all solution. It's important for COOs to carefully assess which processes can be automated without compromising flexibility or quality. In one instance, we automated the packaging process in a plant, which significantly reduced labour costs and cycle time, freeing up staff to focus on more value-added activities.

Cycle time reduction is a focused process optimisation technique that seeks to reduce the time it takes to complete a task or produce a product. Shortening cycle times can improve customer satisfaction by enabling faster delivery, increasing production capacity, and reducing costs. Techniques like SMED (Single-Minute Exchange of Die), which focuses on reducing changeover times between different production runs, can be highly effective. I once implemented SMED in a factory experiencing long changeover times between product lines. By streamlining the process and training staff on quick-change techniques, we cut changeover times by 40%, allowing us to increase production without additional resources.

Data-driven decision-making is essential for effective process optimisation. COOs must rely on real-time data and analytics to monitor production performance and identify areas for improvement. Key metrics like cycle time, defect rates, and machine utilisation provide valuable insights into how efficiently a process is running. Implementing a data collection system, such as an ERP or MES (Manufacturing Execution System), can help COOs track these metrics and make informed decisions. In one of my previous roles, we introduced a real-time data dashboard that allowed us to monitor production in real-time, enabling faster responses to issues and better overall performance.

In conclusion, process optimisation is a continuous effort that involves identifying inefficiencies, streamlining workflows, and leveraging technology to improve operational performance. By focusing on workflow analysis, bottleneck identification, standardisation, automation, and data-driven decision-making, COOs can significantly enhance the efficiency and effectiveness of manufacturing operations. The key is approaching process optimisation as an ongoing journey, where incremental improvements lead to substantial long-term gains.

2.4 - Automation and Technology

In today's rapidly evolving manufacturing environment, automation and technology have become indispensable tools for improving operational efficiency. The integration of advanced technologies, such as robotics, artificial intelligence (AI), machine learning (ML), and the Internet of Things (IoT), has revolutionised the way manufacturing operations are conducted. For COOs, the challenge lies in effectively leveraging these technologies to enhance efficiency, reduce costs, and improve overall business performance without disrupting operations.

One of the most significant advantages of automation is its ability to increase speed and reduce errors. Automation can handle repetitive, labour-intensive tasks with greater precision and consistency than human workers, reducing the likelihood of mistakes. In areas like assembly, packaging, and inspection, automation ensures that processes are carried out consistently, improving speed and quality. I've worked in facilities where we automated entire assembly lines, resulting in a 30% increase in throughput and a significant reduction in defects, all while allowing employees to focus on higher-value tasks.

Robotic Process Automation (RPA) is a rapidly growing technology that automates routine, rule-based tasks. RPA can be used in manufacturing tasks such as data entry, inventory management, and production scheduling. By automating these administrative processes, companies can reduce human error and free up employees for more strategic roles. For example, one factory I worked with used RPA to streamline its order processing system, reducing lead times from order placement to production by 20%. This improved efficiency and enhanced the customer experience by delivering products faster.

Artificial Intelligence (AI) and machine learning (ML) are transforming how manufacturers optimise their operations. AI can analyse vast amounts of data in real-time, identifying patterns and anomalies that would be impossible for humans to detect. This is particularly useful for predictive maintenance, where AI monitors machine performance to predict when equipment will fail. In one instance, we implemented an AI-powered maintenance system that monitored critical equipment and alerted us to potential failures before they occurred. This proactive approach to maintenance reduced downtime by 25% and extended the lifespan of key machinery.

Another significant development is the Internet of Things (IoT), which allows machines, devices, and systems to communicate in real-time. IoT sensors embedded in machinery provide real-time data on performance, enabling COOs to monitor the production process more closely and identify issues before they escalate. IoT can also track inventory levels, monitor supply chains, and optimise energy consumption. In one of my roles, we used IoT to monitor energy usage across our production facility. By identifying peak consumption times and adjusting processes accordingly, we reduced our energy costs by 15% while maintaining full production capacity.

3D printing, or additive manufacturing, is another technology with significant potential to enhance efficiency, particularly in prototyping and custom manufacturing. 3D printing allows manufacturers to produce complex parts quickly and cost-effectively, reducing lead times and eliminating the need for expensive tooling. In industries such as aerospace and automotive, where customisation is critical, 3D printing can streamline production and reduce waste. In one project, we used 3D printing to prototype new product designs, reducing the time to bring a product from concept to market by 40%.

While automation and technology offer tremendous benefits, it's essential to approach their implementation thoughtfully. Not every process is suitable for automation, and over-automating can lead to inflexibility in operations. COOs must assess where automation will have the most significant impact and ensure that it complements, rather than replaces, human workers. A successful automation strategy often involves collaborative robots (cobots), which work alongside human employees to perform tasks that require human skill and robotic precision. Cobots are particularly effective in tasks such as machine tending or assembly, where human judgment and adaptability are still necessary.

Data analytics is another critical component of technology-driven efficiency. Advanced analytics tools allow COOs to make data-driven decisions based on real-time insights across the production floor. By collecting and analysing data on machine performance, production times, defect rates, and other key metrics, COOs can identify inefficiencies, optimise workflows, and improve decision-making. In one of my previous roles, we implemented a real-time data analytics platform that monitored every stage of the production process. This visibility allowed us to identify a bottleneck in one section of the assembly line, which we corrected, resulting in a 12% increase in overall throughput.

Cybersecurity is a crucial consideration when implementing new technologies in manufacturing. As operations become increasingly digital and connected, the risk of cyberattacks grows. A data breach or cyberattack could disrupt production, compromise sensitive information, and damage a company's reputation. COOs must work closely with IT teams to ensure that robust cybersecurity measures are in place, from firewalls and encryption to regular system audits and employee training on cybersecurity best practices.

One key challenge in adopting automation and technology is the skills gap. Many manufacturing workers are not trained to work with advanced technologies, creating a potential barrier to successful implementation. To address this, COOs must invest in employee training and development, ensuring their workforce has the skills to operate and maintain automated systems. Upskilling employees enhances operational efficiency and morale by demonstrating that the company is committed to investing in its workforce.

In conclusion, automation and technology are transformative forces in modern manufacturing, offering significant opportunities to enhance efficiency, reduce costs, and improve quality. However, successfully implementing these technologies requires a thoughtful, strategic approach that considers the unique needs of the business, the workforce, and the broader operational environment. By leveraging tools such as AI, IoT, and robotics and ensuring robust cybersecurity and upskilling initiatives, COOs can harness the power of technology to drive operational excellence and stay competitive in an increasingly digital world.

2.5 - Supply Chain Management

Effective supply chain management is a cornerstone of operational efficiency in manufacturing. The supply chain connects all the elements of production, from sourcing raw materials to delivering finished goods to customers, and any disruption or inefficiency in this chain can have a cascading effect on overall operations. For COOs, optimising the supply chain means ensuring that materials flow smoothly, inventory is managed efficiently, suppliers are reliable, and costs are controlled.

Improving visibility is one of the first steps in optimising the supply chain. Supply chain visibility refers to tracking and monitoring materials, components, and products as they move through the supply chain. With greater visibility, COOs can identify potential disruptions or inefficiencies before they become major problems. Technologies such as RFID (Radio Frequency Identification), IoT, and blockchain can provide real-time insights into the movement of goods, allowing companies to monitor inventory levels, track shipments, and identify bottlenecks. In one organisation I worked with, we implemented a real-time RFID system to track raw materials from suppliers to the production floor. This level of visibility reduced stockouts and improved production scheduling, ultimately enhancing overall efficiency.

Supplier management is another critical aspect of supply chain optimisation. Reliable, high-quality suppliers are essential for maintaining consistent production schedules and reducing costs. COOs must build strong relationships with key suppliers, ensuring clear communication and mutually beneficial partnerships. In one of my roles, we developed a supplier scorecard system, where we rated our suppliers on key performance metrics such as on-time delivery, quality, and cost competitiveness. This system helped us identify the best-performing suppliers and fostered a collaborative environment where underperforming suppliers were encouraged to improve. We reduced lead times and minimised disruptions by working closely with our suppliers.

Lean supply chain management is a popular approach for improving supply chain efficiency. The principles of Lean focused on waste reduction, continuous improvement, and value creation, apply as much to the supply chain as they do to production. One technique often used in Lean supply chain management is Just-in-Time (JIT) inventory. JIT aims to minimise inventory by receiving materials only as they are needed for production. While this approach reduces carrying costs and waste, it requires precise coordination with suppliers and careful demand monitoring. In one company, we shifted to a JIT system for certain high-cost materials, which freed up working capital and reduced the risk of obsolescence.

Risk management is another vital component of supply chain optimisation. The COVID-19 pandemic and other global disruptions have highlighted the fragility of many supply chains, particularly those that rely heavily on a single region or supplier. To mitigate these risks, COOs should consider diversifying their supplier base and creating contingency plans for potential disruptions. In one instance, I worked with a company that had been overly dependent on a single supplier in Asia. When geopolitical tensions caused supply chain delays, we quickly sourced alternative suppliers in Europe and North America, ensuring that production remained uninterrupted.

Another key area of supply chain optimisation is inventory management. Efficient inventory management ensures that the right materials are available when needed without tying up excessive amounts of capital in stock. One technique that has proven effective in many manufacturing environments is ABC analysis, which categorises inventory into three groups: A items (high value, low quantity), B items (moderate value and quantity), and C items (low value, high quantity). By optimising the management of A items, where the greatest value lies, COOs can ensure that inventory levels are aligned with production needs and customer demand. I once implemented an ABC analysis for a manufacturer holding excessive inventory across all categories. By focusing on A items and reducing stock levels for C items, we cut inventory costs by 15% while improving service levels.

Technology also plays a crucial role in optimising the supply chain. Advanced planning and scheduling systems (APS) and enterprise resource planning (ERP) systems help COOs manage supply chain complexity by integrating data across procurement, production, and logistics. These systems provide real-time data and analytics, enabling better forecasting, demand planning, and decision-making. In one of my previous roles, we implemented an ERP system connecting our suppliers directly with our production schedule, allowing real-time adjustments based on demand fluctuations. This integration improved coordination and reduced lead times by 10%.

Collaboration within the supply chain is increasingly important. Traditional supply chains operate in silos, with limited communication between suppliers, manufacturers, and distributors. Today, COOs are shifting toward more collaborative supply chains, where all parties collaborate to share data, align goals, and improve overall performance. In one project, we worked closely with our logistics provider to synchronise delivery schedules with production needs, reducing warehouse storage costs and ensuring that materials arrived just in time for production. This collaborative approach resulted in a 12% reduction in logistics costs.

In conclusion, optimising the supply chain is essential for driving efficiency and maintaining competitive advantage in manufacturing. By improving visibility, fostering strong supplier relationships, managing risks, and leveraging technology, COOs can ensure that their supply chain operates smoothly and efficiently. A well-optimised supply chain reduces costs, enhances productivity, and improves the company's ability to respond to market changes and customer demands.

2.6 - Inventory Management

Effective inventory management is critical to operational efficiency in the manufacturing sector. Mismanagement of inventory can lead to a range of issues, from excessive carrying costs to stockouts, which negatively impact a company's bottom line and operational performance. For COOs, mastering inventory management means striking the delicate balance between having enough stock to meet production demands and minimising the capital in excess inventory. Efficient inventory management can reduce waste, free up cash flow, and enhance the overall agility of the operation.

One of the most fundamental techniques in inventory management is Economic Order Quantity (EOQ). EOQ is a formula that determines the optimal order quantity and minimises ordering and holding costs. The goal is to find the balance between ordering too frequently, which increases ordering costs and ordering in large quantities, which increases carrying costs. EOQ is particularly useful in environments where demand is relatively stable, allowing COOs to optimise their procurement process. In one factory I worked with, we used EOQ to standardise order quantities for frequently used raw materials, reducing carrying costs by 8% while maintaining sufficient stock levels to prevent production delays.

Just-in-Time (JIT) inventory is another popular strategy for effective inventory control. The JIT approach aims to keep inventory levels as low as possible by ordering materials just as they are needed in the production process. This minimises inventory holding costs and reduces the risk of excess stock becoming obsolete. However, JIT requires highly reliable suppliers and a well-coordinated supply chain. In one of my roles, we implemented JIT for high-value components, which allowed us to free up significant capital previously tied up in inventory. While the approach reduced storage costs, it also required us to strengthen supplier relationships to ensure timely deliveries.

ABC analysis is a technique that helps COOs prioritise their inventory management efforts based on the value and importance of different items. Companies can focus on the items that significantly impact the business by classifying inventory into three categories: A, B, and C. Category A consists of high-value items with low volume, B represents moderate-value items, and C includes low-value items typically ordered in high volumes. This segmentation allows COOs to allocate resources more effectively, prioritising managing A items, which often represent the highest financial risk if mismanaged. In one company, we reduced inventory carrying costs by 12% by applying ABC analysis and adjusting our procurement and stock management processes based on the classifications.

Safety stock is another critical component of inventory management. Safety stock acts as a buffer to protect against uncertainties in demand or supply. It is particularly important in environments with unpredictable lead times or customer demand. However, holding too much safety stock can lead to increased carrying costs, so it's essential to determine the right level of buffer inventory based on historical data, demand forecasting, and supplier reliability. In a project I led, we recalculated safety stock levels using more accurate demand forecasts and reduced excess safety stock by 15%, which resulted in significant savings without compromising service levels.

In addition to traditional methods, inventory optimisation software is increasingly important in modern inventory management. These software tools leverage data analytics to provide real-time visibility into inventory levels, track usage patterns, and automate reorder points. Enterprise Resource Planning (ERP) systems with integrated inventory management modules allow companies to track every stock movement, from raw material intake to finished goods shipment. In one manufacturing plant I worked with, we integrated an ERP system that centralised inventory data across multiple warehouses, reducing stock discrepancies and improving replenishment accuracy.

Vendor-managed inventory (VMI) is a collaborative inventory management strategy where suppliers manage inventory levels at the customer's site. This approach allows suppliers to optimise inventory replenishment based on real-time consumption data, reducing stockouts and excess inventory. In one instance, we partnered with a key supplier to implement VMI for a critical component in our production process. This reduced our administrative burden and improved supply chain coordination, resulting in fewer production delays and a 10% reduction in inventory holding costs.

Cycle counting is an inventory auditing technique that involves regularly counting a subset of inventory rather than conducting a full physical inventory count once or twice a year. By counting smaller portions of inventory more frequently, companies can identify discrepancies early and address any issues before they escalate. This method is particularly useful in environments where inventory turnover is high. In one organisation, we switched to a cycle counting approach, which improved the accuracy of our inventory records and reduced the time and labour required for full physical counts by 40%.

Lastly, effective inventory management requires accurate demand forecasting. Forecasting allows COOs to anticipate customer demand and adjust inventory levels accordingly. By leveraging historical data, market trends, and sales forecasts, companies can minimise the risk of stockouts or excess inventory. However, demand forecasting is challenging, especially in volatile markets where customer preferences or external factors like economic conditions can shift rapidly. Companies should use statistical models and real-time data analysis to mitigate these risks to make more informed inventory decisions.

In conclusion, mastering inventory management is essential for operational efficiency in manufacturing. Techniques such as EOQ, JIT, ABC analysis, and safety stock management, coupled with modern inventory optimisation software, allow COOs to strike the right balance between having enough stock to meet production needs while minimising costs. By implementing these strategies and fostering collaboration with suppliers, COOs can ensure that inventory management supports the broader goals of operational excellence and business agility.

2.7 - Quality Management Systems

In manufacturing, quality is non-negotiable. Consistently delivering high-quality products is essential for customer satisfaction, regulatory compliance, and a competitive edge. For COOs, implementing and maintaining a robust Quality Management System (QMS) is critical to ensuring that quality standards are met at every stage of the production process. A well-designed QMS enhances product quality and improves operational efficiency by reducing rework, waste, and defects.

The foundation of any QMS is the Plan-Do-Check-Act (PDCA) cycle, a systematic process for continuous improvement. The PDCA cycle begins with planning, where COOs define quality objectives and set measurable targets. These plans are implemented in the "do" and "check" phases, monitoring and measuring results against the targets. Finally, the "act" phase involves taking corrective actions based on the results, ensuring the process improves continuously. In my experience, implementing the PDCA cycle across all departments has helped identify and eliminate recurring quality issues, creating a culture of continuous improvement.

One of the most widely recognised frameworks for quality management is the ISO 9001 standard. ISO 9001 provides a comprehensive set of criteria for establishing a QMS, focusing on customer satisfaction, process improvement, and regulatory compliance. Achieving ISO 9001 certification requires companies to develop a formal quality policy, define roles and responsibilities, and establish processes for monitoring, measuring, and improving quality. In one of the manufacturing companies I worked with, obtaining ISO 9001 certification was a turning point. The process forced us to re-evaluate our quality control procedures, streamline workflows, and ensure that every employee was aligned with the company's quality goals.

Total Quality Management (TQM) is another approach that emphasises the involvement of all employees in the pursuit of quality improvement. TQM promotes a company-wide culture where every worker, from management to the production floor, is responsible for maintaining and improving quality. One of the core principles of TQM is that quality is built into the process and is not inspected after the fact. In one plant, we introduced cross-functional quality teams involving production, engineering, and quality control employees. These teams regularly reviewed processes and identified areas for improvement, leading to a 15% reduction in defects within the first year.

Statistical Process Control (SPC) is a data-driven method for monitoring and controlling quality during the manufacturing process. It involves using control charts to track process variability and detect deviations from the norm. By identifying trends and variations in real time, SPC allows companies to take corrective action before defects occur. In one of my previous roles, we implemented SPC across several critical production lines. This proactive approach to quality control helped us reduce product variation and scrap rates by 10%, significantly improving overall process reliability.

Another critical element of maintaining quality is root cause analysis (RCA). RCA is used to identify the underlying causes of defects or failures, allowing companies to address the root of the problem rather than just treating the symptoms. Techniques such as the Five Whys and Fishbone diagrams are commonly used to conduct RCA. In one quality crisis I encountered, where we were experiencing a high rate of defects, we used the Five Whys technique to trace the problem back to a supplier's inconsistent material quality. By addressing the issue with the supplier and improving incoming inspection protocols, we reduced defects by 25%.

Poka-Yoke, or mistake-proofing, is another essential technique in quality management. It involves designing processes and tools to prevent errors. For example, in an assembly process, Poka-Yoke might install fixtures that ensure components can only be assembled in the correct orientation. We implemented Poka-Yoke techniques in one plant's packaging department, significantly reducing incorrect labelling and packaging errors.

Maintaining quality standards also requires a robust training and development system. Employees must be properly trained on quality standards, procedures, and expectations. Regular training sessions and refresher courses ensure that workers stay up-to-date with the latest quality control techniques and understand their role in maintaining product quality. In one organisation, we developed a comprehensive training programme that included classroom instruction and hands-on practice, resulting in a measurable improvement in employee adherence to quality standards.

Customer feedback plays an essential role in continuously improving quality management systems. By actively soliciting and analysing customer feedback, companies can gain valuable insights into areas for improvement. This feedback loop allows COOs to align quality standards more closely with customer expectations and address any issues arising after products leave the factory. In one case, we implemented a customer feedback system that gathered insights on product performance in the field. Using this data to inform product design and manufacturing improvements, we saw a 20% decrease in customer complaints within a year.

In conclusion, implementing and maintaining a robust QMS ensures that products meet the highest quality standards. Techniques such as PDCA, ISO 9001, TQM, SPC, and RCA provide a framework for continuously improving quality throughout manufacturing. For COOs, fostering a culture of quality that involves every employee and leverages data-driven decision-making is essential for achieving long-term success and operational excellence.

2.8 - Performance Metrics

In the pursuit of operational efficiency, performance metrics are invaluable tools that allow COOs to assess how well the business is functioning and identify areas for improvement. The right metrics provide clear, actionable insights into the effectiveness of processes, the productivity of workers, and the utilisation of resources. Without these metrics, efforts to improve efficiency are often based on guesswork rather than data-driven decisions, leading to suboptimal results.

One of the most critical performance metrics in manufacturing is Overall Equipment Effectiveness (OEE). OEE measures how effectively a manufacturing operation is utilised by factoring in machine availability, performance, and quality. A plant operating at 100% OEE produces only good parts as fast as possible with no downtime. However, no operation is perfect, and COOs use OEE to pinpoint where losses occur, whether from machine downtime, slow cycles, or product defects. In one facility I managed, our initial OEE was only 65%, indicating significant room for improvement. We increased OEE to 80% over six months by addressing equipment reliability and optimising changeover times, significantly boosting overall productivity.

Another key metric is Cycle Time, which measures the time it takes to produce a single unit from start to finish. Reducing cycle time increases throughput and allows a company to meet customer demand quickly. One of the most effective ways to reduce cycle time is using Lean manufacturing principles, such as eliminating non-value-added activities and improving workflow efficiency. In one instance, we focused on reducing cycle time in a critical production process by reorganising the layout of the production line, resulting in a 15% reduction in the time it took to complete each unit.

First Pass Yield (FPY) is a vital quality metric that measures the percentage of products manufactured correctly the first time without rework or repair. A high FPY indicates that a process is running smoothly and efficiently, while a low FPY suggests that defects or errors are occurring that waste time and resources. By tracking FPY at various stages of production, COOs can quickly identify problem areas and take corrective action. In one plant, we discovered that a particular workstation had a consistently low FPY, leading to excessive rework. After retraining staff and recalibrating equipment, we raised FPY by 10%, significantly reducing waste and improving overall efficiency.

Throughput is another crucial metric, representing the number of units produced within a given time frame. Improving throughput can be achieved by optimising workflows, minimising downtime, and addressing bottlenecks. For example, in one factory where I worked, throughput was limited by a bottleneck in the assembly process. By reallocating resources and staggering shift changes to ensure continuous operation, we increased throughput by 20% without adding additional equipment.

Scrap Rate is an important efficiency measure, especially in industries where raw materials are expensive or hard to come by. High scrap rates indicate that materials are wasted during production through errors, defects, or inefficiencies. Reducing scrap not only saves costs but also improves the environmental sustainability of the operation. In one instance, we identified excessive scrap in a metalworking process due to inconsistent material quality. By working with our suppliers to ensure more stringent quality checks and recalibrating our cutting machines, we reduced scrap by 25%, leading to substantial cost savings.

Capacity Utilisation measures the extent to which a manufacturing operation uses its full production capacity. A low capacity utilisation rate suggests that equipment or resources are underutilised. At the same time, a rate that is too high may indicate that the operation is running too close to its limits, risking burnout or unplanned downtime. For COOs, finding the right balance is critical. In one factory, we consistently operated at over 90% capacity, leading to frequent equipment failures and unplanned downtime. Investing in preventive maintenance and adjusting production schedules reduced capacity utilisation to a more sustainable 85%, stabilising operations and improving overall output.

Labour Productivity is another key metric for measuring efficiency. This metric tracks the output produced per employee or hour worked. Improving labour productivity can be achieved through training, better tools, and optimised workflows. In one plant, we saw a 10% improvement in labour productivity by implementing a cross-training programme that allowed employees to move between workstations as needed, reducing idle time and increasing flexibility on the shop floor.

Lead Time measures the time it takes from receiving a customer order to delivering the finished product. Shorter lead times improve customer satisfaction and reduce the need for large inventories. Lead time is affected by every stage of the supply chain, from raw material procurement to production and shipping. In one project, we focused on reducing lead times by improving coordination between our procurement and production teams, ensuring that materials arrived just as needed on the production line. This reduced lead time by 20%, allowing us to respond to customer orders quickly.

While individual metrics like OEE, cycle time, and FPY are essential, taking a holistic view of performance is also important. Focusing too much on one metric can lead to unintended consequences in other areas. For example, increasing throughput without considering quality can lead to higher defect rates and rework costs. COOs must balance these metrics to ensure that improvements in one area do not negatively impact overall performance.

The use of real-time data is becoming increasingly important in measuring and improving efficiency. Advanced monitoring systems, integrated with production equipment, allow COOs to track performance metrics in real-time and respond immediately to issues as they arise. In one factory I managed, we implemented a real-time dashboard that displayed key performance metrics across the shop floor. This visibility empowered workers to take ownership of their performance and allowed us to make quicker, more informed decisions, leading to a 12% improvement in overall efficiency within six months.

In conclusion, performance metrics are essential for COOs to understand their operations' effectiveness and identify areas for improvement. Metrics such as OEE, cycle time, FPY, throughput, and scrap rate provide valuable insights into the efficiency of production processes. At the same time, capacity utilisation and labour productivity offer a broader view of resource management. By leveraging these metrics, COOs can make data-driven decisions that improve operational efficiency, reduce costs, and enhance the overall performance of the manufacturing operation.

2.9 - Case Study: Efficiency Success Stories

To truly understand the impact of mastering operational efficiency, it's useful to explore real-world examples of companies successfully implementing strategies to improve their performance. In this case study, I will share two examples from my experience in the manufacturing sector, where operational efficiency was dramatically improved, resulting in significant business benefits.

Case Study 1: Reducing Cycle Time in an Automotive Parts Manufacturer

One of the companies I worked with was a mid-sized automotive parts manufacturer facing challenges meeting its production targets due to long cycle times. The factory was consistently running behind schedule, leading to missed delivery deadlines and increased overtime costs. Despite running extra shifts, the company couldn't keep up with customer demand, and morale on the shop floor was low due to the pressure of working long hours.

The first step in addressing this problem was to conduct a *workflow analysis* to identify where bottlenecks were occurring. After mapping out the entire production process, we discovered that much of the delay occurred during changeovers between product lines. These changeovers required machines to be retooled and recalibrated, taking an average of 90 minutes per shift.

To reduce changeover times, we implemented *Single-Minute Exchange of Die (SMED)* techniques, which focus on reducing the time it takes to switch from one production run to the next. This involved training staff to perform parts of the changeover process while the machines were still running (external setup), reorganising tools and parts to reduce search time, and standardising procedures across shifts. Within two months, we reduced the average changeover time from 90 minutes to 35 minutes, a 61% improvement.

The reduction in cycle time dramatically impacted the company's ability to meet production targets. By improving throughput, the factory could fulfil customer orders on time without relying on overtime. This reduced labour costs and boosted employee morale, as workers no longer had to work extended shifts regularly. The improvements also allowed the company to take on new contracts, driving revenue growth.

Case Study 2: Implementing Lean Principles in a Consumer Goods Manufacturer

In another project, I worked with a consumer goods manufacturer struggling with high levels of waste and inefficiency in its production process. The company's scrap rate was 15%, well above industry standards, and significant amounts of raw materials were wasted due to overproduction, defects, and inefficient workflows.

We decided to take a Lean approach, focusing on waste reduction and process optimisation. The first step was to conduct a Value Stream Mapping (VSM) exercise to identify non-value-added activities across the production process. Through VSM, we found that the company was producing too many products in anticipation of customer demand, leading to overproduction and excess inventory. Additionally, we identified frequent rework due to quality issues arising from inconsistent process control.

To address these problems, we implemented a series of Lean initiatives, starting with Kanban, a just-in-time inventory system that aligns production with actual customer demand. Using visual signals to trigger production, the company could reduce overproduction and minimise excess inventory. Next, we applied Kaizen principles to improve quality by involving employees in continuous improvement efforts. Cross-functional teams were formed to address quality issues, focusing on standardising work processes and improving communication between departments.

Within six months, the company saw remarkable results. The scrap rate dropped from 15% to 8%, thanks to better process control and employee involvement in identifying root causes of defects. The Kanban system helped reduce inventory by 20%, freeing up warehouse space and reducing carrying costs. The company also experienced a 10% improvement in overall productivity as employees became more engaged in continuous improvement efforts.

These two case studies highlight the transformative power of operational efficiency. Both companies achieved significant cost savings, improved product quality, and enhanced customer satisfaction by reducing waste, optimising processes, and engaging employees in improvement initiatives. For COOs, these examples demonstrate that even small changes can lead to substantial improvements when operational efficiency is prioritised.

2.10 - Overcoming Efficiency Challenges

Achieving and sustaining operational efficiency is not without its challenges. In the complex and dynamic manufacturing world, COOs often face various obstacles that can hinder their efforts to improve efficiency. These challenges can range from resistance to change to technological limitations, but they can be effectively overcome with the right strategies. This section will explore some of the most common efficiency challenges and practical solutions for addressing them.

One of the most prevalent challenges is resistance to change. Employees, particularly those in the company for a long time, may resist new methods, technologies, or processes. This resistance often stems from a fear of the unknown, concerns about job security, or simply a preference for the status quo. To overcome this obstacle, COOs must focus on change management and communication. Explaining the reasons for the changes, involving employees in the decision-making process, and demonstrating how the changes will benefit the company and workforce can help reduce resistance. In one organisation I worked with, we held town hall meetings where employees could voice their concerns and ask questions about new process changes. We successfully implemented Lean practices with minimal resistance by addressing their fears and providing thorough training.

Another common challenge is the lack of data visibility. In many manufacturing environments, decisions are made based on intuition or historical practices rather than data-driven insights. Without real-time data, it's difficult to accurately assess performance, identify inefficiencies, or predict issues before they arise. To solve this problem, COOs should invest in data analytics and automation tools that provide real-time monitoring and reporting. Implementing systems such as ERP or MES (Manufacturing Execution Systems) allows companies to track key performance metrics in real-time, enabling quicker responses to inefficiencies. In one of my previous roles, introducing a real-time production monitoring system helped us identify machine downtime issues early, leading to a 10% improvement in overall equipment effectiveness (OEE).

Skill gaps can also pose a significant challenge to efficiency improvement efforts. As manufacturing operations become more automated and technology-driven, there is a growing need for workers with technical skills to operate and maintain these systems. However, many manufacturers struggle to find qualified workers, and upskilling existing staff can be lengthy. To address this, COOs should prioritise training and development initiatives. In one plant, we launched a cross-training programme that allowed employees to rotate between different roles, gaining the skills needed to operate new technologies. This filled skill gaps and improved workforce flexibility, enabling us to adjust to changing production needs more efficiently.

Supply chain disruptions are another major challenge derailing even the most efficient manufacturing operations. Global events such as natural disasters, pandemics, or geopolitical tensions can disrupt the flow of materials and components, leading to production delays and increased costs. To mitigate this risk, COOs should focus on building a more resilient supply chain. This could involve diversifying suppliers, building stronger relationships with key vendors, and maintaining a buffer of critical materials. In one company I worked with, we reduced reliance on a single supplier by developing alternative sources in different regions. This reduced the impact of supply chain disruptions and gave us more leverage in negotiating better terms with suppliers.

Finally, outdated technology can be a significant barrier to improving operational efficiency. Many manufacturing operations still rely on legacy systems that are slow, inefficient, and unable to integrate with modern technologies. Upgrading to new, more efficient systems can be costly and time-consuming, but it is often necessary to achieve long-term efficiency gains. To overcome this challenge, COOs should develop a technology roadmap that outlines a phased approach to upgrading systems. By starting with the most critical areas, such as automating repetitive tasks or implementing real-time data monitoring, companies can begin to see the benefits of modernisation without disrupting the entire operation. In one of my roles, we introduced robotic process automation (RPA) to handle manual data entry tasks. This freed up employees to focus on more value-added activities and reduced errors.

In conclusion, while efficiency challenges are common in manufacturing, they are not insurmountable. By addressing resistance to change, investing in data visibility and technology, upskilling the workforce, and building supply chain resilience, COOs can overcome these obstacles and drive sustainable improvements in operational efficiency. The key is to approach each challenge strategically, using a combination of clear communication, data-driven decision-making, and continuous improvement efforts to ensure that the organisation remains agile, competitive, and efficient.

Chapter 3

Financial Acumen for COOs

> "In operations, the smallest improvement can create the biggest impact."
>
> **Robert N. Jacobs**

This chapter introduces COOs to the critical financial skills required for operational success. Understanding key financial metrics, such as gross profit margin, operating margin, and return on investment (ROI), enables COOs to make data-driven decisions that align operational efficiency with the organisation's broader financial goals. The chapter also delves into budgeting, forecasting, and cost control strategies, essential for maintaining profitability and cash flow stability in today's competitive markets. Through detailed examples and case studies, this chapter empowers COOs to enhance their financial acumen, ensuring their operational strategies not only support but also enhance financial performance and long-term business success.

3.1 - Understanding Key Financial Metrics

For COOs, understanding financial metrics is not just about tracking profitability; it's about making informed decisions that impact every aspect of the business. Key financial metrics provide a clear picture of operational health, guide strategic decisions, and allow COOs to measure the effectiveness of their actions in driving efficiency and value creation. While finance may traditionally be viewed as the domain of CFOs, successful COOs must also have a firm grasp of financial principles to ensure operational decisions align with the company's broader financial objectives.

One of the most important financial metrics for COOs is gross profit margin. This metric represents the difference between revenue and the cost of goods sold (COGS) as a percentage of revenue. Essentially, it shows how much money is left after covering the direct production costs, such as raw materials and labour, before accounting for overheads. A declining gross profit margin could indicate rising production costs or pricing pressure, prompting the COO to look for ways to cut costs or increase operational efficiency. I remember working with a manufacturing company where rising material costs eroded the gross profit margin. We restored profitability by renegotiating supplier contracts and improving production processes to reduce waste.

Operating margin, another critical metric, shows the percentage of revenue left after all operating expenses, including administrative and selling costs, have been deducted. This metric provides insight into how efficiently the business is being run from an operational standpoint. Improving the operating margin for a COO could involve streamlining processes, reducing overhead, or enhancing productivity. In one of my roles, we improved the operating margin by automating certain labour-intensive processes, reducing headcount and overtime costs while maintaining output.

Return on Assets (ROA) is essential for assessing how effectively the company uses its assets to generate profits. ROA measures how efficiently management deploys its assets, such as machinery, inventory, and equipment, to produce income. A low ROA might indicate that the company is underutilising its assets or carrying excess capacity. To address this, a COO might improve machine utilisation rates or liquidate underperforming assets. In one project, we improved ROA by identifying and offloading idle machinery and reallocating resources to higher-demand product lines.

Return on Investment (ROI) is a particularly important metric when evaluating the success of capital investments or projects. ROI measures the profitability of an investment relative to its cost. For COOs, it's essential to understand the expected ROI when considering major investments, such as new production lines, automation technologies, or facility expansions. For instance, when I was involved in a project to implement a new automated packaging system, we calculated that the ROI would be realised within 18 months through labour cost savings and increased output. A clear understanding of ROI helped us make a strong business case for the investment.

Another key financial metric is inventory turnover, which measures how often a company sells and replaces its stock of goods. High inventory turnover indicates efficient inventory management and strong sales, while low turnover suggests overstocking or weak demand. Managing inventory turnover is critical for a COO, as excess inventory ties up capital and increases carrying costs, while insufficient inventory can lead to stockouts and lost sales. In one case, we reduced our inventory turnover cycle by implementing a just-in-time (JIT) system, which improved cash flow and reduced storage costs.

Working capital is another vital concept that COOs need to monitor closely. Working capital is the difference between a company's assets (cash, inventory, and receivables) and liabilities (payables and short-term debt). Positive working capital means a company can meet its short-term obligations, while negative working capital indicates potential liquidity issues. For COOs, managing working capital efficiently involves optimising inventory levels, reducing the time it takes to collect receivables, and negotiating favourable payment terms with suppliers. In one business I managed, we improved working capital by reducing the day's sales outstanding (DSO) through better credit control and more aggressive collection efforts.

Earnings Before Interest, Taxes, Depreciation, and Amortisation (EBITDA) is a widely used measure of profitability that focuses on the company's core operational performance, excluding the effects of capital structure, taxes, and non-cash accounting items. EBITDA is a useful metric for COOs because it highlights the company's operational efficiency without being influenced by financial or accounting decisions. By improving EBITDA, COOs can demonstrate the effectiveness of operational improvements. In one organisation, we focused on improving EBITDA by reducing waste in production and increasing efficiency on the shop floor, which led to a 5% increase in operating profit within a year.

In conclusion, understanding and monitoring key financial metrics such as gross profit margin, operating margin, ROA, ROI, inventory turnover, working capital, and EBITDA is crucial for COOs. These metrics provide insights into how effectively the company is running its operations, highlight areas for improvement, and help align operational decisions with financial performance. By developing financial acumen, COOs can make data-driven decisions that enhance efficiency, profitability, and long-term business success.

3.2 - Budgeting and Forecasting

Budgeting and forecasting are essential responsibilities for any COO, as they provide the financial blueprint for operational planning and ensure that the organisation remains on track to meet its financial and strategic objectives. Developing accurate financial plans requires an understanding of past performance and the ability to anticipate future needs, challenges, and opportunities. For COOs, effective budgeting and forecasting involve close collaboration with other departments, especially finance, and a thorough understanding of the factors that drive costs and revenues in the manufacturing sector.

The first step in the budgeting process is to establish clear operational goals. These goals should align with the company's overall strategic objectives and provide a roadmap for the budget. For example, suppose the company is focused on expanding production capacity. In that case, the budget must reflect increased capital expenditures for new machinery or facilities and the associated labour and material costs. Conversely, if the focus is on cost reduction, the budget should prioritise investments in efficiency-enhancing technologies, process improvements, or supplier negotiations.

When developing a budget, COOs must pay close attention to fixed and variable costs. Fixed costs, such as rent, salaries, and insurance, remain constant regardless of production levels, while variable costs, such as raw materials, energy, and labour, fluctuate with production volume. A deep understanding of these cost structures allows COOs to develop more accurate budgets that account for potential fluctuations in demand. We faced a sharp rise in material costs in one project due to supplier issues. By reviewing our cost structure and adjusting procurement strategies, we were able to mitigate the impact on the budget and protect our margins.

Scenario planning is an invaluable tool in the forecasting process, particularly in volatile or uncertain markets. By developing multiple budget scenarios, such as best-case, worst-case, and most likely outcomes, COOs can prepare for various contingencies and ensure the organisation is ready to respond to unexpected challenges. In my experience, this approach proved particularly useful during economic downturns. By preparing a conservative budget that accounted for potential drops in demand and price increases in raw materials, we could adjust quickly when market conditions worsened.

Rolling forecasts are another technique COOs can use to maintain flexibility in their financial planning. Unlike traditional static budgets, typically set annually, rolling forecasts are updated regularly, often quarterly or monthly, to reflect changing conditions. This approach allows COOs to make more informed decisions throughout the year and adjust spending or investment plans as needed. For example, during a period of rapid growth, we implemented rolling forecasts to ensure that we had enough capacity to meet increasing demand while avoiding unnecessary capital expenditures.

A key component of effective budgeting is cross-functional collaboration. COOs must work closely with finance, sales, and other departments to ensure their budget aligns with the organisation's broader objectives and incorporates input from all relevant stakeholders. This collaborative approach ensures that the budget is realistic and that all departments work toward the same goals. In one case, I led a cross-functional budgeting process that involved production, finance, and sales teams. By aligning our forecasts with expected sales growth and production capacity, we developed a budget that supported our expansion plans while maintaining tight cost control.

Monitoring and adjusting the budget throughout the year is essential to staying on track. Unexpected events, such as equipment breakdowns, supplier disruptions, or shifts in customer demand, can quickly throw even the most carefully planned budget off course.

Regular budget reviews and variance analysis help COOs identify where actual performance deviates from the plan and make the necessary adjustments. In one instance, we faced higher-than-expected overtime costs due to a production bottleneck. Reviewing the budget and reallocating resources, we addressed the issue without exceeding our overall labour budget.

Technology plays a critical role in modern budgeting and forecasting. Advanced financial planning software and integrated ERP systems provide COOs with real-time data on costs, revenues, and operational performance. These tools allow for more accurate forecasting and easier tracking of progress against the budget. In one company I worked with, we implemented a new financial planning system that automated much of the budgeting process and provided real-time visibility into key financial metrics. This improved our forecasting accuracy and allowed us to make faster, data-driven decisions.

Cash flow forecasting is another vital element of financial planning. While budgets focus on income and expenses, cash flow forecasting ensures the company has enough liquidity to meet its short-term obligations. This is particularly important in manufacturing, where large capital investments and long lead times can strain cash flow. By forecasting cash inflows and outflows, COOs can ensure that the company remains solvent and avoids liquidity crises. In one situation, we used cash flow forecasting to identify potential shortfalls during a major expansion project, allowing us to secure financing in advance and avoid disruptions.

In conclusion, budgeting and forecasting are critical to any manufacturing business's financial planning and operational success. For COOs, developing accurate, flexible, and data-driven budgets and forecasts is essential in ensuring that resources are allocated efficiently and that the company remains on track to achieve its strategic goals. By understanding cost structures, engaging in scenario planning, and leveraging advanced technology, COOs can create financial plans that reflect current realities and anticipate future challenges and opportunities. Moreover, regular monitoring and collaboration across departments ensure these plans remain dynamic and responsive to the ever-changing business environment.

3.3 - Cost Control Strategies

Cost control is at the heart of operational success, particularly in the manufacturing sector, where margins are often thin, and any inefficiencies can quickly erode profitability. COOs must deeply understand the company's cost structure and implement strategies to manage and reduce costs without compromising quality or operational effectiveness. Successful cost control requires a combination of disciplined spending, continuous process improvement, and strategic investment in efficiency-enhancing technologies.

One of the most fundamental cost control strategies is process optimisation. Streamlining processes can significantly reduce both direct and indirect costs. This might involve eliminating bottlenecks, automating repetitive tasks, or reducing lead times. For example, in one company I worked with, we reduced costs by implementing Lean manufacturing principles, which focused on eliminating waste and reducing the time spent on non-value-added activities. Reengineering workflows and introducing cellular manufacturing cut production time by 20%, directly reducing labour costs and improving productivity.

Labour costs are a major expense in any manufacturing operation, and managing these costs effectively is crucial to maintaining profitability. One way to control labour costs is through workforce optimisation. This involves ensuring that employees are deployed efficiently, with the right people in the right roles at the right time. Cross-training employees so they can perform multiple tasks, for example, can increase flexibility and reduce downtime. In one plant I managed, we introduced a flexible workforce system where employees were trained in several functions, allowing us to reduce overtime by redistributing labour across departments during peak periods.

Energy efficiency is another area where significant cost savings can be achieved. Manufacturing operations often consume large amounts of energy; even small energy-use improvements can lead to substantial cost reductions. Investing in energy-efficient machinery, implementing energy-saving practices, and using data analytics to monitor energy consumption are all effective strategies. In one case, we installed energy-efficient lighting and upgraded our HVAC systems, which resulted in a 15% reduction in overall energy costs. We also implemented a system to shut down non-essential equipment during off-peak hours, reducing energy usage.

Supplier negotiations play a critical role in managing material costs. COOs must work closely with procurement teams to negotiate favourable terms with suppliers, whether securing volume discounts, locking prices through long-term contracts, or exploring alternative suppliers to increase competition. In one instance, we reduced material costs by 8% by consolidating our supplier base and negotiating bulk purchase agreements, which gave us better pricing and improved delivery reliability. Establishing strong relationships with suppliers also allowed us to negotiate more favourable payment terms, improving our cash flow.

Another cost control strategy involves inventory management. Excess inventory ties up working capital and incurs carrying costs, such as storage, insurance, and the risk of obsolescence. Conversely, insufficient inventory can lead to stockouts and production delays. Implementing inventory control techniques, such as Just-in-Time (JIT) inventory or Economic Order Quantity (EOQ), can help optimise stock levels and reduce costs. In one project, we reduced inventory carrying costs by 12% by switching to a JIT system, which aligned material orders with actual production needs and minimised excess stock.

Maintenance costs are another area where COOs can find savings opportunities. While equipment breakdowns are inevitable, a proactive approach to maintenance can help reduce the frequency and cost of repairs. Predictive maintenance uses real-time data from machinery to identify potential issues before they lead to breakdowns, allowing for timely interventions that minimise downtime and repair costs. In one factory, we implemented predictive maintenance using sensors that monitored equipment health. This system allowed us to reduce unplanned downtime by 25%, translating into significant cost savings, particularly in avoiding costly emergency repairs and production stoppages.

Outsourcing non-core activities is another effective way to control costs. For many manufacturers, logistics, IT support, or even some production elements can be outsourced to third-party providers who can perform these functions more efficiently or at a lower cost. When done correctly, outsourcing allows the company to focus on its core competencies while reducing overhead. In one of my roles, we outsourced our non-essential IT functions to a specialist provider, which reduced our IT costs by 30% and improved service reliability. However, it's important to ensure that outsourcing arrangements are carefully managed to avoid issues related to quality control or service disruptions.

Standardising parts and processes can also drive down costs. By using standardised components across different product lines, manufacturers can achieve economies of scale and reduce the complexity of their supply chains. Similarly, standardising work processes across shifts or locations can increase efficiency and lower training costs. In one instance, we standardised the components used in our product designs, which allowed us to consolidate suppliers and negotiate better pricing. This change resulted in a 10% reduction in material costs and simplified our inventory management process.

Lastly, cost-benefit analysis is a critical tool for managing and reducing costs. Before implementing new initiatives or making major investments, COOs should conduct a thorough cost-benefit analysis to ensure that the expected benefits outweigh the costs. This analysis should include direct costs, such as capital expenditures and labour, and indirect costs, such as potential downtime during implementation or training requirements. In one project, we considered implementing a new automation system. Still, after conducting a detailed cost-benefit analysis, we determined that the upfront costs outweighed the potential savings in the short term. This analysis allowed us to delay the investment until we were better positioned to achieve a strong ROI.

In conclusion, effective cost-control strategies are essential for maintaining profitability in manufacturing. By focusing on process optimisation, labour efficiency, energy management, supplier negotiations, inventory control, and preventive maintenance, COOs can drive down costs without compromising quality. Outsourcing, standardisation, and cost-benefit analysis further enhance the ability to manage costs effectively. For COOs, mastering these strategies is crucial to ensuring the business's long-term financial health and operational success.

3.4 - Investment Decisions

Capital investments play a significant role in the long-term success of any manufacturing operation. Whether upgrading machinery, expanding production capacity, or implementing new technologies, investment decisions can impact a company's operational efficiency and profitability. For COOs, evaluating capital investment opportunities requires a deep understanding of operational needs and financial metrics. This ensures that investments align with strategic goals and deliver a strong return on investment (ROI).

The first step in evaluating capital investments is to assess the strategic alignment of the investment. Does the investment support the company's broader objectives, such as expanding into new markets, increasing production capacity, or improving efficiency? For example, if the company's strategy involves diversifying its product offerings, investing in flexible manufacturing systems that can handle multiple product lines may be smart. In one instance, we invested in a new automated production line because it aligned with the company's goal of reducing lead times and increasing output to meet growing customer demand. This investment improved operational efficiency and positioned us to capture additional market share.

Cost-benefit analysis is a critical tool for evaluating capital investment opportunities. This involves comparing the upfront costs of the investment with the expected benefits, such as increased production capacity, reduced labour costs, or improved product quality. The analysis should include both direct and indirect costs, as well as tangible and intangible benefits. For instance, when evaluating a decision to implement a new ERP system, we considered the software and training costs and the potential productivity gains from better data visibility and improved decision-making. While the initial cost was high, the long-term benefits outweighed the investment, and the system paid for itself within two years.

The payback period is another important financial metric when evaluating capital investments. It is the time it takes for the investment to generate enough savings or profits to cover its initial cost. While a shorter payback period is generally preferable, COOs should also consider the long-term benefits of the investment. We invested in energy-efficient equipment with a four-year payback period in one project. Although the payback period was relatively long, the investment significantly reduced our energy costs, leading to substantial savings over the life of the equipment.

Net Present Value (NPV) is a more sophisticated financial metric that considers the time value of money. NPV measures the difference between the present value of cash inflows and the present value of cash outflows over the life of the investment. A positive NPV indicates that the investment is expected to generate more value than it costs, while a negative NPV suggests that the investment may not be worthwhile. In one case, we used NPV analysis to evaluate the purchase of a new automated assembly system. We determined that the investment would generate a positive NPV by discounting future cash flows, making it a financially sound decision.

Internal Rate of Return (IRR) is another key metric for evaluating investment decisions. IRR is the discount rate at which the NPV of an investment becomes zero, effectively representing the expected annual rate of return. A higher IRR indicates a more attractive investment. COOs should compare the IRR of potential investments to the company's cost of capital to determine whether the investment will likely generate a sufficient return. In one instance, we had to choose between two investment opportunities, one with a higher upfront cost but a shorter payback period and a higher IRR. By comparing both options, we chose the investment with the higher IRR, which offered better long-term returns.

Risk assessment is another critical component of capital investment evaluation. All investments carry some risk, whether the risk of cost overruns, implementation delays, or changes in market conditions. COOs should conduct a thorough risk assessment to identify potential challenges and develop mitigation strategies. We invested in a new production line in one project to meet increasing demand. However, before proceeding, we conducted a risk analysis highlighting potential supply chain disruptions as a major risk. As a result, we built contingency plans into the investment, securing alternative suppliers and developing flexible production schedules to minimise the impact of any disruptions.

In addition to financial metrics, COOs should consider operational impact when evaluating capital investments. Will the investment lead to disruptions in production during installation? Will employees need to be retrained to operate new equipment? How will the investment affect existing workflows? For example, when implementing a new automation system in one facility, we carefully planned the installation to minimise downtime and scheduled extensive training for operators. This proactive approach ensured a smooth transition and maximised the benefits of the investment from day one.

In conclusion, evaluating capital investment opportunities is a critical responsibility for COOs. By considering strategic alignment, conducting cost-benefit analysis, and using financial metrics such as payback period, NPV, and IRR, COOs can make informed investment decisions that drive long-term operational efficiency and profitability. Additionally, a thorough risk assessment and consideration of the operational impact ensure that investments are implemented smoothly and deliver the expected returns. For COOs, evaluating and executing smart capital investments is key to maintaining a competitive edge in the manufacturing industry.

Operations align with the company's financial goals. Additionally, clear communication of financial insights to stakeholders is essential for fostering collaboration and ensuring that the organisation remains on track to achieve its objectives.

3.5 - Financial Reporting

Financial reporting is vital to a COO's role, providing the transparency and data needed to make informed decisions that drive operational and financial success. Effective financial reporting enables COOs to monitor the organisation's health, identify trends, and make proactive adjustments to ensure the business remains on track to meet its goals. While financial reports are often seen as the domain of CFOs, COOs must also understand how to interpret these reports to align operational performance with financial outcomes.

Financial reporting involves preparing and analysing key financial statements, including the balance sheet, income statement, and cash flow statement. Each document provides a different perspective on the company's financial position, and COOs must be adept at using them to guide operational decisions.

The income statement (the profit and loss statement) is perhaps the most directly relevant financial report for COOs, as it provides a detailed breakdown of the company's revenues, costs, and profits over a specific period. By closely monitoring the income statement, COOs can identify where operational costs are rising and where efficiencies can be gained. For instance, if labour costs are increasing faster than revenue, this may signal the need for a review of staffing levels or the introduction of automation to reduce dependence on manual labour. In one organisation I worked with, we noticed a steady rise in overtime costs, negatively impacting our gross profit margin. By adjusting production schedules and cross-training staff, we reduced overtime costs and improved profitability.

The balance sheet provides a snapshot of the company's assets, liabilities, and equity at a given time. For COOs, the balance sheet is particularly useful for understanding the company's resource allocation and financial stability. Key figures like inventory levels, receivables, and payables can provide insight into how efficiently the company manages its working capital. For example, if inventory levels are consistently high, it may indicate overproduction or poor inventory management, which ties up capital that could be better used elsewhere. We used a balance sheet analysis in one company to identify excess inventory that had been building up over time. We freed up cash flow and reduced carrying costs by implementing more effective inventory control measures.

The cash flow statement tracks the company's cash inflows and outflows over a period and provides insight into the company's liquidity. For COOs, understanding cash flow is critical, as it directly impacts the ability to fund operations, pay suppliers, and invest in growth. Positive cash flow ensures that the company can meet its obligations and invest in capital improvements, while negative cash flow signals potential liquidity issues that must be addressed. In one case, we faced a period of negative cash flow due to an expansion project. By delaying non-essential capital expenditures and renegotiating payment terms with suppliers, we managed our cash flow more effectively and avoided potential disruptions.

Variance analysis is another important tool in financial reporting that allows COOs to compare actual financial performance against the budget or forecast. Variance analysis helps identify areas where costs exceed expectations or revenues fall short. For example, if production costs are higher than budgeted, the COO can investigate the root causes, such as increased material costs or lower-than-expected productivity, and take corrective action. In one organisation, we identified a significant variance in material costs due to inefficiencies in the supply chain. By renegotiating contracts and streamlining procurement processes, we brought costs back in line with the budget.

Key performance indicators (KPIs) are essential to financial reporting and analysis for COOs. Financial KPIs, such as gross profit margin, return on assets (ROA), and operating margin, provide a high-level overview of the company's financial health and operational efficiency. Non-financial KPIs, such as production cycle time, machine utilisation, and first-pass yield, also offer valuable insights into how well the operation is performing. For COOs, regularly reviewing KPIs with financial reports allows for a more comprehensive business view. In one manufacturing plant, we introduced a KPI dashboard that integrated financial and operational metrics, providing a real-time performance overview across departments. This helped us quickly identify issues and make data-driven decisions to improve operational efficiency and profitability.

Effective financial reporting also involves ensuring accuracy and timeliness. Outdated or inaccurate financial reports can lead to poor decision-making and missed opportunities. COOs must work closely with the finance department to ensure that financial reports are generated regularly, typically monthly or quarterly, and reflect the most current and accurate data. In one case, delays in financial reporting led to missed opportunities to address rising material costs, which impacted our profitability for several months. By improving our reporting processes and ensuring that data was available in real-time, we were able to act more quickly and make informed decisions that protected our margins.

Technology plays a crucial role in modern financial reporting and analysis. Advanced financial reporting software and integrated enterprise resource planning (ERP) systems allow COOs to access real-time financial data and generate reports more efficiently. These systems also provide forecasting, budgeting, and scenario analysis tools, helping COOs plan for the future more accurately. In one organisation, we implemented an ERP system that integrated financial data from across the business, allowing us to automate many of our reporting processes and significantly reduce the time it took to generate reports. This real-time access to financial data allowed us to make quicker, more informed decisions about resource allocation and cost control.

Lastly, effective financial reporting is not just about analysing the numbers; it's about communication. COOs must be able to interpret financial data and communicate it clearly to other stakeholders, including the CEO, board of directors, and department heads. This involves presenting the financial results, explaining the operational drivers behind them, and recommending actions to improve performance. In one of my previous roles, we held monthly financial review meetings where I presented operational insights alongside the financial data. This approach ensured everyone understood how operational decisions impacted the bottom line and fostered collaboration across departments to improve performance.

In conclusion, effective financial reporting and analysis are critical for COOs to monitor the organisation's health, make informed decisions, and drive operational and financial success. By regularly reviewing key financial statements, conducting variance analysis, tracking KPIs, and leveraging technology, COOs can ensure that their operations align with the company's financial goals. Additionally, clear communication of financial insights to stakeholders is essential for fostering collaboration and ensuring that the organisation remains on track to achieve its objectives.

3.6 - Cost-Benefit Analysis

Cost-benefit analysis (CBA) is a powerful decision-making tool that allows COOs to assess the financial implications of various operational strategies and investments. By weighing the expected costs against the anticipated benefits, COOs can make informed decisions that maximise value for the business while minimising risk. CBA helps ensure that resources are allocated efficiently and that investments or process changes provide a strong return on investment (ROI).

At its most basic level, cost-benefit analysis involves calculating the total costs associated with a decision, such as labour, materials, capital expenditures, and any potential downtime, and comparing them to the expected benefits, which may include increased revenue, reduced costs, improved productivity, or enhanced customer satisfaction. However, to be effective, CBAs must go beyond simply tallying numbers; they should also consider intangible benefits and opportunity costs that may not be immediately quantifiable.

One of the first steps in conducting a CBA is identifying and quantifying costs. This includes direct costs, such as capital expenditures for new equipment, and indirect costs, such as training employees to use the new system or the potential disruption to production during implementation. For example, when evaluating whether to invest in a new automated packaging line, we calculated the upfront costs of purchasing the equipment, installing it, and training staff and the potential downtime during installation. Additionally, we considered the ongoing maintenance costs and potential savings from reduced labour.

Next, the COO must estimate the benefits associated with the decision. These benefits might include increased production capacity, reduced labour costs, improved quality, or faster lead times. In the case of the automated packaging line, we estimated that it would lead to a 25% increase in throughput and a 20% reduction in labour costs, as fewer workers would be needed to operate the system. Additionally, the improved speed and accuracy of the packaging process would reduce errors, leading to fewer returns and higher customer satisfaction. These benefits were then quantified based on expected revenue growth and cost savings.

One of the challenges in cost-benefit analysis is accounting for intangible benefits that are difficult to quantify but still valuable to the business. For example, investing in a new employee training programme might not result in immediate financial gains. Still, it could improve employee retention, morale, and productivity. Similarly, investments in sustainability initiatives might enhance the company's reputation and attract new customers, even if the direct financial benefits are harder to measure. In one project I worked on, we invested in an energy-efficient production line to reduce energy costs and position the company as a leader in sustainability, which helped us win contracts with environmentally conscious clients.

Opportunity costs, the benefits forgone by choosing one option over another, are another critical consideration in CBA. For example, if a company upgrades existing machinery, the opportunity cost might be the potential gains from investing in a new product line instead. By considering opportunity costs, COOs can ensure they use the company's limited resources best. In one case, we had to decide between investing in a new production facility or upgrading our current machinery. After conducting a thorough CBA, we determined that the opportunity cost of delaying the new facility was too high, as it would limit our ability to meet future demand. As a result, we prioritised the expansion over the equipment upgrade.

Risk assessment is another important component of cost-benefit analysis. Every decision carries some risk, whether it's the risk of cost overruns, implementation delays, or lower-than-expected returns. COOs must evaluate these risks and consider how they could impact the overall costs and benefits of the decision. In one instance, we were evaluating whether to invest in a new production process that promised significant cost savings. However, after conducting a risk assessment, we identified potential supply chain disruptions that could negate some expected benefits. As a result, we developed contingency plans to mitigate these risks before proceeding with the investment.

Sensitivity analysis is a useful tool for understanding how changes in key assumptions, such as costs, demand, or interest rates, might affect the outcome of the cost-benefit analysis. By testing different scenarios, COOs can determine whether the decision is still viable under less favourable conditions. For example, in one project, we conducted a sensitivity analysis to evaluate how fluctuations in raw material prices would impact the ROI of a new production line. This analysis allowed us to build a buffer to account for potential price increases, ensuring the investment remained profitable even in a volatile market.

In conclusion, cost-benefit analysis is essential for COOs to evaluate the financial impact of operational decisions and investments. By carefully assessing both the costs and benefits, including intangible factors and opportunity costs, COOs can make informed decisions that align with the company's strategic objectives and drive long-term value. Additionally, conducting risk assessments and sensitivity analyses ensures that decisions are robust and resilient in the face of uncertainty. For COOs, mastering the art of cost-benefit analysis is key to ensuring that resources are used efficiently and that the business remains financially healthy and competitive.

3.7 - Profitability Improvement

Improving profitability is a core responsibility of every COO. In the manufacturing sector, where margins can be thin, even small efficiency gains or cost reductions can significantly impact the bottom line. For COOs, enhancing profit margins requires a combination of operational optimisation, cost control, strategic pricing, and continuous improvement.

One of the most effective strategies for improving profitability is process optimisation. By streamlining operations, eliminating bottlenecks, and reducing cycle times, COOs can increase throughput without incurring additional costs. Lean manufacturing principles, such as waste elimination and process standardisation, are powerful tools for driving these improvements. For example, in one factory I managed, we implemented Lean techniques to reduce setup times on our production lines. By adopting Single-Minute Exchange of Die (SMED) methods, we reduced changeover times by 40%, allowing us to increase production capacity without additional resources. This efficiency gain directly improved our profit margins by reducing labour costs and increasing output.

Cost reduction is another critical lever for improving profitability. While reducing costs is important, it's essential to do so in a way that doesn't compromise quality or operational efficiency. One approach is to reduce variable costs, such as raw materials, energy, and labour, without impacting fixed costs. For instance, in one project, we renegotiated supplier contracts to secure better pricing on raw materials, which reduced our cost of goods sold (COGS) by 8%. We also introduced energy-saving initiatives, such as installing energy-efficient lighting and upgrading our heating and cooling systems, reducing operational costs. These savings directly contributed to improved profit margins.

Pricing strategy is a key factor in profitability. COOs must work closely with the sales and finance teams to ensure pricing reflects customer value and production costs. Many companies fall into the trap of underpricing their products to capture market share, which can erode profitability. COOs should analyse the true cost of production and ensure that prices are set at a level that covers costs and generates a healthy margin. In one instance, we conducted a cost analysis that revealed our pricing model was too low, especially given the rising costs of raw materials. By adjusting our prices to reflect these costs, we improved gross margins without losing customers, as we effectively communicated the value of our products.

Product mix optimisation is another powerful strategy for improving profitability. Not all products deliver the same margin, and COOs must understand which products contribute the most to the bottom line. Companies can enhance overall profitability by shifting the focus toward higher-margin products and reducing or discontinuing low-margin offerings. For example, in one business, we identified that certain product lines generated much lower margins due to high production complexity and low customer demand. Reallocating resources to focus on our most profitable products improved profit margins and reduced production complexity, further contributing to operational efficiency.

Supply chain optimisation is another key area where COOs can improve profitability. Efficient supply chain management reduces costs, improves lead times, and enhances customer satisfaction. For example, implementing a Just-in-Time (JIT) inventory system can reduce carrying costs and free up working capital. In one case, we implemented JIT across our supply chain, which reduced inventory holding costs by 15% and improved cash flow. Additionally, by strengthening relationships with key suppliers and consolidating our supplier base, we negotiated better terms, further improving profitability.

Quality management also plays a vital role in profitability. Poor quality products can lead to rework, waste, and customer returns, eroding profit margins. By implementing a robust quality management system, such as Total Quality Management (TQM) or Six Sigma, COOs can reduce defects, improve first-pass yield, and minimise waste. In one factory, we used Six Sigma methodologies to identify the root causes of defects in our production process. By addressing these issues, we reduced defect rates by 20%, improving customer satisfaction and reducing the costs associated with rework and returns.

Another strategy for improving profitability is to invest in automation and technology. Automation reduces reliance on manual labour, increases consistency, and improves throughput. While the upfront cost of automation can be high, the long-term savings in labour costs and productivity gains can significantly improve profitability. In one manufacturing facility, we invested in robotic automation for part of our assembly line, which resulted in a 30% increase in production capacity and a 15% reduction in labour costs. These improvements had a direct and sustained impact on our profit margins.

Employee engagement is an often-overlooked factor in profitability improvement. Engaged employees are more productive, innovative, and committed to improving processes. COOs should focus on creating a culture of continuous improvement, where employees are encouraged to contribute ideas for enhancing efficiency and reducing costs. In one company, we implemented a suggestion programme that incentivised employees to propose cost-saving initiatives. Over a year, this programme led to several small but impactful changes, such as reducing material waste and improving machine setup times, collectively improving our profit margins by 5%.

Capacity utilisation is another key driver of profitability. Underutilised capacity results in wasted resources and higher per-unit costs. COOs must ensure production lines run as close to full capacity as possible without overburdening equipment or staff. This might involve adjusting production schedules, increasing marketing efforts to drive demand, or exploring new markets to increase order volumes. In one project, we improved capacity utilisation by offering discounts on large orders during off-peak production periods. This helped smooth out demand fluctuations and allowed us to keep our production lines running consistently, improving profitability by spreading fixed costs over larger units.

Finally, data-driven decision-making is critical for improving profitability. COOs must have access to real-time data on key performance indicators (KPIs) such as production efficiency, scrap rates, and labour costs. By leveraging this data, COOs can identify areas where profitability is eroded and take corrective action. In one organisation, we implemented a real-time dashboard that tracked operational and financial metrics across all departments. This visibility allowed us to spot inefficiencies and implement targeted improvements, resulting in a 7% improvement in operating profit within the first six months.

In conclusion, improving profitability requires a multifaceted approach encompassing process optimisation, cost control, strategic pricing, and supply chain efficiency. By focusing on quality, leveraging technology, engaging employees, and making data-driven decisions, COOs can drive sustained improvements in profit margins. For COOs, enhancing profitability is not just about cutting costs; it's about creating a more efficient, responsive, and value-driven organisation well-positioned for long-term success.

3.8 - Cash Flow Management

Cash flow management is one of the most critical aspects of financial health for any business, especially in the manufacturing sector, where large capital expenditures, long production cycles, and extended payment terms can strain liquidity. For COOs, ensuring a steady and positive cash flow is essential to maintaining operational stability, funding growth initiatives, and avoiding financial distress. Effective cash flow management involves monitoring cash inflows and outflows and implementing strategies to optimise working capital, improve payment terms, and minimise cash flow gaps.

At the core of cash flow management is accurately forecasting cash flow. This involves predicting the timing and amount of cash inflows (from customer payments) and outflows (for expenses such as payroll, materials, and overhead). COOs must work closely with finance teams to develop cash flow forecasts based on realistic assumptions about sales, production cycles, and payment terms. In one company I worked with, we faced a recurring cash flow crunch due to delayed customer payments. By developing a more detailed cash flow forecast and adjusting our payment terms, we were able to smooth out these fluctuations and maintain a positive cash position.

Optimising working capital is one of the most effective ways to improve cash flow. Working capital is the difference between a company's current assets (cash, inventory, and receivables) and its current liabilities (payables and short-term debt). Positive working capital ensures the company can meet its short-term obligations, while negative working capital can lead to liquidity issues. One key strategy for optimising working capital is to reduce inventory levels. Excess inventory ties up cash that could be used to fund operations or invest in growth. Implementing inventory management techniques such as Just-in-Time (JIT) or Economic Order Quantity (EOQ) can help reduce inventory levels without impacting production. In one project, we implemented JIT and reduced our inventory carrying costs by 12%, which freed up cash and improved our liquidity position.

Managing accounts receivable (AR) is another critical component of cash flow management. Late customer payments can create significant cash flow gaps, putting pressure on the company's ability to meet its obligations. To address this, COOs should work closely with the finance team to implement credit control measures and improve the efficiency of collections. This might involve offering early payment discounts to incentivise faster payments or tightening credit terms for customers with poor payment histories. In one organisation, we reduced our day's sales outstanding (DSO) by 15 days by introducing aggressive collections policies and offering a 2% discount for early payments. This had a direct positive impact on our cash flow, as we received payments more quickly.

Conversely, managing accounts payable (AP) involves negotiating favourable payment terms with suppliers. Extending payment terms allows the company to hold onto cash longer, improving liquidity. However, COOs must balance extending payment terms and maintaining strong supplier relationships. In one project, we negotiated extended payment terms with key suppliers, moving from 30-day to 60-day terms, providing additional working capital to support a major expansion project. At the same time, we ensured that these extended terms did not jeopardise our relationships with suppliers by maintaining open communication and committing to prompt payment within the agreed timeframe.

Minimising capital expenditures (CapEx) during periods of tight cash flow is another important strategy. While capital investments are often necessary for growth, they can strain cash flow, particularly if they require significant upfront spending. COOs should carefully evaluate capital investment decisions to ensure they align with the company's cash flow situation. In some cases, leasing equipment rather than purchasing it outright can help spread the cost over time and reduce the immediate impact on cash flow. In one case, we opted to lease new production machinery rather than purchase it outright, allowing us to preserve cash while upgrading our equipment.

Cash flow financing options, such as revolving credit lines or invoice factoring, can provide short-term liquidity to bridge cash flow gaps. While these options come with costs, they can be valuable tools for managing periods of negative cash flow or financing working capital needs during rapid growth. In one instance, we used invoice factoring to unlock cash tied up in accounts receivable, which allowed us to meet our payroll obligations during a seasonal sales slump. However, using these tools judiciously is important, as over-reliance on external financing can lead to increased financial risk.

Another strategy for improving cash flow is to focus on profitability. Increasing margins through process optimisation, cost control, and strategic pricing improves the company's bottom line and boosts cash flow. For example, we improved profitability in one project by reducing scrap rates and energy consumption, directly impacting our cash position. By increasing our profit margins, we generated more cash from each sale, which helped improve our overall liquidity.

Lastly, monitoring and managing cash flow on an ongoing basis is essential. COOs should regularly review cash flow reports, identify potential cash shortfalls, and take proactive steps to address them. This might involve delaying non-essential expenditures, renegotiating payment terms, or securing short-term financing. In one company, we implemented a weekly cash flow review process that allowed us to identify potential cash flow issues early and take corrective action. This proactive approach helped us avoid cash flow crises and maintain financial stability.

In conclusion, cash flow management is critical to ensuring a manufacturing business's financial health and liquidity. By optimising working capital, managing receivables and payables, controlling capital expenditures, and leveraging financing options, COOs can ensure that their organisations have the cash to operate effectively and fund growth initiatives. For COOs, effective cash flow management is not just about keeping the business afloat; it's about positioning the company for long-term success and financial stability.

3.9 - Financial Risk Management

Effective financial risk management is essential for COOs to safeguard their organisation's operational and financial health. A proactive approach to managing financial risks is crucial in the manufacturing sector, where external market conditions, raw material costs, and fluctuating demand can introduce significant volatility. COOs must identify their organisation's various financial risks, implement strategies to mitigate them and ensure the business remains resilient in the face of uncertainty.

One of the most common financial risks in manufacturing is market risk. This risk arises from changes in market conditions, such as fluctuating commodity prices, interest rates, or currency exchange rates. For example, if a manufacturer relies heavily on imported raw materials, exchange rate fluctuations can significantly impact the cost of those materials, affecting profitability. To manage this risk, COOs can consider implementing hedging strategies. Hedging through financial instruments such as forward contracts or options allows businesses to lock in exchange rates or commodity prices, providing greater cost predictability. In one case, we hedged against rising steel prices by securing contracts with our suppliers and protecting our margins from market volatility.

Another significant financial risk is liquidity risk, which is the possibility that the company may not have enough cash or liquid assets to meet its short-term obligations. Liquidity risk often arises from poor cash flow management, excessive debt, or unforeseen disruptions in operations. To mitigate liquidity risk, COOs must ensure that the company maintains sufficient working capital and access to credit lines. One effective strategy is to build cash reserves during periods of strong financial performance, which can serve as a buffer during downturns. In one organisation, we established a cash reserve policy that ensured we always had a minimum of three months of operating expenses in reserve, which provided a safety net during periods of market volatility.

Credit risk is another financial risk that COOs need to manage, especially in industries with long payment cycles or customers with uncertain creditworthiness. Credit risk refers to the potential that a customer will default on their payment obligations, leading to a loss of revenue. To manage credit risk, COOs should work closely with the finance team to implement credit control measures, such as performing thorough credit checks on new customers, setting appropriate credit limits, and monitoring outstanding receivables. In one project, we reduced our exposure to credit risk by implementing stricter credit terms for customers with poor payment histories. This helped reduce our accounts receivable turnover and improved our cash flow stability.

Operational risk is a broad category encompassing risks related to internal processes, systems, and human factors. For COOs, operational risks include equipment failures, supply chain disruptions, labour shortages, and cybersecurity threats. Managing operational risk involves identifying potential vulnerabilities in the organisation's operations and implementing measures to mitigate those risks. For example, investing in preventive maintenance and predictive analytics can help reduce the risk of equipment breakdowns, while diversifying the supplier base can reduce supply chain risk. In one manufacturing plant, we implemented a comprehensive preventive maintenance programme that reduced unplanned equipment downtime by 25%, mitigating the financial risks associated with production delays.

Supply chain risk is particularly relevant in manufacturing, where disruptions in the supply chain can lead to production delays, increased costs, and loss of revenue. Global events such as the COVID-19 pandemic have highlighted the vulnerability of supply chains to external shocks. COOs should focus on building supply chain resilience to mitigate supply chain risk. This might involve diversifying suppliers to avoid over-reliance on a single source, maintaining a safe stock of critical materials, and developing contingency plans to ensure continuity of supply in the event of disruptions. In one case, we diversified our supply base for key components, sourcing from domestic and international suppliers, which reduced the impact of geopolitical risks and ensured a steady flow of materials during times of crisis.

Interest rate risk is another financial risk that can impact the cost of borrowing and affect a company's financial performance. Rising interest rates can increase the cost of servicing debt, which may strain cash flow and reduce profitability. To manage interest rate risk, COOs should work with the finance team to evaluate the company's debt structure and consider locking in fixed interest rates on loans to avoid exposure to rising rates. In one project, we refinanced a portion of our debt at a fixed rate, which protected us from future interest rate increases and provided greater financial stability.

Regulatory risk is the risk that changes in laws or regulations will negatively impact the company's financial performance. In the manufacturing sector, regulatory risks can include environmental regulations, labour laws, or changes in tax policy. To mitigate regulatory risk, COOs must stay informed about potential regulatory changes and ensure that the organisation complies with all relevant laws and standards. Additionally, engaging with industry associations or lobbying efforts can help shape regulatory policy to benefit the business. In one instance, we proactively invested in environmentally friendly technologies ahead of new environmental regulations, ensuring compliance and positioning the company as a leader in sustainability.

Cybersecurity risk has become an increasingly significant concern for manufacturers as operations become more digitally integrated. A cyberattack can disrupt production, compromise sensitive data, and result in significant financial losses. To mitigate cybersecurity risk, COOs must ensure the company's IT infrastructure is robust and secure. This includes implementing firewalls, encryption, and intrusion detection systems, regularly updating software and conducting cybersecurity training for employees. In one project, we worked closely with the IT department to implement a comprehensive cybersecurity plan that included regular system audits and employee training, which reduced our exposure to cyber threats.

Finally, strategic risk refers to the risk that the company's business strategy may not deliver the expected results due to changes in market conditions, technological advancements, or competitive pressures. To manage strategic risk, COOs must regularly review and adapt the company's strategic plan to changing circumstances. This might involve pivoting to new markets, investing in innovation, or adjusting pricing strategies to stay competitive. In one case, we faced significant competitive pressure from lower-cost manufacturers in emerging markets. By shifting our focus to premium products and investing in advanced manufacturing technologies, we were able to differentiate our offerings and protect our market share.

In conclusion, financial risk management is a critical responsibility for COOs, especially in the volatile and complex environment of the manufacturing sector. By identifying and mitigating market, liquidity, credit, operational, and regulatory risks, COOs can safeguard their organisation's financial health and ensure long-term success. A proactive approach to risk management, combined with hedging, diversification, and contingency planning tools, helps build a more resilient and adaptable business capable of thriving in uncertain times.

3.10 - Case Study: Financial Turnarounds and Success Stories

A successful financial turnaround in manufacturing is often the result of strategic leadership, disciplined cost management, and operational excellence. In this case study, I'll share two real-world examples from my experience demonstrating how financial acumen and operational improvements can lead to significant financial recovery and sustained profitability in manufacturing businesses.

Case Study 1: Turning Around a Failing Automotive Parts Manufacturer

One of the most challenging turnaround projects I managed involved an automotive parts manufacturer on the verge of bankruptcy due to declining sales, rising costs, and poor cash flow management. When I stepped in as COO, the company was experiencing consistent losses, and suppliers were starting to cut off credit due to unpaid bills. The situation was dire, and immediate action was needed to stabilise the business.

The first step in the turnaround was to assess the company's financial health and identify the key drivers of the losses. A thorough analysis of the financial statements revealed that the company's gross profit margin had been steadily declining due to rising raw material costs and inefficiencies in the production process. Additionally, the company was carrying excess inventory, tying up working capital and contributing to liquidity issues.

To address these challenges, we implemented a comprehensive cost-reduction programme that focused on three key areas: material costs, labour efficiency, and inventory management. First, we renegotiated contracts with key suppliers to secure better pricing on raw materials. We also introduced a Just-in-Time (JIT) inventory system, which reduced excess stock levels and freed up cash flow. By aligning material orders more closely with production needs, we reduced inventory carrying costs by 20% and improved liquidity.

Next, we focused on improving labour productivity. We reviewed the production process in detail and identified several bottlenecks causing delays and increasing labour costs. By streamlining workflows and investing in employee cross-training, we reduced overtime and improved overall efficiency. These changes led to a 15% reduction in labour costs within the first six months.

Finally, we implemented a working capital management strategy to improve cash flow. We tightened credit terms for customers and accelerated collections by offering early payment discounts. At the same time, we extended payment terms with suppliers to reduce the pressure on cash flow. These efforts improved our cash position and allowed us to pay down some of the outstanding debt threatening the company's relationships with suppliers.

Within a year, the company had returned to profitability, with gross margins improving by 10% and cash flow stabilising. Financial discipline, operational improvements, and strategic cost management drove the turnaround. The company secured new contracts with major automotive manufacturers, further solidifying its financial recovery.

Case Study 2: Improving Profitability at a Consumer Goods Manufacturer

In another project, I was brought in to help improve profitability at a consumer goods manufacturer struggling with thin margins and high production costs. The company's products were popular in the market. Still, rising raw material costs and inefficient production processes were eating into the profit margins, and the company could not capitalise on its strong sales.

The first step in the turnaround was to conduct a cost-benefit analysis of the production process to identify areas where costs could be reduced without compromising product quality. One key finding was that the company produced several low-margin products, consuming disproportionate resources. By shifting the product mix to focus on higher-margin items, we improved the overall profitability of the product line.

Next, we focused on reducing material waste in the production process. By implementing Lean manufacturing principles, including value stream mapping and kaizen events, we identified several opportunities to reduce scrap and rework. We also invested in equipment that improved production accuracy, reduced defects, and improved first-pass yield. These changes resulted in a 25% reduction in material waste and significantly improved the company's gross profit margin.

We also implemented a pricing strategy that better reflected the company's costs and market position. By conducting a detailed cost analysis, we identified that the company's pricing model had not kept pace with rising material and labour costs. We worked with the sales team to adjust prices for key products, which improved margins without negatively impacting sales. Additionally, we introduced a premium product line that commanded higher prices and offered better margins, further improving profitability.

Finally, we focused on improving supply chain efficiency. By consolidating suppliers and renegotiating contracts, we reduced lead times and secured better pricing on raw materials. We also implemented a vendor-managed inventory (VMI) system with key suppliers, which reduced inventory carrying costs and improved cash flow.

Within 18 months, the company's gross profit margin had improved by 15%, and net profitability had increased significantly. The combination of product mix optimisation, waste reduction, pricing strategy, and supply chain improvements allowed the company to improve its financial performance and position itself for long-term growth.

Chapter 4

Leading and Developing High-Performance Teams

> "A great COO turns complexity into clarity and challenges into opportunities."
>
> **Robert N. Jacobs**

In the fast-paced business world, high-performance teams are the backbone of any successful organisation. This chapter explores the essential elements required to build and nurture teams that can consistently deliver outstanding results. This chapter examines key leadership strategies, the role of trust and psychological safety, and the impact of clear communication on team performance. With practical insights from real-world experience, it emphasises how COOs can create an environment where teams are empowered, diverse, and fully aligned with the organisation's goals, leading to sustained success and innovation.

4.1 - Building High-Performance Teams

Building high-performance teams is fundamental to success in any organisation, especially in the fast-paced and demanding manufacturing world. A high-performance team is more than just a group of talented individuals; it's a cohesive unit where members collaborate effectively, trust each other, and are fully committed to shared goals. In my 30 years of experience, I've seen firsthand how a well-functioning team can make the difference between mediocrity and excellence.

The first key trait of high-performance teams is clarity of purpose. Every member must understand the team's goals, how their work contributes to the overall objectives, and what success looks like. Without a clear purpose, teams can lose focus or misalign their efforts.

One approach I've consistently used is setting SMART (Specific, Measurable, Achievable, Relevant, and Time-bound) goals for the team. This provides a clear roadmap for what needs to be achieved and helps the team stay aligned. When I was COO of a mid-sized manufacturing company, we used SMART goals to guide our cross-functional teams during a major product launch, ensuring that every department, from engineering to production, worked toward the same end goal. This clarity allowed us to meet our ambitious production targets ahead of schedule.

Trust and psychological safety are also critical for high-performance teams. Team members must feel safe expressing their ideas, asking questions, and challenging assumptions without fear of ridicule or retaliation. In one of the manufacturing plants I managed, we had a diverse team working on a complex project to integrate new technology into our production lines. By fostering an environment where every voice was valued, even the more reserved team members felt comfortable contributing their insights, leading to several innovative solutions we would have missed otherwise. Google's research into what makes teams successful reinforces this; psychological safety was identified as the number one factor in high-performing teams.

Effective communication is another cornerstone of successful teams. In high-performance teams, communication is open, frequent, and purposeful. Members share information, give feedback, and collaborate without hesitation. I've found that setting up regular team check-ins and feedback loops is essential for keeping communication channels open. For instance, during a major facility expansion project I led, we instituted daily briefings to ensure every team member was current on progress and potential roadblocks. This simple yet structured communication practice reduced delays and allowed us to identify issues early, keeping the project on track.

Accountability is also vital. In high-performance teams, every member is accountable for their responsibilities and the team's success. This doesn't mean micromanaging; instead, it's about creating a culture where individuals take ownership of their tasks and feel personally responsible for the team's outcomes. I remember a key supplier failing to deliver crucial components for a new product line. Rather than shifting blame, our procurement and production teams worked together, proactively adjusting schedules and finding alternative suppliers. This sense of shared accountability was instrumental in meeting our launch deadline despite the setback.

Diversity of skills and perspectives also contributes to high-performance teams. A team with a mix of skills, experiences, and viewpoints is better equipped to tackle complex problems and innovate. Diversity fosters creativity and leads to more well-rounded decision-making. I recall a project where we faced a production challenge that initially seemed unsolvable. By bringing together a cross-functional team that included engineers, production workers, and quality control specialists, we were able to come up with a solution that none of us would have developed alone. The diversity of thought and expertise allowed us to approach the problem from multiple angles, ultimately leading to a breakthrough.

Effective communication is perhaps the most critical trait of all. Even the most talented team will struggle without clear, open, and frequent communication. High-performance teams communicate regularly through formal meetings, quick check-ins, or digital collaboration tools. This ensures everyone is aligned and that issues can be addressed quickly before they become bigger problems. In one organisation, we implemented a daily stand-up meeting for our production teams, which allowed us to identify bottlenecks early and reallocate resources as needed. This simple communication practice significantly improved our overall efficiency.

Resilience and adaptability are also hallmarks of high-performing teams. In today's dynamic business environment, teams must adapt to changing circumstances, whether a shift in customer demand, a new technology, or an unexpected challenge. High-performance teams thrive on this kind of agility. They quickly regroup, pivot, and find new ways to achieve their goals. I once led a team through a major operational change when we decided to automate a significant portion of our production line. While there were initial concerns about the impact on jobs, the team's resilience and willingness to adapt enabled us to implement the new system smoothly and with minimal disruption.

Lastly, leadership plays a crucial role in shaping high-performance teams. A strong leader sets the vision and direction and empowers team members to take ownership of their work. As a COO, I've always believed in giving teams the autonomy to make decisions while providing the support and resources necessary to succeed. In one company, I worked with a team leader who excelled at balancing oversight with empowerment. He trusted his team to make key decisions, but he was always available for guidance and support. This leadership style fostered a sense of empowerment, and the team consistently outperformed expectations.

Building high-performance teams requires clarity of purpose, trust, accountability, diversity, effective communication, resilience, and strong leadership. When cultivated and nurtured, these traits create a team environment where individuals are motivated to excel, collaborate effectively, and drive the organisation toward success.

4.2 - Leadership Styles

In my three decades of experience as a COO, I've come to understand that one-size-fits-all leadership doesn't work. Every team is unique, with different dynamics, strengths, and challenges. It would be best if you adapted your leadership style to fit your team's needs to get the best out of your team. Leadership isn't about rigidly following a prescribed approach; it's about being flexible, empathetic, and strategically guiding your team.

One of the most effective leadership styles in the manufacturing sector is situational leadership, a concept developed by Paul Hersey and Ken Blanchard. This model suggests that leaders should adapt their style based on the development level of their team members, whether they need more direction, coaching, or autonomy. For example, a directive leadership style might be necessary when working with a new team on a process or project. This involves providing clear instructions, setting specific goals, and closely monitoring progress. I recall a project where we were introducing a new technology on the production floor. The team was unfamiliar with the system, so I took a more hands-on approach, ensuring everyone needed the training and support. Over time, as the team became more comfortable, I shifted to a more hands-off, supportive role, allowing them to take ownership of the process.

Conversely, with more experienced and capable teams, a delegation leadership style can be highly effective. This approach involves giving team members the autonomy to make decisions and take responsibility for their work. It's a style that fosters trust and empowerment, enabling people to perform at their best. I once led a highly skilled engineering team responsible for optimising production processes. Rather than micromanaging their efforts, I empowered them to identify problems and propose solutions. This level of autonomy motivated the team and led to more innovative ideas and solutions.

Another important leadership style is transformational leadership. This style focuses on inspiring and motivating the team to achieve their full potential, often by encouraging them to embrace change, think creatively, and take on new challenges. In a fast-moving manufacturing environment where continuous improvement is key, transformational leadership can be particularly powerful. I remember leading a team through a major organisational shift, transitioning from traditional manufacturing methods to a fully automated production system. By emphasising the long-term benefits of the change and involving the team in shaping the vision, I was able to inspire a sense of purpose and enthusiasm, even among those who were initially resistant to the transformation.

Transactional leadership is another style that can be useful in certain situations. This approach is based on a system of rewards and penalties, setting clear expectations and providing feedback based on performance. In highly regulated or safety-critical environments, transactional leadership ensures that processes are followed precisely and standards are met. While it may not foster the same level of innovation as other leadership styles, it's effective in maintaining consistency and compliance. In one plant I managed, safety was a top priority, and a transactional approach helped ensure that all safety protocols were adhered to without exception. The clear structure and direct feedback helped us maintain a flawless safety record.

Servant leadership is a style I've found particularly effective in building trust and fostering a collaborative culture. This approach flips the traditional leadership hierarchy on its head, with the leader's role being to serve and support the team rather than directing from above. Servant leaders create an environment where individuals feel valued and motivated by focusing on the team's needs and empowering them to succeed. I've seen this approach work wonders when teams are under pressure. When leading a team through a challenging period of tight deadlines and high expectations, I adopted a servant leadership approach by ensuring I could remove obstacles, offer support, and provide resources. This created a sense of camaraderie and shared purpose, and the team exceeded expectations.

Finally, coaching leadership is particularly valuable when developing talent and nurturing future leaders. This style involves guiding team members toward their long-term professional goals, offering feedback, and providing growth opportunities. Coaching can help employees build the skills they need to advance in manufacturing, where skilled talent is crucial. I once worked with a young production manager who showed great potential but lacked confidence in certain areas. Through regular one-on-one coaching sessions, I helped him develop his leadership skills and broaden his understanding of operational strategy. Within a year, he had grown into a highly capable leader, taking on more responsibility and contributing significantly to the organisation's success.

In conclusion, the key to effective leadership lies in adapting your style to the needs of your team and the specific circumstances you face. Whether you're taking a directive approach with a new team, empowering experienced employees through delegation, or inspiring transformation during times of change, the ability to flex your leadership style is crucial. Leadership is not about enforcing a rigid methodology; it's about understanding your team, responding to their needs, and creating an environment where they can thrive.

4.3 - Talent Acquisition and Retention

Talent acquisition and retention are critical to sustaining operational excellence in today's highly competitive manufacturing sector. The ability to attract, develop, and retain skilled professionals directly influences the organisation's productivity, innovation, and long-term success. Over my 30 years in manufacturing, I've learned that creating a robust strategy for attracting new talent and retaining top performers requires a multifaceted approach. It's not enough to offer competitive salaries; companies must foster an engaging, rewarding environment where employees feel valued and supported in their career growth.

One of the key strategies for attracting top talent is to build a strong employer brand. The best candidates are drawn to companies with a reputation for innovation, excellence, and a positive workplace culture. As a COO, you must ensure that your company's values, mission, and work environment are communicated internally and externally. During my time at a mid-sized manufacturing company, we revamped our employer branding strategy to emphasise our commitment to sustainability, continuous improvement, and employee development. We highlighted these elements on our website, job descriptions, and social media. This helped attract candidates aligned with our values and differentiated us from competitors struggling to find skilled workers.

Competitive compensation and benefits packages remain an essential component of talent acquisition. However, today's top talent seeks more than just a good salary. Flexible working arrangements, professional development opportunities, and comprehensive healthcare benefits can be major differentiators in attracting the best candidates. I've found that tailoring benefit packages to meet the needs of different employee groups can be particularly effective. For instance, younger professionals may value career advancement opportunities, while more experienced workers might prioritise work-life balance and retirement benefits. In one instance, we introduced a flexible benefits programme allowing employees to customise their packages based on their needs. This flexibility significantly improved our ability to attract and retain top talent.

To truly stand out in talent acquisition, it's important to tap into non-traditional talent pools. Many manufacturing businesses focus too narrowly on candidates with specific industry experience, overlooking other talented individuals who can bring fresh perspectives. At one point in my career, we faced a significant skills shortage in a highly technical production area. Rather than continuing to search for experienced hires, we partnered with a local technical college to develop a customised training programme. This initiative allowed us to bring in promising candidates with transferable skills and train them for the roles we needed to fill. Over time, this talent pipeline became a key source of skilled workers for our operation.

Once you've attracted top talent, the next challenge is retaining them. Retention begins on day one with a strong onboarding process. A comprehensive, well-structured onboarding programme helps new employees understand the company culture, their role, and how they can contribute to the organisation's success. It also ensures they have the necessary resources and support to hit the ground running. In one company I worked with, we noticed that new hires took too long to become fully productive. After reviewing our onboarding process, we made several changes, including assigning each new hire a mentor, providing more in-depth training on internal systems, and offering clear 30-, 60-, and 90-day objectives. These adjustments dramatically improved new hire retention and reduced employees' time needed to reach full productivity.

Career development is another critical factor in retention. Talented professionals want to know that they have opportunities for growth within the company. This means providing clear career paths, offering training and development opportunities, and ensuring employees feel supported in their long-term goals. I've always believed that an investment in employee development pays dividends in the long run. In one organisation, we implemented a formal career development programme that included regular skills assessments, training budgets, and opportunities for advancement. This helped us retain high performers and created a culture of continuous learning, which benefitted the entire organisation.

Employee engagement plays a significant role in retention. Engaged employees are likelier to stay with the company, be more productive, and contribute positively to the workplace culture. As a COO, fostering a culture of engagement means actively seeking out employee feedback, recognising achievements, and creating a work environment where employees feel their contributions are valued. In one company, we introduced quarterly "town hall" meetings where employees could voice their concerns, offer suggestions, and hear directly from leadership about the company's goals and challenges. This open line of communication helped build trust and engagement across the organisation, reducing turnover rates and improving overall morale.

Recognition and rewards are another key component of retention. Employees want to know that their hard work is appreciated. This doesn't always have to come in the form of financial incentives, recognising achievements publicly, offering additional time off, or providing development opportunities can be just as impactful. In one plant I managed, we introduced a peer-recognition programme where employees could nominate colleagues for their contributions. This fostered a sense of camaraderie and reinforced a culture of excellence and mutual respect. The programme had a noticeable impact on retention, as employees felt more appreciated and connected to the company's mission.

Finally, work-life balance is increasingly important to today's workforce, and companies prioritising it are more likely to retain top talent. This can mean offering flexible working hours, remote work options where possible, or providing wellness programmes that support physical and mental health. I've seen firsthand how flexible scheduling and wellness support initiatives can lead to higher retention rates. In one instance, we introduced a wellness programme that included gym memberships, mental health resources, and flexible work hours for parents. This profoundly affected employee satisfaction and significantly reduced turnover in critical roles.

In conclusion, attracting and retaining top talent in the manufacturing sector requires a comprehensive approach beyond competitive salaries. By building a strong employer brand, offering flexible benefits, creating career development opportunities, and fostering a culture of engagement and recognition, COOs can ensure they not only attract the best talent but also keep them engaged and committed for the long term.

4.4 - Training and Development

One of the most important investments a COO can make is employee training and development. In the manufacturing industry, where technology constantly evolves, staying ahead means ensuring that your workforce has the skills and knowledge necessary to adapt to new processes, equipment, and industry trends. Over my years as a COO, I've seen how a well-designed training and development programme can transform a company's performance by improving productivity, enhancing employee engagement, and fostering innovation.

The first step in creating an effective training and development strategy is to assess the current skills of your workforce and identify any gaps. This can be done through regular performance reviews, skills assessments, and feedback from team leaders. Once you clearly understand where the gaps are, you can design targeted training programmes to address them. For instance, in one organisation I worked with, we identified a significant skills gap in using new digital manufacturing technologies. We created a customised training programme that included classroom instruction and hands-on learning. Within six months, our teams were not only proficient in the new technology but also actively finding ways to use it to improve efficiency and reduce costs.

On-the-job training is one of the most effective methods for upskilling employees, especially in manufacturing, where practical, hands-on experience is invaluable. While classroom-based learning can provide a theoretical foundation, the most impactful learning often happens on the shop floor. I've always encouraged a blend of both, ensuring employees can apply what they've learned in real-world situations. We implemented a mentoring system in one plant where experienced employees were paired with newer team members. This facilitated skill transfer and helped build a sense of community and collaboration.

In addition to technical skills, focusing on soft skills development is essential. Communication, leadership, teamwork, and problem-solving are all critical competencies contributing to a high-performing workforce. I've found that investing in leadership development programmes for mid-level managers can have a ripple effect throughout the organisation, improving team dynamics, boosting morale, and enhancing productivity. In one case, we implemented a leadership training programme focused on emotional intelligence, conflict resolution, and effective communication. This improved management's ability to lead their teams, reduced workplace conflicts, and improved overall employee satisfaction.

Continuous learning should be a core principle of any development strategy. In today's fast-changing business environment, employees must be encouraged to develop a mindset of lifelong learning. This means providing opportunities for employees to pursue additional qualifications, attend workshops or conferences, and access online learning platforms. I once worked with a company that offered tuition reimbursement for employees who wanted to pursue further education in areas related to their roles. This initiative improved our overall skill base and increased employee retention, as workers felt that the company was invested in their personal growth.

Cross-training is another valuable development tool that can enhance employee skills and operational flexibility. Cross-training involves training employees to perform multiple roles within the organisation. This increases the workforce's versatility and helps the company manage workloads more efficiently during peak times or in the event of absenteeism. In one factory I managed, we implemented a cross-training programme where machine operators were trained on multiple machines. This reduced downtime during maintenance periods and improved production flow, as we could easily shift workers to where they were needed most.

Training and development initiatives should also be aligned with the organisation's broader strategic goals. For example, if the company plans to introduce new technology or expand into new markets, employees must have the necessary skills to support these initiatives. In one instance, our company was preparing to launch a new product line that required advanced technical knowledge. We developed a comprehensive training programme, including internal workshops and external certifications. As a result, the transition to the new product line was seamless, and we could meet production targets ahead of schedule.

It's also important to measure the impact of training and development initiatives. This can be done through post-training assessments, tracking key performance indicators (KPIs) improvements, and gathering feedback from trainees and managers. In one organisation, we used a combination of surveys and performance data to assess the effectiveness of our training programmes. By analysing this data, we could identify the most effective training methods and adjust future programmes.

Finally, creating a culture of learning is essential for long-term success. This means fostering an environment where continuous improvement and skill development are valued and encouraged at all levels of the organisation. In one company, we established a "learning day" once a quarter, where operations were paused for a full day of training, workshops, and knowledge sharing. This helped employees stay up-to-date on the latest industry trends and technologies and reinforced the importance of learning as a core organisational value.

In conclusion, investing in training and development is critical to maintaining a competitive edge in the manufacturing industry. By focusing on both technical and soft skills, offering opportunities for continuous learning, and aligning development initiatives with strategic goals, COOs can ensure that their workforce is equipped to meet the challenges of today's dynamic business environment. A well-trained workforce improves operational efficiency and enhances employee engagement, innovation, and long-term success.

4.5 - Performance Management

Effective performance management is a cornerstone of any high-functioning organisation. For a COO, it's not just about setting targets and tracking metrics, it's about aligning individual and team performance with the organisation's broader strategic goals. In my experience, performance management is most successful when approached as an ongoing process of communication, feedback, and development rather than a rigid, annual exercise.

The foundation of effective performance management lies in setting clear and measurable goals. These goals should align with the business's overall objectives and must be specific, achievable, relevant, and time-bound (SMART). One of the most common mistakes I've seen in performance management is setting vague or unrealistic goals, which only frustrate employees and create confusion. In one of my roles, we prepared to scale production to meet increased demand. Instead of setting a general goal to "increase output," we established a series of specific objectives, such as reducing machine downtime by 10% and increasing first-pass yield by 5% within six months. These clear, measurable goals gave the team a tangible target to work towards and provided a basis for tracking progress.

Continuous feedback is another critical component of performance management. While annual performance reviews are important, they should not be the only time employees receive feedback. Regular, informal check-ins provide an opportunity for course corrections, encouragement, and alignment. I've always believed that waiting until the end of the year to address performance issues or celebrate successes is a missed opportunity. For example, in one manufacturing plant, we implemented a quarterly feedback process where team leaders met one-on-one with each member. This allowed us to address issues early, provide recognition for achievements, and adjust individual goals as needed.

Objective and transparent evaluation metrics are crucial for ensuring that performance evaluations are fair and consistent. This often involves tracking key performance indicators (KPIs) such as productivity, quality, safety, and efficiency in manufacturing. However, it's important to remember that numbers don't tell the whole story. In one company, we had a production team that consistently met their output targets but struggled with quality issues. By taking a more holistic approach to performance management, which considered production numbers, teamwork, problem-solving, and initiative, we addressed the underlying issues and improved overall team performance.

Employee development should be a core focus of performance management. Rather than just focusing on past performance, the process should also look forward, identifying opportunities for growth and development. This is where a forward-thinking COO can truly make a difference. When employees see that performance management is not just about meeting targets but also about their personal growth, they are more likely to be engaged and motivated. We introduced a career development framework in one organisation that linked performance evaluations to training and development opportunities. This encouraged employees to view performance management as a tool for their career advancement, leading to improved motivation and retention.

Recognition and rewards play a key role in reinforcing positive performance. While financial incentives like bonuses are often the most visible form of recognition, non-financial rewards such as public acknowledgement, extra time off, or development opportunities can be just as impactful. I recall one plant where we introduced a "Top Performer of the Month" award, which recognised team members for hitting production targets and demonstrating leadership and teamwork. This small initiative greatly impacted morale and helped create a culture where people were motivated to go the extra mile.

Addressing underperformance is one of the more challenging aspects of performance management but is crucial for maintaining high standards. When someone is not meeting expectations, it's important to address the issue promptly and constructively. In my experience, most performance issues stem from a lack of clarity around expectations, insufficient training, or personal challenges that may affect the employee's work. The key is to approach underperformance as an opportunity for improvement rather than simply a problem to be punished. In one case, we had an employee consistently missing production targets. After a thorough review, we discovered the root cause was inadequate training on new equipment. By providing additional training and support, we were able to turn the situation around, and the employee went on to become one of our top performers.

Collaboration and teamwork should also be factored into performance management. In high-performing teams, individual success often depends on how well team members work together. In one organisation, we shifted part of our performance evaluation process to include peer feedback, allowing team members to assess each other's contributions to the team's overall success. This improved teamwork and helped identify employees quietly making significant contributions that might have gone unnoticed.

Lastly, technology can play a significant role in modernising performance management. Digital performance management tools allow real-time tracking of individual and team performance metrics, making the process more transparent and data-driven. In one plant, we implemented a digital dashboard that tracked KPIs for each production line. This allowed managers and employees to monitor performance in real-time and adjust as needed. The system's transparency also reduced the potential for evaluation bias and provided a clear, objective basis for performance discussions.

In conclusion, effective performance management is more than tracking metrics and conducting annual reviews. It's about setting clear goals, providing continuous feedback, fostering development, recognising achievements, and constructively addressing underperformance. When done well, performance management drives individual and organisational success by aligning personal objectives with the broader goals of the business.

4.6 - Motivating Your Team

One of the most important responsibilities of a COO is to keep the team motivated and engaged. A motivated workforce is more productive, creative, and committed to achieving the organisation's goals. Over the years, I've learned that motivation is not a one-size-fits-all approach. Different people are motivated by different factors, and as a leader, it's critical to understand these differences and use various techniques to inspire your team.

At the heart of motivation is purpose. People want to feel that their work is meaningful and that they are contributing to something larger than themselves. In manufacturing, where day-to-day tasks can sometimes feel repetitive, connecting individual roles to the company's broader mission and goals is crucial. I remember working with a team in an aerospace manufacturing plant, where precision and quality were critical. We made it a point to regularly remind employees that the components they were producing were not just parts; they were contributing to the safety and success of aircraft carrying thousands of passengers. This sense of purpose significantly increased engagement and pride in their work.

Recognition and appreciation are powerful motivators. Everyone wants to feel that their efforts are valued, and regular, genuine recognition can go a long way in keeping employees motivated. While financial rewards like bonuses and incentives are important, I've found that simple, heartfelt acknowledgement is often just as impactful. In one company, we implemented a "Thank You" programme where managers were encouraged to recognise employees' contributions daily through a quick email, a public acknowledgement during a meeting, or a handwritten note. This culture of appreciation fostered a positive atmosphere, and we saw a noticeable increase in employee engagement.

Growth and development opportunities are another key motivator, especially for ambitious, high-performing employees. People want to know that their hard work will lead to new opportunities through promotions, new responsibilities, or skills development. I've always made it a priority to provide clear career pathways for employees and to invest in their growth. In one organisation, we created a mentorship programme where high-potential employees were paired with senior leaders who helped guide their development. This programme motivated the employees involved and helped us build a strong pipeline of future leaders for the company.

Autonomy is another powerful motivator. People are more motivated when they have control over how they do their work and are trusted to make decisions. This can sometimes be challenging in manufacturing, as processes are often tightly controlled to ensure consistency and quality. However, I've found that giving employees more autonomy within clear guidelines can lead to increased motivation and innovation. For instance, in one plant, we allowed production teams to take ownership of certain process improvements. The teams were free to identify inefficiencies and propose solutions, which improved productivity and significantly increased employee engagement and job satisfaction.

Work-life balance has become an increasingly important motivator, especially in today's fast-paced, always-on work environment. Offering flexible working arrangements, such as flexible shifts or remote, can help employees feel more in control of their personal and professional lives. In one company, we introduced flexible working hours for employees with family commitments, and the result was not only improved morale but also increased productivity, as employees were less stressed and more focused at work.

Teamwork and collaboration also play a crucial role in motivation. People are more motivated when they feel a sense of belonging and camaraderie with their colleagues. Creating a culture of teamwork, where employees feel supported, and collaboration is encouraged, can significantly boost morale. I once led a cross-functional team tasked with solving a major production bottleneck. By bringing together employees from different departments and encouraging open communication, we solved the problem. We created a strong unity and shared purpose that lasted well beyond the project.

Incentives and rewards are traditional but effective motivational tools. However, the key is to tailor incentives to what genuinely matters to your employees. While monetary bonuses are always appreciated, non-monetary rewards such as additional time off, professional development opportunities, or even simple public recognition can be just as motivating. In one instance, we introduced a reward system where employees who consistently exceeded their targets were given a day off or the opportunity to attend a conference of their choice. This motivated employees to perform at their best and reinforced the message that we valued their hard work and well-being.

Listening and responding to employee feedback is another critical aspect of motivation. Employees are more engaged when they feel their voices are heard, and their opinions matter. In one plant, we held regular "listening sessions" where employees could share their thoughts, concerns, and ideas with management. By taking their feedback seriously and acting on it, we created a culture of trust and engagement, which led to increased productivity and lower turnover.

Finally, creating a positive work environment is essential for keeping employees motivated. A positive work culture, where employees feel supported, valued, and part of a team, is a key driver of engagement. This includes everything from maintaining open communication and encouraging collaboration to fostering a culture of respect and inclusivity. In one factory, we noticed tensions between shifts created a negative atmosphere. To address this, we implemented team-building activities and inter-shift collaboration projects. These initiatives helped break down barriers and improve relationships, leading to a more harmonious and motivated workforce.

In conclusion, motivating your team requires a thoughtful, personalised approach that considers your employees' individual needs and aspirations. By providing purpose, recognition, growth opportunities, autonomy, and a supportive work environment, COOs can create a motivated, engaged workforce committed to driving operational success.

4.7 - Conflict Resolution

In any organisation, conflicts are inevitable, particularly in fast-paced, high-pressure environments like manufacturing. While conflict can be disruptive if left unchecked, it also presents an opportunity for growth and improvement when managed effectively. As a COO with decades of experience, I've learned that resolving conflicts quickly and constructively is critical to maintaining a healthy workplace and sustaining team performance. Effective conflict resolution isn't just about quelling disputes; it's about fostering open communication, trust, and collaboration so that conflicts lead to better outcomes for both individuals and the organisation.

The first step in managing conflict is to address issues early. Often, conflicts start as small disagreements or misunderstandings that, if ignored, can escalate into larger, more disruptive problems. In one manufacturing plant I managed, we noticed the tension between the quality control and production teams. The issue's root was a disagreement over quality standards, but it had grown into personal conflicts between team members. By addressing the issue early and bringing both teams together to clarify expectations and discuss their challenges, we could prevent the conflict from escalating and find a mutually agreeable solution.

Active listening is an essential skill in conflict resolution. Creating an environment where all parties feel heard and understood is important when conflicts arise. I've often found that conflicts persist because one or both sides feel their concerns are not acknowledged. As a leader, your role is to listen without judgment, ask clarifying questions, and ensure everyone can express their viewpoint. In one case, we had two team leaders who were clashing over how to allocate resources for a new project. Instead of issuing a directive, I facilitated a discussion where both sides could explain their perspectives. By simply giving them the space to communicate openly, we found a compromise that worked for both teams.

Focusing on the issue, not the person, is another key principle in conflict resolution. Personal attacks or blaming individuals for the problem can escalate tensions and make it harder to find a solution. Instead, encourage team members to focus on the issue and how it can be resolved. I had two employees in a heated dispute over a production error in one situation. Instead of letting the conversation turn into finger-pointing, I redirected the discussion toward understanding the process failure that led to the error and how to improve our systems to prevent future mistakes. This shift in focus helped both employees move beyond their frustrations and work together to develop a solution.

Encouraging collaboration to find a resolution is another effective strategy. Rather than imposing a solution from the top down, involve the parties in developing a resolution that works for everyone. This collaborative approach leads to better outcomes and increases the likelihood that all involved will accept and implement the solution. I recall a time when two departments conflicted with scheduling priorities. Instead of stepping in to decide for them, I facilitated a joint meeting where both teams could share their concerns and propose solutions. By involving everyone in the decision-making process, we reached a solution that balanced both departments' needs and reduced future scheduling conflicts.

In some cases, conflicts can arise from differences in communication styles or cultural backgrounds. As a leader, it's important to know these dynamics and help team members navigate them. In one plant, we had a diverse workforce with employees from different cultural backgrounds, sometimes leading to misunderstandings and tension. By providing training on cross-cultural communication and encouraging team members to be mindful of different communication preferences, we were able to reduce conflicts and improve overall team cohesion.

Neutral mediation can also be a helpful tool in resolving more serious or entrenched conflicts. As a COO, you may sometimes need to step in as a neutral mediator to facilitate discussions between conflicting parties. Mediation aims to create a safe, impartial environment where both sides can discuss their issues and work toward a resolution. In one organisation, two senior managers were locked in a dispute, affecting their teams and creating a toxic work environment. By bringing them into a neutral space and acting as a mediator, I was able to help them express their frustrations and find common ground. While the resolution didn't happen overnight, the mediation helped rebuild trust and set the stage for better collaboration in the future.

Establishing clear policies around conflict resolution is also important. Employees should know what to do if they encounter a conflict and understand that there are established procedures for addressing issues. This ensures that conflicts are handled consistently and gives employees confidence that their concerns will be taken seriously. In one company, we developed a formal conflict resolution process that included clear steps for reporting conflicts, guidelines for mediation, and procedures for escalating issues when necessary. This policy helped create a more transparent and supportive work environment, where conflicts were seen as opportunities for growth rather than as threats to be avoided.

Finally, it's important to remember that not all conflicts must be resolved immediately or directly by the COO. Empowering team leaders to handle conflicts is essential for fostering a culture of accountability and collaboration. In one instance, a production supervisor approached me with a conflict between two team members, affecting the line's productivity. Rather than stepping in myself, I coached the supervisor on facilitating a resolution. This helped resolve the conflict and empowered the supervisor to handle similar situations in the future, reducing the need for escalation.

In conclusion, conflict resolution is vital for any leader, particularly in high-pressure environments like manufacturing. By addressing issues early, listening actively, focusing on the issue rather than the person, and fostering collaboration, COOs can turn conflicts into opportunities for improvement. Effective conflict resolution strengthens teams through mediation, clear policies, or empowering team leaders and contributes to a more cohesive, productive work environment.

4.8 - Creating a Collaborative Culture

A collaborative culture is one where teamwork, communication, and shared responsibility are embedded in the organisation's DNA. In manufacturing, where efficiency and coordination are paramount, fostering collaboration across departments and functions can significantly improve productivity, innovation, and morale. Throughout my years in leadership, I've seen that a truly collaborative culture doesn't happen by chance; it must be nurtured intentionally, with leaders playing a key role in setting the tone and creating the right environment.

Leading by example is one of the first steps in building a collaborative culture. As a COO, your actions speak louder than words. When team members see leaders actively collaborating, sharing information, and supporting cross-functional initiatives, they are likelier to adopt these behaviours. I recall when we were rolling out a new ERP system across multiple departments, which required close cooperation between production, IT, and finance. Rather than simply delegating the project, I was actively involved in cross-functional meetings and demonstrated a willingness to listen and compromise. This set the tone for the rest of the organisation and showed that collaboration wasn't just encouraged; it was expected.

Breaking down silos is essential for fostering collaboration. In many organisations, departments operate in isolation, leading to a lack of communication and coordination. This can result in inefficiencies, duplicated efforts, and missed opportunities for innovation. One of the most effective ways to break down silos is to create cross-functional teams that bring together employees from different departments to work on specific projects or solve problems. We introduced cross-functional problem-solving teams in one company to address recurring production issues. By bringing together engineers, operators, and quality control specialists, we could identify root causes and develop solutions more quickly than if each department had worked independently.

Open communication is the foundation of any collaborative culture. Employees must feel they can freely share information, ideas, and feedback without fear of judgment or retribution. This requires creating an environment of psychological safety where team members are encouraged to speak up and offer their perspectives. In one plant, we implemented regular "town hall" meetings where employees from all levels of the organisation could ask questions, share concerns, and suggest improvements. This open forum improved communication and helped build trust between leadership and frontline workers, which is essential for effective collaboration.

Recognising and rewarding collaboration is another important step in building a collaborative culture. Too often, organisations focus on individual achievements rather than team successes, which can inadvertently discourage teamwork. In one company, we shifted our recognition programme to focus more on team-based accomplishments. For example, instead of recognising only the top-performing individual in a department, we began celebrating the achievements of teams that worked together to meet production targets or solve complex problems. This shift in focus helped reinforce the importance of collaboration and encouraged employees to work more closely with their colleagues.

Cross-training is another powerful tool for fostering collaboration. When employees understand each other's roles and responsibilities, they can better appreciate their colleagues' challenges and collaborate more effectively. In one factory I managed, we introduced a cross-training programme that allowed employees to spend time working in other departments. Not only did this improve operational flexibility, but it also gave employees a broader understanding of the business and strengthened relationships between departments. This led to better communication and more effective problem-solving across the organisation.

Technology can also play a crucial role in supporting collaboration. In today's digital age, collaboration tools like shared project management platforms, real-time communication apps, and cloud-based data systems make it easier for teams to work together, even when they are geographically dispersed. In one project, we used a cloud-based project management tool to coordinate the efforts of multiple departments working on a new product launch. The tool allowed everyone to track progress, share updates, and collaborate on tasks in real-time, which streamlined the process and improved overall efficiency.

Empowering employees to take ownership of collaboration is key to creating a sustainable collaborative culture. Leaders can set the stage, but true collaboration happens when employees take the initiative and work together without constant oversight. One way to encourage this is by giving teams more autonomy over their projects and decision-making processes. In one company, we introduced a system of "autonomous work teams," where each team managed its workflow and solved problems independently. This not only improved collaboration within the teams but also increased employee engagement and accountability.

Finally, celebrating diversity of thought is essential for fostering a collaborative culture. A collaborative organisation values diverse perspectives and encourages employees to bring unique experiences and ideas. In one company, we assembled diverse teams for important projects, drawing on employees with different backgrounds, skill sets, and areas of expertise. This led to more creative solutions and helped build a more inclusive and collaborative culture where everyone felt valued and heard.

In conclusion, creating a collaborative culture requires intentional effort from leadership and the right structures, tools, and incentives to encourage teamwork. By leading by example, breaking down silos, fostering open communication, and empowering employees to take ownership of collaboration, COOs can build a culture where teamwork and shared success are the norm. The result is a more cohesive, innovative, and high-performing organisation.

4.9 - Succession Planning

Succession planning is an essential aspect of organisational sustainability. It ensures that key leadership positions are filled with competent, prepared individuals when the time comes for transitions. In the manufacturing sector, where operations are complex and specialised knowledge is often required, succession planning can be the difference between a seamless transition and a major disruption. As a COO, ensuring that your organisation has a strong pipeline of future leaders is crucial to maintaining operational continuity and driving long-term success.

One of the first steps in effective succession planning is identifying *critical roles* within the organisation. While the focus is often on the top leadership positions, such as the CEO or COO, it's equally important to consider other key roles, particularly those that require specialised skills or institutional knowledge. In my experience, some of the most challenging leadership transitions occur at the mid-management level, where technical expertise and operational experience are often concentrated. For instance, in one manufacturing company, we identified that our plant managers, maintenance leads, and engineering supervisors were all in critical roles that would be difficult to replace quickly. By recognising these key positions early, we were able to develop tailored succession plans that ensured continuity in these vital areas.

Assessing potential candidates for leadership roles is another critical component of succession planning. This involves evaluating both current performance and future potential. In my view, leadership potential is not always immediately apparent, and it's essential to look beyond current job performance to identify individuals who can grow into more senior roles. This might involve looking at how employees handle challenges, their ability to think strategically, and their interpersonal skills. In one plant I managed, we introduced a talent review process where department heads met quarterly to discuss the development and potential of their teams. This process helped us identify high-potential employees early and allowed them to take on more responsibility and leadership training.

Development programmes are key to succession planning, as they provide future leaders with the skills and experience they need to succeed in more senior roles. These programmes should be tailored to the specific needs of the organisation and the individual. For example, if a potential successor lacks experience in a particular area, such as financial management or team leadership, the development plan should include targeted training. We created a leadership development programme in one organisation, including job rotations, mentorship, and external leadership courses. This programme allowed us to prepare multiple high-potential employees for future leadership roles and gave them a well-rounded understanding of the business.

Job shadowing and mentorship are particularly effective tools in succession planning. By pairing potential successors with experienced leaders, companies can ensure that institutional knowledge is passed down and that future leaders clearly understand their challenges and responsibilities. We established a mentorship programme in one company where senior managers mentored high-potential employees. This helped prepare the mentees for future leadership roles and strengthened organisational relationships. I've seen firsthand how this type of programme can provide invaluable real-world insights that are difficult to gain through formal training alone.

Cross-functional experience is another critical aspect of developing future leaders. In manufacturing, future leaders must understand the broader context in which their department operates. Cross-functional rotations, where employees spend time working in different business areas, can provide valuable experience and help them develop a more strategic perspective. In one plant I worked with, we implemented a rotational leadership programme where high-potential employees spent six months in different departments, including production, quality control, and supply chain management. This broadened their skill sets and improved their ability to collaborate with other teams, which is crucial for effective leadership.

Feedback and evaluation are essential for refining succession plans and ensuring that the right individuals are prepared for leadership roles. Regularly evaluating potential successors and providing them with feedback on their progress helps keep development plans on track. In one organisation, we held semi-annual reviews where potential successors met with their mentors and supervisors to discuss their development. These sessions provided valuable feedback and allowed us to adjust the development plans as needed. This ongoing evaluation ensured that the individuals stepping into new roles were well-prepared when leadership transitions occurred.

It's also important to *create a culture of transparency* around succession planning. When employees understand that the company is invested in their development and that there are clear opportunities for advancement, they are more likely to be engaged and committed to the organisation. In one company, we made succession planning a part of our regular communication with employees. We discussed the importance of leadership development in town halls and encouraged employees to take ownership of their career paths by seeking development opportunities. This transparency helped retain top talent and created a shared responsibility for the organisation's future success.

Dealing with unplanned transitions is another critical aspect of succession planning. While it's ideal to have a planned transition where a successor is fully prepared to step into a leadership role, there will be times when transitions happen unexpectedly due to illness, resignation, or other unforeseen circumstances. To mitigate the risks associated with these unplanned transitions, it's essential to have an interim plan in place. In one case, we faced the unexpected departure of a key plant manager. Fortunately, we had already identified a potential successor in their development plan's early stages. While they were not yet fully ready to take on the role, we were able to appoint them as interim manager while continuing their development. This allowed us to maintain stability in the plant while we worked through the leadership transition.

Finally, succession planning should be seen as an ongoing process, not a one-time event. The organisation's needs will evolve, and so will the potential successors within it. By regularly revisiting and updating succession plans, COOs can ensure that the company remains prepared for future leadership transitions, no matter when or where they occur.

In conclusion, succession planning is a vital aspect of long-term organisational success. By identifying critical roles, developing high-potential employees, and creating a transparent and structured approach to leadership development, COOs can ensure that their organisation is prepared for future leadership transitions. A well-executed succession plan provides continuity and strengthens the organisation by building a deep bench of talented, capable leaders ready to step up when needed.

4.10 - Case Study: Success Stories of Outstanding Leadership

There are countless examples of how strong leadership can transform a team's performance and drive an organisation's success. In this case study, I will share two examples from my experience demonstrating the power of effective leadership in building high-performance teams and navigating complex challenges.

Case Study 1: Leading a Production Team through a Major Operational Change

One of the manufacturing companies I worked with faced a major operational change when we decided to implement a new automated production line. The ambitious project involved replacing several manual processes with advanced automation technologies, significantly increasing production capacity and requiring the team to adapt to new working methods.

The first challenge we faced was resistance to change. Many employees had been with the company for years and were comfortable with the existing processes. There was a palpable fear that automation would lead to job losses and low morale. As the COO, I knew that successful implementation of the new system would require technical training and a major shift in mindset.

The key to overcoming this resistance was open communication and transparency. From the outset, I clarified to the team that automation was not about replacing jobs but about making the company more competitive and creating growth opportunities. We held several town hall meetings where employees could ask questions, express concerns, and understand the long-term vision behind the project. By being transparent about the challenges and benefits of the change, we built trust and reduced anxiety.

Next, we focused on comprehensive training and development. We knew employees needed to feel confident working with the new technology, so we invested heavily in training programmes that included classroom learning and hands-on experience with the new equipment. We also introduced a mentorship system where more experienced employees who were quick to adapt could help their colleagues. This approach increased the team's technical competence and fostered a sense of collaboration and mutual support.

The result was a successful transition to the new production system with minimal disruption. Not only did we achieve the desired increase in production capacity, but we also improved team morale. The employees, who had initially been sceptical of the change, became strong advocates for the new system, and many of them took on leadership roles in training new hires.

Case Study 2: Building a High-Performance Engineering Team to Solve a Critical Supply Chain Issue

In another organisation, we faced a critical supply chain issue that threatened to halt production. A key supplier had unexpectedly left us without an essential component for one of our most important product lines. The pressure was immense, as any significant delay in production would result in missed orders and a loss of customer trust.

The first step in addressing the issue was to assemble a *cross-functional team* of engineers, supply chain experts, and procurement specialists. My leadership approach was to empower the team to take ownership of the problem while providing them with the resources and support they needed to succeed. We held daily meetings to review progress, brainstorm solutions, and adjust strategies as needed.

One of the key decisions we made early on was to *encourage creativity and risk-taking*. We knew traditional solutions wouldn't work, so we encouraged the team to think outside the box. In one meeting, an engineer proposed slightly modifying the product's design so that it could be manufactured with an alternative, more readily available component. While this was a bold move, we decided to move forward with it, and the team worked tirelessly to test the new design and ensure that it met all quality standards.

The second key to our success was *collaboration and open communication*. This was not a time for silos; everyone needed to work together, share information, and support one another. To facilitate this, we set up an open forum where team members from different departments could freely communicate their progress, challenges, and ideas. This ensured that there were no bottlenecks in information flow and allowed us to pivot if something wasn't working quickly. Each department brought unique insights, whether engineering solving design issues or procurement sourcing alternative suppliers. This open line of communication allowed us to stay agile and responsive to rapidly changing circumstances.

One of the challenges we faced during this process was the *fear of failure*. Some team members were understandably concerned that the alternative component might not meet the rigorous quality standards required or that the changes would not pass customer inspections. I reinforced the importance of failing fast and learning quickly to address this. Instead of spending too much time debating potential problems, we focused on testing assumptions and learning from results. If a particular idea didn't work, we swiftly moved on to the next one. This approach kept the team motivated and focused on progress rather than being paralysed by the fear of failure.

Another critical element to our success was having a clear *sense of urgency*. With production deadlines looming and customer orders at risk, we couldn't afford unnecessary delays. I worked closely with the team to establish short-term, actionable milestones. We reviewed our progress against these targets daily, ensuring we stayed on track. This sense of urgency kept everyone focused and aligned, but I also emphasised the importance of maintaining *quality*; we weren't just solving the problem for today but developing a solution that had to stand up to long-term scrutiny.

We also focused on supplier relationships in parallel with the design and engineering modifications. Our procurement team worked around the clock to source potential new suppliers who could provide the alternative component at the required quality and volume. This process involved negotiations, due diligence, and even site visits to ensure that any new supplier would meet our standards and align with our production needs. By leveraging the relationships we had built over time, we secured a new supplier within a tight timeframe, avoiding a major production stoppage.

During the final stages of the project, I made it a priority to ensure that *all stakeholders were kept informed*. Customers, in particular, needed to know that we managed the issue effectively and that their orders would not be significantly delayed. We provided regular updates on our progress, and because we were transparent about the challenges we faced and how we addressed them, we maintained their trust throughout the process. Ultimately, the swift action and innovative approach allowed us to deliver the orders on time and strengthened our relationships with key customers.

The project was a testament to the power of *cross-functional collaboration and innovative problem-solving*. By fostering a culture that embraced risk-taking, open communication, and accountability, we overcame a potentially catastrophic supply chain issue and delivered exceptional results. Moreover, the experience deepened the trust between departments and reinforced the value of creative thinking under pressure.

We didn't just revert to business as usual in the following months. We conducted a *post-mortem* review to identify lessons learned from the experience. This helped us refine our processes, particularly in supply chain management and product design. We also formalised many practices we had developed during the crisis, such as more frequent cross-functional meetings and stronger contingency planning for critical components.

In conclusion, building a high-performance team to tackle a critical supply chain issue required more than technical expertise; it required strong leadership, open communication, and a willingness to think creatively. By empowering the team to take ownership of the problem and fostering an environment that encouraged innovation and collaboration, we were able to turn a potential crisis into an opportunity for growth. This experience solved the immediate problem and prepared us better to handle future challenges with confidence and agility.

Chapter 5

Enhancing Customer Focus

> "In operations, you don't just react; you anticipate, innovate, and elevate."
>
> **Robert N. Jacobs**

This chapter will delve into the critical strategies and practices necessary for operational leaders, especially COOs, to foster a customer-centric organisation. The chapter emphasises the pivotal role of the COO in understanding and addressing customer needs through active listening, segmentation, and collaboration. It also highlights the importance of improving the customer experience by mapping the customer journey, ensuring consistency, and empowering employees. The chapter concludes by exploring feedback mechanisms, building strong customer relationships, and maintaining high-quality standards. This chapter is a comprehensive guide for COOs aiming to enhance customer focus as a key driver for long-term success.

5.1 - Understanding Customer Needs

Understanding and addressing customer needs is the foundation of sustainable success in the manufacturing sector. As COO, one of your primary responsibilities is ensuring that your organisation delivers not just a product but the right one that meets or exceeds the customer's expectations. Over my 30 years of experience, I've seen that truly understanding customer needs requires a mix of deep engagement, data-driven insights, and a willingness to adapt quickly to changing market conditions.

The first step in understanding customer needs is active listening. Your role as a COO is crucial in this process. Customers are often vocal about what they want and need, but too often, organisations fail to capture these insights fully. It's important to have mechanisms to gather customer input, whether through surveys, face-to-face meetings, or customer advisory panels. Early in my career, I managed a product line for an automotive parts manufacturer, and one of the turning points came when we initiated a series of in-depth interviews with our key customers. We discovered that while our products were technically sound, they were not optimised for the latest vehicle designs. This realisation allowed us to shift our development efforts and retain important contracts.

In addition to gathering feedback, it's essential to analyse market trends and customer behaviour to anticipate future needs. One of the most valuable lessons I've learned is that customers often don't articulate what they will need in the future; they focus on current problems. As a leader, it's your job to look ahead and anticipate how changing technologies, regulations, or market dynamics might impact your customers. For example, in one of my roles, we anticipated a shift towards electric vehicles long before our competitors, allowing us to develop components suited to the emerging market. This foresight secured long-term contracts and positioned us as an innovative partner in the industry.

A crucial aspect of understanding customer needs is segmentation. Not all customers are the same, and their requirements may vary significantly based on size, industry, or region. By segmenting your customer base and tailoring your products or services to meet the specific needs of each segment, you can provide more value and foster stronger relationships. In one instance, I worked with a company that served large multinational corporations and smaller regional businesses. We realised that while the large corporations prioritised cost savings and high-volume production, the smaller businesses valued flexibility and faster turnaround times. We could meet both needs more effectively by developing different service models for each segment.

Collaboration with customers can also help you stay ahead of their needs. Co-development projects, where you work alongside your customers to create products that address specific challenges, are an excellent way to build deeper insights into their requirements. In one case, we collaborated with a key customer to design a bespoke component that solved a specific problem in their production line. This strengthened our relationship with that customer and led to the development of a new product that we could offer to others in the industry.

Once customer needs are identified, the next step is to ensure that the entire organisation is aligned with meeting these requirements. This involves creating clear communication channels between sales, product development, and operations teams. Too often, I've seen situations where the sales team promises something to a customer that the production team can't deliver within the required timeframe. To avoid these disconnects, we implemented cross-functional planning meetings in one of my previous organisations. These meetings ensured that all departments clearly understood customer requirements and could work together to meet them efficiently.

Finally, it's important to remain agile in addressing customer needs. Market conditions and customer priorities can change quickly, and adapting is key to staying competitive. In one example, our major customer underwent a significant restructuring and shifted their priorities toward cost reduction. By rapidly adjusting our production processes to reduce waste and pass the savings on to the customer, we were able to maintain the relationship and secure additional business during a challenging period.

In conclusion, understanding customer needs requires a proactive, multifaceted approach. You can deliver products and services that meet and exceed expectations by actively listening to your customers, anticipating future trends, segmenting your customer base, collaborating on solutions, and ensuring organisational alignment. A customer-focused approach builds long-term loyalty and positions your organisation as a trusted partner, essential for sustained growth and success.

5.2 - Customer Experience Management

Customers experience management (CEM) is about more than just delivering a good product or service; it's about managing every interaction a customer has with your organisation to create a seamless, positive experience from start to finish. In my three decades as a COO, I've learned that consistently improving the customer experience is a key differentiator, especially in manufacturing, where fierce competition and customer loyalty can be fragile.

The first step in improving customer experience is to map the customer journey. This means looking at every touchpoint a customer has with your organisation, from initial contact to after-sales support, and identifying areas where the experience can be improved. Early in my career, I worked for a company with excellent products but struggled with customer retention. After mapping the customer journey, we realised that the onboarding process was confusing, and customers often felt abandoned after making a purchase. By redesigning the onboarding process to include more touchpoints, such as follow-up calls, user guides, and dedicated account managers, we improved customer satisfaction and increased retention rates.

A crucial part of CEM is ensuring consistency across all channels. Whether a customer interacts with your company online, over the phone, or in person, they should receive the same high level of service. In one organisation, we found that while our sales team provided excellent service, our online ordering platform was cumbersome and difficult to use. This inconsistency was frustrating for customers and resulted in lost sales. By investing in a user-friendly digital platform and ensuring that our service levels were consistent across all channels, we significantly improved the overall customer experience.

Personalisation is another powerful tool for improving customer experience. Customers want to feel that their needs are understood and that the service they receive is tailored to them. This can be as simple as remembering a customer's previous orders or preferences or as complex as providing customised solutions based on their specific requirements. In one case, we implemented a CRM system that allowed our sales and service teams to access detailed information about each customer's history and preferences. This enabled our team to offer more personalised recommendations and solutions, which improved customer satisfaction and increased sales.

Responsiveness is another critical factor in managing customer experience. Customers value timely communication and quick resolution of issues and are more likely to remain loyal to a company that promptly addresses their concerns. In one company, we implemented a 24-hour response policy, ensuring that all customer inquiries, whether positive or negative, received a response within a day. This simple policy change significantly impacted customer satisfaction, as customers felt their concerns were promptly addressed.

Another important aspect of CEM is empowering employees to deliver exceptional service. Too often, front-line employees feel constrained by rigid policies and procedures, preventing them from providing the best possible service. In one of my roles, we restructured our customer service protocols to give employees more autonomy to solve problems on the spot. For example, employees were empowered to offer discounts, replacements, or other solutions instead of escalating every issue to a manager. This improved the customer experience and increased employee satisfaction, as they felt more trusted and capable in their roles.

Proactive communication can also enhance the customer experience. Don't wait for customers to contact you with a problem; anticipate potential issues and reach out before they escalate. In one instance, we were facing a delay in production due to a supply chain issue. Rather than waiting for customers to complain about late deliveries, we proactively contacted them to explain the situation, provided regular updates, and offered alternative solutions. This transparency helped maintain customer trust and prevented frustration, even though the delay was beyond our control.

Lastly, it's important to measure customer experience continuously. Using tools such as Net Promoter Score (NPS), customer satisfaction surveys, and regular feedback channels allows you to gauge how well you're meeting customer expectations and where improvements are needed. In one organisation, we implemented a quarterly NPS survey that gave valuable insights into how customers perceived their interactions with us. By tracking these scores over time and acting on the feedback, we made targeted improvements that enhanced the overall experience.

In conclusion, customer experience management is about creating a seamless, consistent, and personalised journey for every customer. By mapping the customer journey, ensuring consistency across all channels, empowering employees, and maintaining proactive communication, COOs can create a customer experience that fosters loyalty, enhances satisfaction, and drives long-term business success. In today's competitive market, managing the customer experience is not just a nice-to-have; it's a critical business strategy.

5.3 - Feedback Mechanisms

Customer feedback is one of the most valuable assets a business can have. It provides direct insight into how your products, services, and operations are perceived by those who matter most: your customers. Over my 30 years in manufacturing, I've seen that organisations that actively gather and use customer feedback can continuously improve their offerings and maintain a competitive edge. However, simply collecting feedback is not enough. The real value comes from systematically analysing, understanding, and acting on that feedback to drive meaningful change.

The first step in implementing effective feedback mechanisms is to ensure that multiple channels are available for customers to provide input. Different customers prefer different methods of communication; some may prefer online surveys, while others might feel more comfortable sharing their opinions over the phone or during in-person meetings. In one company I worked with, we initially relied solely on online surveys to gather feedback, which resulted in limited responses. After expanding our feedback mechanisms to include phone interviews, on-site visits, and email feedback forms, we saw a significant increase in customer input quantity and quality. This holistic approach gave us a complete picture of our customers' experiences.

Post-sale surveys are an excellent way to capture immediate feedback after a transaction or service interaction. These surveys can be designed to gauge customer satisfaction, identify areas for improvement, and even highlight opportunities for additional sales. I once led a manufacturing organisation where we introduced post-sale surveys as part of our standard process. After every major order, we asked customers about their satisfaction with the product, the ease of the ordering process, and the quality of our customer service. By tracking this feedback over time, we could spot trends and address recurring issues before they escalated.

Beyond surveys, customer interviews or focus groups are among the most powerful feedback mechanisms. These sessions allow one to dive deeper into customer experiences and gather qualitative insights often missed in more structured surveys. In one project, we invited key customers to participate in a focus group about a new product we planned to launch. Their candid feedback helped us refine the product design and improve its usability. The result was a better product and stronger customer relationships, as customers appreciated being involved in the development process.

Monitoring social media and online reviews can also provide valuable, unfiltered feedback. In today's digital age, many customers voice their opinions publicly through platforms like LinkedIn, Facebook, or review websites. While this feedback may not always be solicited directly, it offers real-time insight into customer sentiment. I've found that monitoring these platforms is an excellent way to stay attuned to how customers perceive your brand and products. In one company, we noticed a pattern of complaints about delivery delays on social media. This alerted us to an issue in our logistics process, which we were able to address before it significantly affected our customer satisfaction scores.

However, gathering feedback is only half the battle. The real challenge is to analyse and act on it. Customer feedback should not just be collected and filed away; it must drive continuous improvement. In one organisation, we set up a cross-functional "feedback task force" that was responsible for reviewing customer feedback every month and identifying actionable insights. This team included sales, operations, and product development representatives, ensuring that feedback was analysed from multiple perspectives. One of the insights we gained from this process was that customers were experiencing difficulty with our packaging, leading to product damage during shipping. By redesigning our packaging based on this feedback, we reduced product returns by 15%.

Closing the loop with customers after acting on their feedback is a critical step many companies overlook. When customers see that their input leads to real change, it strengthens their trust and loyalty. In one instance, after implementing a suggestion from a customer regarding a more efficient component design, we reached out to that customer to let them know how their feedback had been incorporated. This gesture reinforced their loyalty to our brand and encouraged other customers to provide more detailed feedback, knowing that their voices would be heard and acted upon.

Customer advisory boards are another valuable tool for gathering strategic feedback. You create an ongoing dialogue with your most important clients by forming a board of key customers. This lets you gain insights into industry trends, customer challenges, and emerging needs, helping you stay ahead of the competition. In one manufacturing firm I worked with, we formed a customer advisory board to help shape our long-term product strategy. The insights we gained from these industry leaders were invaluable in guiding our R&D efforts and ensuring we were developing products that met future market demands.

Analysing feedback trends over time is crucial for identifying recurring issues and opportunities for improvement. It's not enough to react to individual pieces of feedback; you need to look for patterns that indicate systemic problems or consistent strengths. In one company, we noticed through long-term feedback analysis that there was a recurring theme around the complexity of our product manuals. This prompted us to overhaul our user documentation, making it more intuitive and user-friendly. This change resulted in fewer customer support inquiries and higher satisfaction ratings.

Finally, it's important to remember that feedback should be shared across the organisation. Too often, feedback is siloed within customer service or sales teams when, in fact, it has valuable insights for every department. In one company, we implemented a monthly "customer feedback report" that was shared with all teams, from operations to product development. This transparency ensured everyone understood the customer's voice and could align their work to meet customer needs more effectively.

In conclusion, gathering and utilising customer feedback is not a one-off exercise; it should be an integral part of your operational strategy. By using multiple feedback mechanisms, analysing the data, and acting on insights, COOs can ensure their organisations remain responsive to customer needs and continuously improve. Moreover, closing the loop with customers and sharing feedback across teams strengthens relationships and creates a culture of customer-centric innovation.

5.4 - Building Strong Customer Relationships

Strong customer relationships are the bedrock of long-term business success, especially in manufacturing, where the stakes are high, and customer switching costs can be substantial. Over my career, I've witnessed that fostering loyalty and trust requires more than delivering a high-quality product. It demands consistent, meaningful customer engagement and a deep understanding of their unique challenges and needs. A customer relationship is a partnership, not a transaction, built on mutual respect, transparency, and value.

The first step in building strong customer relationships is to personalise your interactions. Customers want to feel that they are more than just a number or a purchase order; they want to know that you understand their business, challenges, and goals. In one manufacturing organisation I worked with, we implemented a key account management system where dedicated account managers were assigned to our top customers. These account managers were responsible for developing a deep understanding of the customer's business and providing tailored solutions that met their specific needs. This personalised approach strengthened our relationships with key clients and increased sales, as customers felt more confident in our ability to deliver value.

Regular, proactive communication is another essential component of building trust. Too often, companies wait until there's a problem to engage with customers, but strong relationships are built through consistent, proactive outreach. In one of my roles, we established a practice of quarterly business reviews (QBRs) with our major customers. These reviews allowed one to discuss past performance, plans, and potential challenges. Regularly checking in with customers, we addressed issues before they escalated and identified new collaboration opportunities.

Transparency is critical to fostering trust, especially when things go wrong. No company is perfect, and problems will inevitably arise, whether it's a delayed delivery, a product defect, or a miscommunication. How you handle these situations can make or break a customer relationship. In one instance, we faced a major production delay due to a supplier issue that would impact a key customer's order. Rather than trying to downplay the situation, we were upfront with the customer about the problem. We worked closely with them to find a solution, including offering alternative product options and adjusting delivery schedules. The customer appreciated our honesty and commitment to resolving the issue, and we maintained their trust despite the setback.

Adding value beyond the product is another powerful way to build strong customer relationships. In manufacturing, the product is only part of the equation; customers also seek partners who can provide expertise, innovation, and support. In one organisation, we offered our customers regular training sessions on optimising the use of our products in their operations. This helped improve their efficiency and reinforced our position as a trusted partner invested in their success.

Another key to fostering loyalty is demonstrating flexibility. Customers' needs and circumstances can change, and being flexible and responsive to those changes is essential to maintaining strong relationships. In one instance, our long-time customer experienced a sudden drop in demand due to an economic downturn. Rather than rigidly enforcing our original contract terms, we worked with them to adjust order volumes and payment schedules. This flexibility helped them navigate a challenging period and ensured that they remained loyal to us when business picked back up.

Engaging with customers on multiple levels within their organisation is another important strategy for building strong relationships. Having a good relationship with just one point of contact is not enough; you must build rapport with decision-makers, influencers, and end-users. In one case, we tried to connect with our customer's procurement team and their engineering and operations teams. By engaging with stakeholders at all levels, we were able to gain a deeper understanding of the customer's needs and build a stronger, more resilient relationship.

Customer loyalty programmes can also strengthen relationships. While these are more common in consumer-facing businesses, they can be equally effective in B2B environments. In one manufacturing firm I worked with, we introduced a loyalty programme that offered discounts, priority service, and exclusive access to new products for our long-term customers. This programme incentivised repeat business and made customers feel valued and appreciated.

Lastly, celebrating shared success is a powerful way to build long-term loyalty. When your products or services help a customer achieve a significant milestone or win a major contract, acknowledge and celebrate that success with them. In one instance, our customer secured a major industry award thanks partly to a product we had developed for them. We made a point of congratulating them publicly and featured the achievement in our marketing materials. This reinforced the strength of our partnership and deepened their loyalty to us.

In conclusion, building strong customer relationships requires a commitment to personalisation, proactive communication, transparency, flexibility, and value creation. By engaging with customers at all levels, being responsive to their changing needs, and consistently delivering more than just a product, COOs can foster deep, lasting relationships that drive customer loyalty and long-term business success.

5.5 - Quality Assurance

In manufacturing, quality assurance is not just about meeting technical specifications but consistently delivering products that meet or exceed customer expectations. Quality is a key differentiator, especially in industries where the cost of defects or failures can be enormous in terms of reputation and operational downtime. Over my three decades in manufacturing, I've seen firsthand how a robust quality assurance (QA) system can strengthen customer trust, drive repeat business, and create a competitive advantage.

The first step in ensuring quality is defining clear standards that align with customer expectations. These standards must be established early in the product development and communicated clearly to all stakeholders, from engineers to production teams. In one company, we worked closely with our top customers during the design phase of a new product to ensure that our quality benchmarks reflected their requirements. This collaborative approach ensured we were aligned, reducing the risk of quality issues later in production.

Quality management systems (QMS), such as ISO 9001, are critical to enforce these standards. A strong QMS provides a structured approach to managing quality throughout the manufacturing process, from raw material procurement to final inspection. I led a manufacturing company early in my career through its first ISO 9001 certification. While the process was intensive, the benefits were clear, our processes became more consistent, we reduced waste, and we saw fewer product defects. Customers noted our commitment to quality, which became a key selling point for winning new contracts.

In addition to formal systems, quality culture is pivotal in ensuring consistent product quality. Quality should not be the sole responsibility of a dedicated QA team; it must be ingrained in every aspect of the organisation, from the factory floor to the boardroom. In one plant, we implemented a "Quality First" programme where every employee, regardless of their role, was trained on quality control principles and encouraged to take ownership of the quality of their work. We also introduced a system where employees could flag potential quality issues in real-time without fear of retribution. This empowered the team to take proactive steps to prevent defects before they occurred, significantly improving our overall product quality.

In-process quality control is another critical element of an effective QA system. Waiting until the end of the production line to inspect for defects is too late; the goal should be to catch and correct issues as early as possible. In one project, we integrated in-line quality checks at multiple stages of the manufacturing process, including automated inspections for key tolerances and manual checks for more nuanced quality aspects. By detecting issues early, we reduced rework and scrap rates, saving time and money while improving overall quality.

Supplier quality management is also crucial in ensuring that the materials and components you receive meet your standards. In one instance, we faced a recurring issue with a key supplier whose components consistently failed to meet our specifications. Rather than simply rejecting the parts and causing production delays, we took a more proactive approach by working closely with the supplier to improve their processes. We implemented joint quality audits, shared our best practices, and provided additional training to their team. This collaborative effort resulted in a significant improvement in the quality of their components, which in turn helped us maintain our production quality.

Customer-specific quality requirements must also be taken into account. Customers may have unique requirements based on their industry, regulatory environment, or product application. For instance, in one company I worked with, our customers in the aerospace industry had much stricter quality requirements than those in other sectors. To meet these heightened expectations, we developed specialised QA protocols, including more frequent inspections, tighter tolerances, and additional documentation for traceability. Meeting these rigorous standards allowed us to position ourselves as a trusted supplier to some of the largest aerospace companies in the world.

Post-delivery quality tracking once a product is shipped helps ensure that it continues to meet customer expectations in real-world applications. In one case, we introduced a post-delivery quality assurance programme where we followed up with customers shortly after they received their products to check for any issues. This helped us identify potential problems early and demonstrated our commitment to customer satisfaction. One of our customers noted that our follow-up calls and willingness to address minor issues quickly were key factors in their decision to continue doing business with us.

Data-driven continuous improvement is essential for maintaining and enhancing product quality over time. Every quality issue, no matter how small, presents an opportunity to learn and improve. In one factory, we implemented a system where every defect identified in production or by a customer was logged and analysed for root causes. This data allowed us to identify patterns and trends, which led to process improvements that reduced the incidence of similar defects in the future. Over time, this focus on continuous improvement helped us achieve a near-zero defect rate, which became a significant competitive advantage.

Finally, it's important to foster open communication with customers about quality. In one organisation, we introduced quarterly quality review meetings with our key customers, where we would review any quality issues that had occurred and discuss steps we were taking to address them. These meetings helped build trust and provided valuable insights into our products' performance in the field. By involving customers in the quality assurance process, we aligned our efforts more closely with their expectations and continually improved our performance.

In conclusion, ensuring product quality is more than meeting technical specifications; it is about consistently delivering products that meet customer expectations and build trust over time. By implementing strong quality management systems, fostering a quality culture, and maintaining open communication with suppliers and customers, COOs can ensure that their organisations consistently deliver high-quality products that drive customer satisfaction and loyalty.

5.6 - Customer Service Excellence

Customer service excellence goes beyond answering questions or resolving complaints, creating a seamless and positive experience at every customer journey stage. In the manufacturing sector, where customer relationships can span years and even decades, consistently delivering exceptional service is critical to building loyalty, fostering trust, and ensuring long-term business success. Over my 30 years as a COO, I've learned that excellence in customer service requires a combination of responsiveness, proactive problem-solving, and a commitment to continuous improvement.

The first principle of customer service excellence is responsiveness. In today's fast-paced business environment, customers expect quick answers and resolutions to their problems. Delayed responses can frustrate customers and erode their trust in your company. Early in my career, I worked for a manufacturing company where customer service response times were inconsistent, leading to dissatisfaction among key clients. To address this, we implemented a "24-hour response policy," every customer inquiry or issue received an initial response within 24 hours, even if the issue couldn't be fully resolved within that time frame. This simple change immediately impacted customer satisfaction, as clients felt their concerns were acknowledged and addressed promptly.

Proactive communication is another key aspect of delivering exceptional customer service. Don't wait for customers to come to you with problems; reach out with updates, insights, and solutions before they even realise an issue. In one company, we faced a supply chain disruption that would delay the delivery of a critical component. Rather than waiting for the customer to call us when the product didn't arrive on time, we proactively contacted them, explained the situation, and offered alternative solutions. This level of transparency helped maintain their trust and allowed us to work together to find a solution that minimised the impact on their operations.

Training and empowering customer service teams is crucial for delivering consistent service. Front-line employees must have the skills, knowledge, and authority to resolve issues quickly and effectively. In one organisation, we recognised that our customer service team was spending too much time escalating issues to management because they had no autonomy to make decisions. We addressed this by providing additional training and giving the team more discretion to resolve issues on the spot, such as offering discounts or expedited shipping without the manager's approval. This improved customer satisfaction and reduced the time it took to resolve issues, benefiting both the customer and the company.

Building a relationship of trust is fundamental to customer service excellence. When customers feel that you have their best interests in mind, they are likelier to remain loyal despite occasional problems. In one instance, our long-time customer experienced a series of minor product issues over six months. While the problems were not severe, they were frustrating for the customer. Rather than simply addressing each issue in isolation, we invited the customer to our facility for a full tour and a detailed discussion of our steps to prevent future issues. This transparency and openness helped rebuild their confidence in our brand, and they continued to place large orders with us for years afterwards.

Service consistency is critical in manufacturing, where the stakes can be high if things go wrong. Customers must know they can rely on your company to deliver high-quality products and consistent, dependable service. One of the most effective ways to ensure consistency is to establish and document clear service-level agreements (SLAs) that define response times, resolution times, and escalation procedures. In one company, we introduced SLAs for our customer service team that included specific targets for resolving issues based on the severity of the problem. By formalising these expectations, we could track performance more effectively and ensure that customers received the same level of service regardless of the issue they were facing.

Customer feedback loops are essential for continuously improving service quality. In one organisation, we implemented a post-service feedback system where customers could rate their experience and comment after every interaction with our service team. This feedback allowed us to identify areas where we excelled and needed improvement. Over time, we used this data to refine our training programmes, improve response times, and introduce new services that better met our customers' needs.

One of the most important elements of customer service excellence is personalisation. Customers appreciate it when companies take the time to understand their specific needs and tailor their service accordingly. In one manufacturing firm, we developed personalised service plans for our top customers, which included dedicated account managers, customised reporting, and priority support. These personalised services helped us stand out from competitors and led to long-term contracts with many clients.

Finally, customer service excellence requires a culture of continuous improvement. It's not enough to deliver good service once; you must constantly look for ways to improve and innovate. In one company, we held quarterly "service innovation" meetings where the customer service team could share ideas for improving processes, introducing new services, or enhancing customer engagement. These meetings generated several successful initiatives, including introducing a customer service chatbot that reduced response times and improved overall efficiency.

In conclusion, consistently delivering exceptional customer service is more than resolving problems; it involves building trust, being responsive, and continuously seeking ways to improve the customer experience. By empowering their team, maintaining proactive communication, and prioritising personalisation, COOs can ensure that their organisations deliver world-class service that drives loyalty and long-term business success.

5.7 - Managing Customer Expectations

Managing customer expectations is a delicate balancing act, particularly in manufacturing, where operational limitations and unexpected challenges can sometimes make it difficult to meet every customer demand. Setting and managing these expectations effectively is critical for maintaining trust, satisfaction, and long-term business relationships. With over 30 years of experience in the manufacturing sector, I've learned that the key to successfully managing customer expectations lies in clear communication, transparency, and proactive problem-solving.

Setting realistic expectations is the first and most fundamental aspect of managing customer expectations. Too often, businesses fall into the trap of overpromising to secure contracts only to underdeliver when it comes to execution. While it may be tempting to agree to aggressive timelines or product specifications to win a customer's business, doing so can lead to disappointment and strained relationships if the promises can't be fulfilled. In one company I worked with, we strategically shifted our focus from aggressive sales targets to operational feasibility. This meant being more upfront with customers about what we could deliver regarding lead times, product capabilities, and pricing. While this initially felt risky, we found that customers appreciated our honesty, and we built stronger, longer-term relationships based on trust.

Effective communication plays a crucial role in managing expectations throughout the customer relationship. It's not enough to set expectations during the initial negotiation; customers need regular updates and transparency about the status of their orders or projects. In one case, a large customer placed an order that involved multiple complex components that required specialised production processes. We knew the timeline would be tight, but we implemented a proactive communication plan rather than reassuring the customer that we would meet the deadline. We provided weekly updates, including progress reports and any potential risks we saw on the horizon. This transparency allowed the customer to adjust their planning and were already prepared when an unforeseen delay occurred. Ultimately, the customer was satisfied because of the final delivery and because we managed their expectations and kept them in the loop throughout the process.

Another important strategy in managing expectations is to understand the customer's priorities. Not all demands are created equal; some may be critical to the customer's success, while others may be more flexible. By identifying which aspects of a project or order are most important to the customer, speed, cost, quality, or service, you can focus your efforts on delivering in the areas that matter most. In one manufacturing project, we had a customer who focused on cost control but was flexible with delivery times. By understanding their priority, we were able to offer a solution that met their budgetary needs, even though it required a longer lead time. This approach satisfied the customer and allowed us to allocate resources more efficiently within our operations.

Transparency about limitations is another key aspect of managing expectations. Customers must know if constraints could impact delivery times, production capacity, or product specifications. In one company, we faced a major challenge with a global raw material shortage, affecting our ability to meet lead times. Rather than trying to navigate the issue quietly, we immediately communicated with our customers about the situation, explaining the reasons for the delays and outlining the steps we were taking to mitigate the impact. We could maintain trust by being upfront about the limitations, even though the delays were beyond our control.

When customer expectations do not align with operational capabilities, it's essential to negotiate and find compromises. In one instance, a customer requested a highly customised product with a short lead time that our current production capacity could not support. Instead of outright rejecting the request, we worked closely with the customer to find a compromise that simplifies some customisations to reduce complexity while meeting the most critical design requirements. This solution allowed us to meet the deadline and ensured that the customer received a product that met their core needs.

Flexibility and adaptability within your operations can also help manage customer expectations. While setting realistic expectations is important, being responsive when customer needs change is equally important. In one case, a major customer unexpectedly increased their order volume halfway through production. Although we had already allocated resources based on the original order, we quickly reallocated production schedules and brought in additional shifts to accommodate the new demand. We exceeded the customer's expectations and strengthened our relationship by remaining flexible and responsive.

Data and analytics can also play a role in managing customer expectations. By leveraging data to forecast production times, identify potential bottlenecks, and anticipate supply chain issues, COOs can provide customers with more accurate timelines and updates. In one factory, we implemented a data-driven production management system that allowed us to track real-time progress and predict delays with greater accuracy. This system enabled us to provide customers with more precise delivery estimates and reduced the number of surprises. As a result, we saw increased customer satisfaction because our projections were more reliable, and we managed expectations more effectively.

When problems arise, they inevitably will; addressing them swiftly and offering solutions is crucial. Customers may not expect everything to go perfectly, but they expect prompt and effective problem-solving when things go wrong. In one case, a key piece of equipment broke down, threatening to delay a large order. Rather than simply informing the customer of the delay, we immediately outlined three potential solutions: outsourcing part of the production to a trusted partner, expediting a repair, or prioritising key components of the order for partial delivery. By offering solutions instead of just presenting the problem, we were able to keep the customer satisfied and minimise the impact of the delay.

Lastly, managing internal expectations is just as important as managing customer expectations. Your sales, marketing, and product development teams must be aligned with your operational capabilities. Too often, disconnecting between these functions leads to overpromising and operational strain. In one organisation, we introduced cross-functional planning sessions where sales teams, product managers, and operations leaders could discuss upcoming projects and align on feasible ones. This practice helped prevent unrealistic promises from being made to customers and ensured everyone was on the same page about what could be delivered.

In conclusion, managing customer expectations requires clear communication, transparency, and a deep understanding of your customer's priorities and operational capabilities. By setting realistic expectations, being proactive in your communication, and offering solutions when problems arise, COOs can build trust and foster long-term customer relationships. Balancing customer demands with what your organisation can realistically deliver ensures that you not only meet but often exceed customer expectations, driving satisfaction and loyalty.

5.8 - Case Study: Customer-Centric Success Stories

In the manufacturing sector, customer-centric innovation is a driving force behind long-term success. When companies focus on understanding and addressing their customers' unique needs, they can develop products, services, and processes that meet and exceed expectations. In this case study, I'll share two examples from my experience where customer-centric innovation led to significant business success and strengthened customer relationships.

Case Study 1: Developing a Custom Solution for a Key Customer in the Aerospace Industry

One of my most memorable customer-centric projects involved a large aerospace manufacturer, one of our top clients. They approached us with a complex problem: they needed a lightweight, high-strength component for their next-generation aircraft. However, the available materials on the market either didn't meet their performance requirements or were too expensive to produce at scale.

The challenge was daunting, but we knew that solving this problem would strengthen our relationship with the customer and position us as an industry leader in innovation. Rather than taking a traditional approach, we decided to work closely with the customer's engineering team to co-develop a solution. We held multiple joint workshops where we shared our expertise in materials science and manufacturing processes while the customer provided detailed insights into their specific performance requirements and constraints.

Through this collaborative process, we developed a proprietary composite material that met all the customer's needs: lightweight, strong, cost-effective, and could be scaled using our existing production lines. The new material solved the customer's immediate problem and opened up new opportunities for us to market the innovation to other aerospace companies.

The key takeaway from this project was the importance of deep customer collaboration. By involving the customer in the development process, we created a solution tailored to their needs. This project reinforced our reputation as a customer-focused innovator, and the customer continued to partner with us on future projects, further cementing our long-term relationship.

Case Study 2: Enhancing Customer Satisfaction through a Service Innovation

In another instance, we were working with a large industrial equipment manufacturer experiencing significant delays in receiving spare parts from us. These delays were disrupting their operations and leading to costly downtime. Although we had been meeting our contractual obligations regarding lead times, the customer's needs had evolved, and they required faster, more flexible service to keep their production lines running smoothly.

Rather than apologising for the delays and continuing with business as usual, we saw this as an opportunity to innovate our service offering. We developed a new just-in-time (JIT) delivery system specifically for this customer, which involved maintaining a dedicated inventory of their most frequently ordered parts at a nearby warehouse. This allowed us to deliver parts within 24 hours, drastically reducing their downtime and operational disruptions.

The implementation of this JIT system required significant investment on our part, including setting up new logistics infrastructure and refining our inventory management processes. However, the results were well worth the effort. The customer's satisfaction levels soared, and they continued to do business with us and expanded the scope of our partnership to include additional product lines.

This case highlighted the importance of listening to customers' evolving needs and being willing to adapt your service offerings accordingly. By providing a more tailored and responsive solution, we turned a potential issue into an opportunity for deeper engagement and long-term growth.

These case studies illustrate the power of customer-centric innovation. By working closely with customers, listening to their challenges, and proactively developing solutions that address their specific needs, COOs can foster stronger relationships, drive business growth, and position their organisations as industry leaders.

5.9 - Handling Customer Complaints

While often seen as a negative aspect of business, customer complaints present an invaluable opportunity for learning and improvement. How a company handles complaints can either salvage a customer relationship or damage it irreparably. As a COO, managing customer complaints effectively is not just about solving the immediate issue but also about demonstrating commitment to customer satisfaction and ensuring that the root causes of the problem are addressed. Over the years, I've found that a structured, empathetic, and solution-oriented approach is key to turning complaints into positive outcomes.

The first step in handling customer complaints is to acknowledge the issue promptly and empathetically. Customers want to feel heard and understood, especially when they are frustrated. A quick, honest acknowledgement of their complaint helps diffuse tension and shows that you take their concerns seriously. In one instance, our major customer was dissatisfied with a batch of products with quality defects. Rather than waiting for a formal investigation to be completed, we immediately reached out to express our regret and assure them we were actively working on a solution. This immediate response helped ease their frustration and allowed us to investigate the issue thoroughly.

Listening actively to the customer's concerns is critical. Too often, companies focus on defending themselves or explaining why the issue occurred rather than truly understanding the customer's perspective. In my experience, asking clarifying questions and listening carefully can reveal important insights that may not be immediately obvious. In one case, a customer was unhappy with the lead times for their orders, but after probing further, we discovered that the real issue was not the lead time itself but a lack of regular communication on our part. The customers felt they were being kept in the dark, causing them frustration. We resolved the underlying issue by addressing this communication gap and restoring their confidence in our company.

Ownership and accountability are essential when handling complaints. Regardless of the cause of the issue, it's important to take responsibility and avoid shifting blame. Customers are not interested in internal excuses; they want to know that the company is taking full ownership of the problem and is committed to resolving it. I recall a product defect being traced back to a supplier error. While it would have been easy to blame the supplier, we took full responsibility for the defect, assured the customer that we would rectify the situation, and worked with the supplier behind the scenes to prevent a recurrence. This approach strengthened our relationship with the customer, as they appreciated our transparency and accountability.

Another critical element in handling complaints is acting swiftly to resolve the issue. Customers are more likely to forgive mistakes if they see the company taking immediate action to resolve the problem. In one company, we implemented a rapid response protocol for customer complaints, ensuring any issues were escalated and addressed within 24 hours. This included assigning a dedicated team to investigate the complaint, determine the root cause, and implement corrective actions. By resolving issues quickly, we prevented small problems from escalating into larger, more damaging situations.

Providing clear solutions is essential to restoring customer trust. Once the cause of the problem has been identified, it's important to offer a clear, actionable solution that addresses the customer's concerns. This might involve replacing faulty products, offering discounts or refunds, or providing expedited service to compensate for lost time. In one instance, a customer received a shipment damaged in transit, which caused a production delay on their end. We replaced the damaged products at no cost and offered to cover the expedited shipping for future orders to help them recover lost time. This proactive approach reassured the customer that we were committed to making things right and exceeded their expectations.

Preventing future issues is a key aspect of effective complaint resolution. After resolving the immediate issue, conducting a thorough root cause analysis is important to understand why the problem occurred and how it can be prevented. In one company, we had a recurring issue with a particular component, causing product failures. After investigating the issue, we found that the problem stemmed from a supplier's manufacturing process flaw. We worked closely with the supplier to implement new quality control measures and prevent further defects. Once these measures were in place, we followed up with the affected customers to inform them what steps we had taken to ensure the issue wouldn't happen again. This resolved the immediate complaint and helped build long-term trust by showing we were committed to continuous improvement.

Following up with the customer after resolving a complaint is equally important. It demonstrates that the company values the relationship and is invested in the customer's long-term satisfaction. In one case, after resolving a shipping delay for a key client, we scheduled a follow-up call a few weeks later to ensure they were satisfied with the solution and to see if there was anything else we could do to support their business. This simple gesture went a long way in reinforcing the customer's confidence in our service and made them feel valued.

Learning from customer complaints and integrating those lessons into the company's processes is also essential. In one of the organisations I worked with, we set up a system where every complaint was logged and analysed as part of our continuous improvement efforts. By tracking trends in complaints, we identified recurring issues and addressed them at their source. For example, we noticed a pattern of complaints about late deliveries, leading us to review and optimise our logistics processes. As a result, we significantly reduced the number of complaints and improved overall customer satisfaction.

Lastly, fostering a culture of customer-centricity within the organisation is crucial. Employees at all levels should understand the importance of handling complaints effectively and view them as opportunities for improvement rather than problems to be avoided. In one plant, we introduced a customer satisfaction training programme that emphasised the role of every employee in ensuring positive customer outcomes. This shift in mindset helped create a more responsive and proactive approach to complaint resolution across the entire organisation.

In conclusion, handling customer complaints effectively requires empathy, swift action, clear solutions, and a commitment to preventing future issues. By taking ownership of problems, acting quickly, and ensuring that lessons learned are integrated into the company's operations, COOs can turn complaints into opportunities to strengthen customer relationships and drive continuous improvement. When handled well, complaints can transform dissatisfied customers into loyal advocates for the business.

5.10 - Creating a Customer-Centric Culture

Creating a customer-centric culture means embedding customer satisfaction into every aspect of the organisation's operations, values, and decision-making processes. It's about ensuring that the customer's needs are not just the concern of the sales or customer service teams but are prioritised across the entire company, from product development to production and logistics. As a COO, fostering a customer-centric culture is critical for maintaining a competitive edge and building long-term loyalty.

The first step in creating a customer-centric culture is to lead by example. Leadership sets the tone for the entire organisation, and if senior leaders are committed to prioritising customer satisfaction, that commitment will filter down through every level of the company. In one manufacturing company I worked for, we directly involved the leadership team in customer interactions through regular customer visits, participation in quarterly business reviews, or even sitting in on customer service calls. This visible involvement demonstrated to the entire organisation that customer satisfaction was a top priority, and it reinforced the message that everyone, from the factory floor to the boardroom, had a role to play in delivering a positive customer experience.

Aligning incentives with customer outcomes is another key strategy for fostering a customer-centric culture. Employees are more likely to prioritise customer satisfaction if they see that their efforts are recognised and rewarded. In one company, we introduced a customer satisfaction bonus scheme where employees across all departments, whether in production, engineering, or logistics, could earn bonuses based on improvements in customer satisfaction scores. This motivated employees to take ownership of customer issues and reinforced the message that customer success was central to the company's overall success.

Embedding customer feedback into decision-making processes is another critical step in building a customer-centric culture. In many organisations, customer feedback is siloed within the sales or customer service departments, while other parts of the company are less connected to what customers say. To address this, we implemented a system in one organisation where customer feedback was shared across all teams, from product development to operations. This ensured that everyone clearly understood what customers valued, their pain points, and how we could improve. By involving cross-functional teams in the review of customer feedback, we were able to make more customer-focused decisions across the entire business.

Training and development also play a crucial role in creating a customer-centric culture. Employees need to understand the importance of customer satisfaction and how their roles contribute to the overall customer experience. In one company, we implemented a comprehensive customer service training programme for all employees, regardless of their department. This training helped employees see the direct impact of their work on the customer experience, whether they were part of the production line ensuring product quality or in the logistics team coordinating on-time deliveries. This organisation-wide focus on customer satisfaction helped build a culture where everyone was aligned to exceed customer expectations.

Customer-centric innovation is another aspect of building a culture that prioritises customer satisfaction. Rather than developing products or services based solely on internal capabilities or assumptions, organisations with a customer-centric culture involve customers directly in the innovation process. We established a customer advisory board in one manufacturing firm that provided regular feedback on our product development efforts. This allowed us to tailor our products more closely to customer needs and anticipate future requirements. The result was better products and stronger customer relationships, as customers felt that their input was valued and that we were invested in their success.

Empowering employees to make decisions that prioritise customer satisfaction is essential. Front-line employees, in particular, need the authority to resolve customer issues quickly and effectively without going through layers of approval. In one organisation, we implemented a "customer-first" policy that empowered customer service and production employees to make decisions that would benefit the customer, whether offering a discount, expediting an order, or adjusting a product specification. This empowerment improved the speed and quality of our customer service and boosted employee morale, as employees felt trusted to do what was best for the customer.

Creating a feedback loop between employees and customers can also strengthen a customer-centric culture. Employees who regularly interact with customers through customer service calls, sales visits, or product support often have valuable insights into what customers need and how the company can improve. In one organisation, we set up a system where front-line employees could submit customer insights directly to senior management, ensuring their feedback was considered in strategic decision-making. This practice improved our responsiveness to customer needs and helped employees feel more connected to the company's mission of delivering outstanding customer experiences.

Finally, celebrating customer success stories can reinforce a customer-centric culture. In one company, we made it a point to regularly share stories of how our products or services had helped customers achieve their goals. These stories were shared in company meetings, newsletters, and internal communications, reminding us of our impact and motivating employees to continue prioritising customer satisfaction. By celebrating these successes, we reinforced the importance of our customer-focused approach and built a stronger sense of purpose throughout the organisation.

In conclusion, creating a customer-centric culture requires commitment from leadership, alignment of incentives, continuous training, and empowerment of employees at all levels. By embedding customer satisfaction into every aspect of the organisation, from decision-making to innovation, COOs can ensure that their companies consistently deliver exceptional customer experiences. A customer-centric culture drives satisfaction and loyalty and creates a competitive advantage that is difficult for competitors to replicate.

Chapter 6

Driving Innovation and Embracing Change

> "Innovation isn't a luxury in operations; it's the engine that keeps progress running."
>
> **Robert N. Jacobs**

This chapter explores innovation's critical role in maintaining competitiveness within the manufacturing sector. It emphasises how continuous improvement, driven by creative thinking and strategic adoption of new technologies, can enhance efficiency, reduce costs, and meet evolving customer demands. The chapter highlights the importance of fostering a culture of innovation, encouraging collaboration, and addressing resistance to change. Practical case studies illustrate how innovation and change management can help manufacturing organisations adapt to market shifts and disruptive challenges, ensuring long-term business success.

6.1 - The Role of Innovation in Manufacturing

Innovation is the engine that drives growth, efficiency, and competitiveness in the manufacturing sector. Manufacturers must continuously improve their processes, products, and technologies as industries evolve. In my three decades as a COO in the manufacturing industry, I have seen firsthand how innovation has transformed businesses, enabling them to improve productivity, reduce costs, and meet changing customer demands.

At its core, innovation in manufacturing involves finding new ways to solve problems or improve existing processes. This can range from adopting new technologies, such as automation or artificial intelligence, to redesigning workflows or implementing lean manufacturing principles. Innovation is not just about creating something new; it can also involve incremental improvements that gradually increase efficiency and quality. In one organisation I led, we applied lean principles to a long-standing production process. Although it was an established process, the innovation came from rethinking how to eliminate waste and optimise every step. The result was a 15% improvement in production speed and a 10% reduction in material costs. One of the most significant impacts of innovation in manufacturing is the potential for cost reduction. Manufacturers can reduce waste, improve energy efficiency, and cut labour costs by adopting new technologies or improving processes. For example, in one of my roles, we introduced automation to handle a previously labour-intensive task. While there was an initial capital investment in the machinery, we quickly recouped the cost through savings in labour and increased production capacity. Over time, the automation allowed us to scale the business and meet growing customer demand without significantly increasing headcount.

In addition to cost reduction, innovation allows manufacturers to improve product quality. By introducing advanced manufacturing techniques or adopting new materials, companies can produce higher-quality products that meet stricter customer and regulatory standards. In one of the companies I worked with, we invested in a new precision machining process that allowed us to produce parts with tighter tolerances and fewer defects. This innovation improved product quality and enhanced our reputation as a reliable supplier in a highly competitive industry.

Innovation also drives competitiveness. As markets become more global, companies that fail to innovate risk falling behind their competitors. Customers constantly seek more efficient, cost-effective solutions, and those who can't deliver risk losing business. In one instance, we faced stiff competition from a lower-cost manufacturer overseas. Rather than competing solely on price, we focused on innovation to differentiate our offering. We developed a new, lightweight material that met the customer's needs more effectively than the competition's product, allowing us to win the contract without lowering our prices.

However, innovation is not without its challenges. It requires investment, both financially and in terms of time and resources. Many manufacturers hesitate to invest in innovation due to the perceived risks, especially in industries with tight margins. In my experience, the key is to approach innovation strategically. Starting with smaller pilot projects that demonstrate value before scaling up is important. For instance, we piloted a new robotics system on one production line in one company. After proving that the system reduced downtime and increased output, we expanded it across the facility. This measured approach helped mitigate the risk and ensured a successful roll-out.

Another key challenge is the cultural shift required to embrace innovation. Many manufacturing companies have long-established processes and a risk-averse culture that can resist change. As a leader, fostering a culture that encourages innovation by promoting experimentation and rewarding creative problem-solving is essential. In one organisation, we introduced an innovation programme that allowed employees to submit ideas for improving processes or products. The best ideas were given resources and support to be tested and implemented. This programme generated valuable innovations and empowered employees to think creatively and take ownership of continuous improvement.

Finally, innovation plays a critical role in adapting to changing market conditions. Manufacturers must be agile and innovative to thrive, whether responding to new regulations, shifting customer preferences, or global supply chain disruptions. In one case, our key customer shifted their focus toward more sustainable products. By quickly innovating our processes to incorporate recycled materials and reduce our carbon footprint, we were able to retain customers and win additional business from other sustainability-focused clients.

In conclusion, innovation is essential for the long-term success of any manufacturing business. It enables companies to reduce costs, improve quality, and remain competitive in an increasingly global market. By strategically investing in innovation, fostering a culture that encourages creative thinking, and remaining agile in the face of change,

COOs can ensure that their organisations continue to thrive and grow in a rapidly evolving industry.

6.2 - Fostering a Culture of Innovation

Creating a culture of innovation within a manufacturing organisation is not just about adopting new technologies or processes; it's about empowering employees to think creatively, take risks, and contribute to continuous improvement. In my 30 years as a COO, I've found that fostering this culture requires a deliberate, sustained effort to break down silos, encourage collaboration, and reward experimentation.

The foundation of an innovative culture is leadership commitment. As a leader, it's crucial to demonstrate that innovation is a priority, not just a buzzword. This means setting the tone from the top, consistently communicating the importance of innovation, and providing the resources and support needed for new ideas to take root. In one organisation I led, we established an "innovation council" composed of leaders from different departments. This council reviewed and prioritised new ideas, ensuring that innovation was treated as a core business function rather than a side project. Senior leadership involvement signalled that innovation was the company's strategic priority.

Encouraging creative thinking at all levels of the organisation is also essential. Innovation should not be limited to the R&D or engineering teams; every employee, from the factory floor to the front office, has the potential to contribute valuable insights. In one company, we introduced regular "innovation workshops," where cross-functional teams were brought together to brainstorm new ideas for improving processes, products, or customer service. These workshops provided a structured environment for employees to think outside the box and collaborate with colleagues from different business areas. One of the most successful innovations of these workshops was a simple redesign of our packaging process, which reduced material waste by 20%.

Experimentation is at the heart of innovation. However, many organisations are held back by a fear of failure. To foster a true culture of innovation, it's important to create an environment where experimentation is encouraged and failure is seen as a learning opportunity rather than a setback. In one case, we introduced a "fail fast" philosophy, where teams were encouraged to test new ideas quickly and learn from the results. The goal was not to avoid failure but to fail quickly, learn, and iterate. This approach led to more successful innovations and built a culture of resilience and continuous improvement.

Another key to fostering innovation is collaboration and breaking down silos. In many manufacturing organisations, different departments, such as engineering, production, and sales, operate in isolation, limiting the flow of ideas and slowing down the innovation process. In one company, we implemented cross-functional innovation teams that brought together employees from different departments to work on specific challenges. By combining the technical expertise of engineers with the sales team's customer insights and the production team's operational knowledge, we were able to develop more holistic, innovative solutions. One of the outcomes was introducing a new product line that met previously unaddressed customer needs, which increased our market share by 15%.

Rewarding innovation is another important aspect of building an innovative culture. Employees need to see that their efforts to innovate are recognised and valued. In one organisation, we introduced an "Innovation of the Year" award, where employees who contributed the most impactful innovations were celebrated at an annual company-wide event. This motivated employees to think creatively and reinforced the message that innovation was central to the company's success.

Providing the right tools and resources is also critical. Innovation requires time, space, and resources, and employees need to know they have the support they need to experiment and explore new ideas. In one of my roles, we set up an "innovation lab" where employees could test new concepts, try new technologies, and prototype ideas without the pressure of immediate commercial success. This lab became a breeding ground for new ideas, leading to several breakthrough innovations we later rolled out across the business.

A culture of innovation also requires openness to external ideas and perspectives. In one company, we realised that while we had a strong internal focus on innovation, we were missing out on valuable insights from outside the organisation. We introduced a programme encouraging collaboration with external partners, such as suppliers, academic institutions, and industry experts, to address this. This "open innovation" approach allowed us to tap into a broader pool of knowledge and expertise, leading to more creative solutions and faster innovation cycles.

Finally, fostering a culture of innovation requires patience and persistence. Innovation is not a one-time event; it's an ongoing exploration, learning, and adaptation process. In one of the organisations I worked with, it took several years for our innovation efforts to take root and deliver significant results fully. However, by staying committed to the process, we built a culture where innovation became a natural part of our operations, leading to sustained competitive advantage.

In conclusion, fostering a culture of innovation requires a commitment from leadership, a willingness to embrace experimentation, and a focus on collaboration and cross-functional thinking. By providing the right resources, recognising and rewarding innovative efforts, and maintaining an openness to new ideas, COOs can create an environment where innovation thrives and drives long-term business success.

6.3 - Change Management

In the fast-paced and ever-evolving manufacturing sector, change is inevitable. Whether it's the adoption of new technologies, shifts in market demand, or regulatory updates, organisations must be able to adapt quickly to survive and thrive. However, managing change effectively is one of the most challenging aspects of leadership, especially when it disrupts long-established processes and practices. Over 30 years as a COO, I've led many change initiatives, from large-scale operational transformations to more focused process improvements. A structured, people-centric approach to change management was the key to success in each case.

The first step in managing change is creating a clear vision of why the change is necessary. Employees must understand the "why" behind the change before fully committing to it. It's not enough to announce a new initiative; you need to communicate the benefits it will bring to the organisation, the customers, and, importantly, to the employees themselves. In one instance, we transitioned from a traditional production model to a more flexible, lean manufacturing system. This shift required significant changes in how teams operated, and there was understandable resistance at first. To address this, we held a series of town hall meetings where we explained how the new system would reduce waste, improve efficiency, and ultimately secure the long-term competitiveness of the business. By connecting the change to the company's broader vision and explaining how it would benefit everyone involved, we were able to win over even the most sceptical employees.

Engaging stakeholders early is another critical aspect of effective change management. Change initiatives often fail when key stakeholders, employees, managers, or external partners feel excluded. It's important to involve these stakeholders from the outset, seeking their input and addressing their concerns. We implemented a major overhaul of our supply chain management system in one company. Before making any changes, we conducted workshops with key stakeholders, including production teams, procurement, and logistics. These workshops allowed us to gather valuable insights, identify potential challenges, and ensure the final solution was practical and workable for everyone involved. By involving stakeholders early in the process, we not only improved the quality of the change initiative but also increased buy-in from those who would be affected.

Communication is vital throughout the change process. In my experience, a lack of information is one of the most common reasons for resistance to change. Employees fear what they don't understand, and unclear or inconsistent communication can lead to rumours, misinformation, and increased resistance. I've always prioritised maintaining transparent and regular communication during any change initiative to avoid this. In one company, we implemented a new enterprise resource planning (ERP) system, which involved significant changes to how departments shared information and managed workflows. To keep everyone informed and reduce anxiety, we established a dedicated change management communication team that provided regular updates, answered questions, and promptly addressed concerns. This ongoing communication helped create a sense of stability and kept employees engaged throughout the transition.

Training and support are crucial for ensuring employees have the skills and knowledge to adapt to the new working method. Even the best-designed change initiatives will fail if employees don't feel confident succeeding in the new environment. In one instance, we introduced a new digital manufacturing platform that automated many tasks previously done manually. While the platform promised significant efficiency gains, it also required employees to learn new skills. We invested in comprehensive training programmes that included classroom instruction and hands-on learning to ensure a smooth transition. We also assigned "change champions" within each department, employees who had undergone additional training and could provide on-the-job support to their colleagues. This approach accelerated the adoption of the new system and boosted employee morale, as people felt supported rather than overwhelmed by the change.

Another important aspect of change management is addressing resistance head-on. Resistance is a natural part of any change process, and it's important to approach it with empathy and understanding. Rather than dismissing concerns or pushing through the change without addressing underlying issues, I've always taken the time to listen to employees' fears and frustrations. In one case, we were implementing a shift to more automated processes in a manufacturing plant, and there was significant concern among employees that the changes would lead to job losses. Rather than ignoring these concerns, we held a series of open forums where employees could express their worries, and we worked with them to clarify how the changes would create new opportunities for upskilling and career advancement. By acknowledging their concerns and providing a clear path forward, we reduced resistance and built a more positive attitude toward the change.

Pilot testing and phased rollouts can also be effective strategies for managing change, particularly for large-scale initiatives. Rather than implementing a major change all at once, starting with a smaller pilot project to test the new process or system is often beneficial. In one organisation, we were implementing a new production scheduling software that promised to improve efficiency but also required significant changes to how production teams operated. Rather than rolling out the system across the entire company, we started with a pilot in one production line. This allowed us to identify issues, gather feedback, and adjust before scaling the solution to the rest of the organisation. The phased rollout reduced the risk of disruption and helped build confidence in the new system as employees saw the benefits firsthand.

Finally, it's important to measure the change initiative's success and make adjustments as needed. Change management is not a one-time event but an ongoing process requiring monitoring and fine-tuning. In one case, after rolling out a new lean manufacturing system, we conducted regular post-implementation reviews to assess its impact on productivity, quality, and employee satisfaction. By tracking key performance indicators and gathering employee feedback, we identified areas where the system worked well and areas needing further improvement. This continuous feedback loop, which involves all levels of the organisation, is integral to the initiative's long-term success and reinforces the organisation's commitment to ongoing improvement.

In conclusion, effective change management requires a clear vision, early stakeholder engagement, open communication, comprehensive training, and a willingness to address resistance. By taking a structured, people-centric approach to managing change, COOs can smoothly guide their organisations through transitions and ensure that changes are embraced and sustained over the long term.

6.4 - Implementing New Technologies

In today's rapidly evolving manufacturing landscape, implementing new technologies is essential for staying competitive. However, the success of any technological implementation depends not only on the technology itself but also on how well it is integrated into the organisation. Over my career as a COO, I've led numerous technology implementation projects, from robotics and automation to advanced data analytics systems. Success lies in a thoughtful, strategic approach that balances technical feasibility with organisational readiness.

The first step in implementing new technologies is evaluating the potential impact on the business. This step is crucial as not every new technology is the right fit for every organisation. You can make more confident decisions by assessing whether a particular technology aligns with your company's goals and capabilities. In one instance, we were considering the introduction of automated guided vehicles (AGVs) to streamline material handling in our factory. Before making any decisions, we conducted a thorough cost-benefit analysis to determine whether the technology would provide a strong return on investment. We also considered the broader impact on production flow, employee roles, and the potential for future scalability. By carefully evaluating the business case for the technology, we were able to make a more informed decision that aligned with our long-term strategic goals.

Involving key stakeholders early in the evaluation process is also crucial. Too often, technology decisions are made in isolation by IT or senior management without input from the employees who will be using the new systems. In one company, we were implementing a new digital manufacturing platform, and it was essential to involve production teams, engineers, and maintenance staff from the outset. Their input helped us identify potential challenges and ensure that the system would meet the practical needs of the shop floor. We secured buy-in and reduced resistance to the new technology by involving stakeholders early.

Assessing the organisation's readiness is another important factor in successful technology implementation. Even the most advanced technology will fail if the organisation is unprepared to adopt it. This includes technical readiness, such as infrastructure and systems compatibility and cultural readiness. In one case, we introduced an advanced data analytics system to improve predictive maintenance. While the technology was sound, we quickly realised that our teams lacked the data literacy skills to fully leverage the system's capabilities. To address this, we implemented a comprehensive training programme to upskill our employees, ensuring they were ready to use the new tools effectively. This preparation was critical to the project's success, allowing us to extract maximum value from the technology once implemented.

Piloting new technologies before full-scale implementation is a best practice that I have found to be invaluable. A pilot project allows you to test the technology in a real-world environment, identify any issues, and make necessary adjustments before rolling it out across the organisation. In one company, we considered using collaborative robots (cobots) to work alongside our human operators on the production line. Rather than deploying the cobots across the entire facility, we started with a pilot on one production line. This allowed us to observe how the technology interacted with existing processes, gather operator feedback and adjust the cobots' programming before expanding their use. The pilot project reduced the risk of disruption and helped build employees' confidence that the new technology would enhance their work rather than replace it.

Change management is a critical component of any technology implementation. Employees need to understand why the new technology is being introduced, how it will impact their roles, and how they will be supported through the transition. In one organisation, we were introducing a new enterprise resource planning (ERP) system, which involved significant changes to how departments shared information and managed workflows. To ensure a smooth transition, we provided extensive training, created detailed user guides, and established a support team that employees could turn to for help during the implementation phase. By providing the right resources and support, we were able to reduce the anxiety that often accompanies major technological changes and ensure that the new system was adopted smoothly.

Measuring the success of the technology post-implementation is essential for understanding whether it is delivering the expected benefits. In one instance, after implementing an automated inspection system, we tracked key performance indicators such as defect rates, production speed, and downtime to assess the impact. While the system initially reduced defect rates, we noticed that it was causing a slight increase in downtime due to maintenance issues. We identified the problem early by tracking these metrics and worked with the supplier to improve the system's reliability. This ongoing monitoring ensured that we achieved the full benefits of the new technology.

Finally, staying flexible and open to iteration is important during technology implementation. No technology implementation is perfect from day one, and it's important to be willing to make adjustments as needed. In one company, we introduced a new manufacturing execution system (MES) that promised to improve production scheduling and real-time monitoring. However, after the initial implementation, we discovered that the system's user interface was not as intuitive as we had hoped, leading to operators' confusion. Rather than abandoning the system, we worked closely with the software provider to customise the interface and improve its usability. This willingness to iterate and adapt ensured that the technology met our needs in the long term.

In conclusion, implementing new technologies in manufacturing requires careful evaluation, stakeholder involvement, and a strong focus on organisational readiness. By piloting new technologies, managing change effectively, and continuously measuring and refining the implementation, COOs can ensure that their organisations reap the full benefits of technological innovation. Successful technology implementation improves operational efficiency and positions the organisation to stay competitive in an increasingly digital and automated world.

6.5 - Innovation Strategies

Innovation in manufacturing is not just about breakthroughs; it's about fostering a culture of continuous improvement that permeates the entire organisation. Over my 30 years as a COO, I've seen that the most successful companies continuously seek ways to improve their processes, products, and services. They don't wait for disruptions to force them into action; they proactively innovate in small, consistent ways that add significant competitive advantage over time. Developing and implementing strategies that drive continuous improvement is essential for keeping pace with the ever-evolving market demands.

One of the most effective strategies for driving continuous improvement is the implementation of lean manufacturing principles. Lean is all about eliminating waste and optimising processes to improve efficiency and quality. In one organisation, we introduced lean methodologies on the shop floor, starting with value stream mapping to identify bottlenecks and areas where resources were underutilised. By systematically addressing these issues, we reduced lead times, improved on-time delivery, and cut costs by 12% without sacrificing quality. Lean also encourages a mindset of continuous improvement, the Japanese call kaizen, where employees at all levels are encouraged to look for small, incremental improvements daily.

Another powerful technique for driving innovation is using cross-functional teams to solve specific challenges. In many manufacturing organisations, different departments operate in silos, which can stifle innovation and slow down progress. By bringing together people from different business areas, such as engineering, production, quality control, and customer service, you can generate more creative solutions to problems. In one company, we created cross-functional "innovation teams" to address specific operational challenges, such as reducing downtime on the production line or improving product quality. These teams worked together over several weeks to analyse the problem, brainstorm solutions, and implement changes. One of the most successful outcomes was introducing a new quality control process that reduced defects by 20%, thanks to the collaboration between production and quality control teams.

Benchmarking against industry leaders is another important strategy for driving continuous improvement. By studying what the best companies in your industry are doing, you can identify best practices that can be adapted to your organisation. In one case, we benchmarked our production processes against competitors known for their speed and efficiency. We visited their facility, studied their workflows, and identified several areas to improve our operations. One of the key insights was real-time data monitoring to track production performance, which we then implemented in our facility. This improved our efficiency and gave us a better understanding of where potential bottlenecks could occur, allowing us to address them proactively.

Employee involvement is crucial for driving continuous improvement. The people who work on the shop floor daily often have the best insights into how processes can be improved, but too often, their ideas go unheard. In one organisation, we introduced an employee suggestion programme where workers were encouraged to submit ideas for improving processes, reducing waste, or enhancing safety. To incentivise participation, we offered small financial rewards for implemented ideas, and we recognised employees whose suggestions made a difference publicly. One of the most impactful suggestions came from a machine operator who proposed a simple change to how raw materials were loaded into the machine, reducing cycle times by 8%.

Data-driven decision-making is another key element of innovation in manufacturing. Today's manufacturing environments generate vast amounts of data, from machine performance metrics to quality control data and customer feedback. The challenge is turning that data into actionable insights. In one company, we implemented an advanced data analytics system that allowed us to monitor key performance indicators (KPIs) in real-time. By analysing this data, we were able to identify trends and make more informed decisions about where to focus our improvement efforts. For example, one of our production lines consistently experienced higher downtime than the others. After investigating the data further, we discovered that a specific machine was causing the delays due to frequent maintenance issues. By addressing this problem, we reduced downtime and increased overall productivity.

Another effective strategy for driving continuous improvement is the use of pilot projects. Rather than implementing a large-scale change across the entire organisation, starting with a small pilot project to test the new process or technology is often more effective. This allows you to identify issues, gather feedback, and adjust before scaling up. In one instance, we piloted a new robotics system on one production line to automate a repetitive task. After monitoring the results for several months and gathering operator feedback, we made several modifications to the system before rolling it out to other lines. The pilot project allowed us to refine the technology and ensure smooth organisational implementation.

Collaboration with external partners is another way to drive innovation. No organisation has all the answers, and by collaborating with suppliers, customers, or even competitors, you can gain new insights and ideas. In one organisation, we worked closely with a key supplier to develop a new material that met the specific needs of one of our major customers. The collaboration resulted in a better product and strengthened our relationship with the supplier and the customer, creating new opportunities for future innovation.

Continuous improvement requires a mindset of experimentation and iteration. Rather than waiting for the "perfect" solution, it's important to test new ideas quickly, learn from the results, and iterate. This "fail fast" mentality allows organisations to innovate more rapidly and reduce the risk of large-scale failures. In one case, we were developing a new production process that promised to reduce energy consumption. Instead of waiting until every detail worked out, we implemented the process on a small scale and monitored the results. While the initial implementation didn't deliver the full energy savings we had hoped for, we learned valuable lessons that allowed us to make adjustments and ultimately achieve the desired outcome.

Finally, leadership support is essential for driving continuous improvement. Employees need to see that innovation and improvement are priorities for senior leadership and know they have the support and resources to experiment and try new things. In one organisation, we celebrated improvement successes at every company level, from small process improvements on the shop floor to larger strategic innovations. This visible commitment from leadership helped create a culture where continuous improvement was ingrained in everything we did.

In conclusion, driving continuous improvement requires a combination of lean principles, cross-functional collaboration, benchmarking, data-driven decision-making, and a willingness to experiment and iterate. By involving employees at all levels, testing new ideas through pilot projects, and fostering external partnerships, COOs can create a culture of continuous improvement that drives innovation and ensures long-term success.

6.6 - Benchmarking and Best Practices

Benchmarking is a powerful tool for driving improvement and innovation in manufacturing. By comparing your organisation's processes, performance, and practices against those of industry leaders, you can identify gaps, uncover best practices, and set realistic goals for improvement. Over my years as a COO, I have seen how effective benchmarking can be when approached strategically and how it can lead to transformative changes in operations.

The first step in effective benchmarking is identifying the key areas you want to improve. Not every aspect of your operation needs to be benchmarked, and trying to compare too many areas at once can dilute the effectiveness of the process. In one organisation, we decided to focus our benchmarking efforts on improving our supply chain efficiency, as we were experiencing delays and bottlenecks impacting our delivery times. By narrowing our focus to this critical area, we conducted a more in-depth analysis and implemented targeted improvements.

Choosing the right benchmarks is also crucial. It's important to benchmark against companies that are truly leaders in the area you are focusing on, even if they are outside your industry. In one case, we wanted to improve our production scheduling and capacity planning processes. Instead of only benchmarking against other manufacturing companies, we also studied the practices of leading logistics companies, as they often excel in complex scheduling and resource management. By learning from industries that faced similar challenges, we were able to adapt best practices to our context and achieve significant improvements in our scheduling efficiency.

Data collection is a key component of benchmarking. You need accurate and relevant data from your organisation and the companies you are benchmarking against to make meaningful comparisons. In one instance, we partnered with a benchmarking consortium to share and compare data with other companies in our sector. This gave us a wealth of anonymised data on production efficiency, quality control, and cost structures. By comparing our performance metrics against this data, we identified areas where we were lagging and set clear, data-driven goals for improvement.

Learning from best practices is the next step in the benchmarking process. Once you've identified areas where your organisation is underperforming, it's important to study the best practices of industry leaders and understand how they achieve their superior performance. In one organisation, we benchmarked our maintenance processes against a leading automotive manufacturer known for its uptime and equipment reliability. By studying their use of predictive maintenance technologies and their approach to proactive equipment servicing, we could adapt these practices to our operations, resulting in a 20% reduction in unplanned downtime.

However, it's important to remember that benchmarking is not about copying. Every organisation is unique, and what works for one company may not be directly transferable to another. Benchmarking aims to learn from others and adapt their best practices to fit your company's needs and context. In one case, we were benchmarking our quality control processes against those of a high-tech electronics manufacturer. While we couldn't adopt their exact processes due to differences in product complexity and regulatory requirements, we could implement several of their practices, such as real-time data monitoring and automated quality checks, in a way that made sense for our industry.

Setting realistic and achievable goals based on benchmarking data is crucial for driving improvement. In one organisation, after benchmarking our production efficiency against industry leaders, we realised that while our goal of achieving a 30% improvement in productivity was ambitious, it was not realistic given our current resources and infrastructure. Instead, we set incremental goals of 5-10% improvement over several phases. This approach allowed us to achieve steady progress rather than becoming discouraged by setting goals that were too far out of reach.

Benchmarking also fosters a culture of continuous improvement. In one company, we made benchmarking a regular part of our strategic planning process. Every year, we benchmark our performance against internal targets and external best practices, identifying new areas for improvement and setting new goals. This created a sense of momentum and encouraged employees at all levels to think about how they could contribute to the company's improvement efforts.

Collaboration with external partners can enhance the benchmarking process. In one instance, we joined an industry benchmarking group where we could share best practices and performance data with other manufacturers in a confidential setting. This gave us access to valuable data and allowed us to build relationships with other companies facing similar challenges. The insights we gained from this collaboration helped us improve our supply chain processes and reduce lead times by 15%.

Finally, it's important to review and update your benchmarks regularly. The competitive landscape is always evolving, and what constitutes "best in class" today may not be the same in a few years. In one case, we had been benchmarking our production efficiency against a competitor for several years, only to discover that they had fallen behind industry leaders due to internal challenges. By regularly reviewing our benchmarks and adjusting our focus to align with the true leaders in the field, we were able to stay ahead of the curve and continue improving.

In conclusion, benchmarking is a powerful tool for driving continuous improvement and innovation in manufacturing. By identifying key areas for improvement, collecting accurate data, learning from best practices, and setting realistic goals, COOs can ensure that their organisations remain competitive and continue to evolve. Benchmarking fosters a culture of continuous learning and helps companies stay agile in an ever-changing industry.

6.7 - Managing Disruptions

Disruptions in the manufacturing sector are inevitable. Manufacturing companies must adapt quickly to stay competitive and operational, whether it's economic downturns, supply chain disruptions, geopolitical tensions, or unforeseen crises like the COVID-19 pandemic. Over my 30 years as a COO, I've faced numerous disruptions. I've learned that the key to successfully managing them lies in preparedness, agility, and strategic thinking. Organisations that can pivot quickly, leverage innovation, and make data-driven decisions emerge stronger from disruptions.

The first step in managing disruptions is anticipating and planning for potential risks. While predicting every disruption is impossible, businesses can create contingency plans for various scenarios. This proactive approach is known as risk management, and it involves identifying key vulnerabilities in your operations, such as dependencies on single suppliers or reliance on just-in-time inventory systems. In one of the companies I worked with, we conducted a comprehensive risk assessment of our supply chain. This process helped us identify suppliers in high-risk regions where political instability or natural disasters could impact their ability to deliver on time. As a result, we diversified our supplier base, reducing our dependency on a single region. This foresight proved invaluable when one of our key suppliers was affected by a natural disaster, as we could switch to alternative sources and avoid production delays quickly.

Agility is another critical factor in navigating disruptions. When disruptions occur, making quick decisions and adapting your operations in real-time is often necessary. In one case, we were hit with a sudden and unexpected spike in raw material costs due to geopolitical tensions. Rather than passing these costs directly to our customers, we implemented a rapid response strategy that involved renegotiating contracts with suppliers, adjusting our production schedules to optimise resource usage, and temporarily shifting production to lower-cost materials. This ability to adapt quickly not only allowed us to maintain our margins but also reassured us about our financial stability without losing business to competitors.

In addition to agility, innovation is a key player in managing disruptions. Companies willing to embrace new technologies, processes, and business models are better equipped to respond to disruptive events and inspire others to do the same. For example, during the COVID-19 pandemic, many manufacturing companies had to pivot rapidly to remote work, digital tools, and new production methods. In one organisation I led, we accelerated the implementation of digital manufacturing technologies, such as IoT-enabled monitoring systems and remote diagnostics. These innovations allowed us to maintain production continuity even when on-site staff was limited due to lockdowns and social distancing measures. They increased our overall operational efficiency, giving us a competitive advantage in the post-pandemic landscape. This success story can inspire others to embrace innovation in their operations.

Effective communication is also critical during times of disruption. Clear, consistent communication with employees, customers, suppliers, and stakeholders helps reduce uncertainty and builds trust. During one significant supply chain disruption, we established a dedicated communication team to keep all stakeholders informed. This team provided daily updates to our key customers, explaining how the disruption affected their orders and the steps we took to mitigate delays. By maintaining transparency and showing that we were actively managing the situation, we could maintain customer confidence even when dealing with the challenges.

Another important aspect of managing disruptions is building operational resilience. Resilience is about having the flexibility and redundancy built into your operations to withstand shocks without significant disruption. In one organisation, we implemented a dual-sourcing strategy for critical components, ensuring we had alternative suppliers available in case our primary suppliers could not deliver. We also invested in automation and cross-training our workforce, which allowed us to maintain production capacity even when faced with labour shortages or unexpected spikes in demand. By building resilience into our operations, we were better able to weather disruptions without sacrificing quality or delivery times.

Scenario planning is a strategic tool that can help organisations prepare for and navigate disruptions. This involves creating hypothetical scenarios based on potential disruptions and developing strategies for how the company would respond. In one company, we conducted scenario planning exercises that considered trade wars, currency fluctuations, and major supplier bankruptcies. These exercises helped us think through the potential impacts on our business and identify the actions we would need to take. When a real disruption did occur, such as a major supplier going out of business, we were already prepared with a plan of action, which allowed us to respond swiftly and effectively.

Collaboration and partnerships are also valuable when managing disruptions. By working closely with suppliers, customers, and industry peers, companies can pool resources and knowledge to navigate challenges more effectively. In one instance, we faced a critical key component shortage due to a global supply chain disruption. Rather than competing with other manufacturers for limited supplies, we formed a strategic alliance with several other companies in our industry. Together, we negotiated better terms with suppliers and shared logistical resources, which helped all of us maintain production and meet customer demand.

Financial flexibility is another important consideration in managing disruptions. Having a strong balance sheet and access to capital allows companies to absorb the financial impact of disruptions and invest in the necessary resources to recover. In one case, we faced a sharp decline in demand during an economic downturn. Because we had maintained healthy cash reserves and kept our debt levels manageable, we avoided layoffs and continued investing in R&D and process improvements. This financial stability strengthened us from the downturn while many competitors were forced to scale back operations.

Finally, learning from past disruptions is critical to improving future responses. After every major disruption, it's important to conduct a post-mortem analysis to identify what worked, what didn't, and how the organisation can improve its resilience in the future. We thoroughly reviewed our response after navigating a significant supply chain disruption in one organisation. We identified several areas where we could have acted faster and more decisively and implemented changes to our contingency planning and communication protocols. This continuous improvement helped ensure we were better prepared for future disruptions.

In conclusion, managing disruptions requires a proactive, strategic approach that combines risk management, agility, innovation, and strong communication. By building resilience into their operations, leveraging technology, and learning from past experiences, COOs can guide their organisations through even the most challenging disruptions and emerge stronger on the other side.

6.8 - Case Study: Successful Innovations in Manufacturing

Innovation is at the heart of any successful manufacturing business. Over my three decades in the industry, I've seen countless examples of innovative thinking and bold decision-making transforming operations, improving efficiency, and opening new markets. In this case study, I'll share two examples of successful innovations I led, demonstrating how strategic thinking, cross-functional collaboration, and technological adoption can drive real business results.

Case Study 1: Introducing Automation to Improve Production Efficiency

One of the manufacturing companies I worked with was under increasing pressure to reduce production costs while maintaining high product quality. Competitors were moving toward lower-cost regions, and while we considered outsourcing some operations, we decided instead to invest in automation as a long-term solution for improving efficiency and remaining competitive.

The challenge was that our workforce was accustomed to traditional, manual production methods, and there was significant resistance to introducing robotics and automated systems. Many employees feared that automation would lead to job losses, while others were concerned about the technical complexity of the new machines. As the COO, I knew that the success of the automation project would depend not only on selecting the right technology but also on managing the human side of the transition.

We began by conducting a comprehensive review of our production processes to identify areas where automation could deliver the greatest benefits. This analysis identified several repetitive, labour-intensive, and prone to human-error tasks, such as material handling and quality inspections. We selected a suite of collaborative robots (cobots) that could work alongside human operators, automating these tasks while allowing employees to focus on higher-value activities.

To address employee concerns, we implemented a robust change management programme. This included extensive training on operating and maintaining the new machines and clear communication about how automation would create new opportunities for upskilling and career development. We also created an automation task force, including managers and front-line employees, to oversee the implementation and address any issues during the transition.

The results were significant. Automation reduced labour costs in the affected areas by 30%, improved product consistency, and increased our production capacity by 25%. Additionally, by involving employees in the process and providing opportunities for reskilling, we maintained high morale and created a more technically skilled workforce. This project improved operational efficiency and positioned us as an industry leader in adopting advanced manufacturing technologies.

Case Study 2: Developing a New Product Line to Meet Changing Market Demand

In another company, we identified a growing market opportunity in sustainable packaging. Customers increasingly demanded eco-friendly products, and we saw this as an opportunity to differentiate ourselves from competitors. However, developing a new sustainable packaging line presented significant challenges, particularly in sourcing environmentally friendly materials that met our customers' performance requirements.

To address these challenges, we took a collaborative, innovation-driven approach. We established a cross-functional team that included R&D, procurement, production, and sales experts. This team worked closely with external partners, including suppliers and environmental experts, to explore different material options and develop new production processes.

Through this collaboration, we developed a line of packaging made from 100% recycled materials that met all of our customers' performance and sustainability requirements. The new product line was well-received in the market, and within two years, it accounted for 20% of our total sales. Additionally, by positioning ourselves as a leader in sustainable packaging, we attracted new customers who prioritised sustainability, further expanding our market share.

The success of this innovation project was due to our willingness to invest in R&D, collaborate across departments, and stay attuned to changing market trends. It demonstrated the importance of agility and customer-centric innovation in driving business growth.

6.9 - Balancing Risk and Innovation

Innovation is critical to maintaining a competitive edge in manufacturing but comes with inherent risks. Whether it's the risk of financial loss, operational disruptions, or employee resistance, every innovation initiative has potential downsides. As a COO, part of my role has been to find the right balance between fostering innovation and managing the risks that come with it. Over the years, I've developed strategies for assessing, mitigating, and managing these risks while driving the business forward through innovative practices.

The first step in balancing risk and innovation is to *conduct a thorough risk assessment before any new initiative*. Every innovation project should be evaluated not only for its potential benefits but also for the risks it introduces to the organisation. These risks can range from financial, such as the costs of developing new products or implementing new technologies, to operational, such as disruptions to current workflows or potential failures of new systems. In one instance, we considered implementing a new enterprise resource planning (ERP) system to streamline operations. While the potential benefits were significant, we also recognised the risk of disruption to our ongoing production during the implementation phase. To mitigate this risk, we conducted a detailed risk assessment that helped us identify specific areas of vulnerability and plan for contingencies.

Identifying and quantifying risks is key. One of the most effective ways to evaluate innovation risks is to categorise them by type, financial, operational, strategic, and reputational, and assign a probability and impact score. In one company, when we were developing a new product line, we used a risk matrix to map out potential risks such as cost overruns, delays in product development, and market rejection. This helped us prioritise the risks that were most likely to occur and would have the greatest impact on the business. Once these risks were identified, we developed specific mitigation strategies for each, such as securing additional funding to cover potential cost overruns and conducting market research to reduce the likelihood of product rejection.

Piloting innovations before scaling them is another effective way to manage risk. Instead of implementing a new technology or process across the entire organisation, starting with a small-scale pilot project is often safer. This allows you to test the innovation in a controlled environment, identify any issues, and make adjustments before rolling it out more broadly. We piloted a new automated quality control system in one organisation on just one production line. This allowed us to see how the technology performed in real-world conditions, gather employee feedback and refine the system before expanding it to other lines. The pilot project reduced our overall risk and gave us the confidence to move forward with the full implementation.

Building flexibility into your innovation strategy is another important approach to managing risk. No innovation project goes as planned, and preparing for changes is important. In one case, we were developing a new, more sustainable material for our packaging products. During the R&D process, we discovered that the original material we had chosen was not performing as expected in terms of durability. Rather than scrapping the entire project, we quickly pivoted to an alternative material that met our sustainability goals and performance requirements. By remaining flexible and open to change, we could mitigate the risk of failure and achieve the desired outcome.

Engaging stakeholders early in innovation is crucial for identifying and mitigating risks. Often, the people closest to the work, such as engineers, operators, or front-line managers, have valuable insights into potential challenges or risks that may not be immediately obvious to senior leadership. In one company, we introduced a new production scheduling software that promised to improve efficiency but posed significant risks of disrupting current workflows. By involving production managers and operators in the planning process, we identified potential bottlenecks and adjusted our implementation plan to address them before the system went live. This early engagement reduced the risk of operational disruptions and ensured a smoother transition.

Financial risk management is another critical consideration when evaluating innovation projects. Innovation often requires significant investment, whether it's in R&D, new technologies, or infrastructure. Creating a detailed budget and ensuring a clear return on investment (ROI) plan is important to manage financial risk. In one instance, we considered investing in a new automated assembly line that promised to increase production capacity. Before moving forward, we conducted a comprehensive financial analysis to assess the total cost of ownership, including upfront capital expenditures, ongoing maintenance, and potential savings from increased efficiency. By carefully evaluating the financial risks and benefits, we could make an informed decision and proceed confidently.

Monitoring and measuring the performance of innovations once they are implemented is essential for managing ongoing risk. Innovation is not a set-it-and-forget-it process, once a new system, product, or process is introduced, it's important to continuously monitor its performance to ensure it delivers the expected results. After implementing a new robotics system in one organisation, we tracked key performance indicators (KPIs) such as production output, defect rates, and downtime to assess the impact. When we noticed that the system was causing occasional delays due to maintenance issues, we worked with the supplier to address these problems and optimise the system's performance. Regular monitoring allowed us to catch issues early and adjust before they become bigger problems.

Balancing risk and innovation also requires a cultural shift within the organisation. Many manufacturing companies have a risk-averse culture, which can stifle innovation. As a leader, fostering a culture encouraging calculated risk-taking while managing potential downsides is important. In one organisation, we introduced an "innovation lab" where employees could experiment with new ideas and technologies in a low-risk environment. This lab allowed employees to test new concepts without the pressure of immediate commercial success. By encouraging experimentation and reducing the fear of failure, we were able to drive more innovation while still maintaining control over the risks involved.

Lastly, it's important to remember that *not all risks are bad.* Innovation inherently involves risks, but these risks can often lead to significant rewards if managed properly. In one case, we were developing a new product for a rapidly growing market. While significant risks were involved, such as uncertainty about customer adoption and the need to invest heavily in new manufacturing capabilities, the potential rewards were equally significant. We proceeded with the project after conducting a thorough risk assessment and developing a solid mitigation plan. The result was a highly successful product launch that opened up new revenue streams and positioned the company as a leader in a burgeoning industry.

In conclusion, balancing risk and innovation requires a careful, strategic approach that involves thorough risk assessment, stakeholder engagement, financial planning, and continuous monitoring. By taking calculated risks, piloting new initiatives, and fostering a culture that encourages experimentation, COOs can drive innovation while effectively managing the risks that come with it. Ultimately, the goal is not to eliminate risk but to manage it to maximise the potential for success.

6.10 - Future Trends

As the manufacturing sector evolves, anticipating and preparing for future trends and emerging technologies is critical for staying competitive. Over my 30 years as a COO, I have witnessed several technological revolutions, from the rise of automation and robotics to the advent of data-driven decision-making through the Industrial Internet of Things (IIoT). In today's fast-changing environment, it's more important than ever for manufacturing leaders to stay ahead of the curve by keeping a close eye on emerging trends and technologies that have the potential to disrupt the industry.

One of the most significant trends shaping the future of manufacturing is the *increasing adoption of digital technologies*. The rise of Industry 4.0, combining the power of automation, data analytics, artificial intelligence (AI), and connectivity, is transforming manufacturers' operations. We implemented IIoT technologies in one organisation to monitor machine performance in real-time. By collecting data from sensors embedded in our production equipment, we could predict maintenance needs before machines broke down, reducing downtime by 25%. Looking ahead, technologies like AI and machine learning will become even more integrated into manufacturing, enabling predictive analytics, real-time optimisation, and smarter decision-making at every level of the organisation.

Automation and robotics will continue to play a central role in manufacturing's future, but the focus is shifting toward greater flexibility and collaboration. In the past, industrial robots were used primarily for repetitive, high-volume tasks. Still, today's collaborative robots (cobots) are designed to work with human operators more flexibly and adaptively. In one company, we introduced cobots on the assembly line to handle repetitive tasks such as material handling and component assembly. This freed human workers to focus on more complex, value-added tasks while improving productivity. Looking ahead, advancements in robotics, such as increased agility, mobility, and AI-driven decision-making, will further enhance the ability of robots to perform a wider range of tasks and adapt to changing production needs.

3D printing and additive manufacturing are also set to revolutionise the manufacturing sector. These technologies allow for the production of complex, customised parts with less material waste and shorter lead times. While traditionally used for prototyping, additive manufacturing is increasingly adopted for full-scale production, particularly in aerospace, automotive, and healthcare industries. In one organisation, we began experimenting with 3D printing to produce spare parts for our machinery. This reduced lead times and allowed us to reduce inventory costs, as we could produce parts on demand rather than maintaining large stocks. As 3D printing technology advances, it will likely play a key role in reducing costs, improving customisation, and enabling more agile production processes.

Sustainability is another major trend shaping the future of manufacturing. Consumers, regulators, and investors are placing increasing pressure on companies to reduce their environmental impact, and manufacturers are responding by adopting more sustainable practices. In one company, we focused on reducing waste and energy consumption by implementing lean manufacturing principles and investing in energy-efficient machinery. We also began sourcing more sustainable materials for our products, reducing our environmental footprint and improving our brand reputation with customers who valued sustainability. Sustainable manufacturing will become even more important as governments introduce stricter regulations and customers increasingly prioritise environmentally friendly products. Technologies such as renewable energy, circular economy models, and carbon capture will drive the industry toward a more sustainable future.

Artificial intelligence and machine learning will also be transformative. These technologies enable manufacturers to analyse vast amounts of data, optimise production processes, and make real-time decisions that improve efficiency, quality, and safety. We implemented AI-driven analytics in one organisation to optimise our supply chain management. The AI system could predict demand fluctuations by analysing historical data and market trends and optimise inventory levels accordingly. This resulted in a 15% reduction in inventory costs and improved our on-time delivery rates. As AI continues to evolve, its applications in manufacturing will expand to include more advanced capabilities, such as autonomous decision-making and fully automated production lines.

The reshoring and regionalisation of supply chains are other trends that have gained traction, particularly after recent global disruptions. Many manufacturers are re-evaluating their reliance on global suppliers and shifting toward more regional or local supply chains to reduce risk and improve resilience. We began diversifying our supply chain in one company by sourcing more materials from regional suppliers. While this initially increased costs, it paid off in the long term by reducing our exposure to global supply chain disruptions and improving our agility. As supply chain risks evolve, we expect to see more companies reshoring or near-shoring their operations to mitigate risk and improve supply chain resilience.

Human-machine collaboration is another emerging trend that will define the future of manufacturing. As automation and AI become more integrated into production processes, there will be a growing emphasis on how humans and machines can work together to achieve optimal outcomes. In one company, we invested in training programmes to upskill our workforce, ensuring employees could work alongside new technologies such as AI and cobots. This focus on human-machine collaboration improved productivity and created new opportunities for employee development and career growth. As technologies evolve, manufacturers must continue investing in their workforce to ensure employees thrive in an increasingly automated environment.

Finally, *resilience and adaptability* will be key factors in the future of manufacturing. As the world becomes more interconnected and disruptions more frequent, manufacturers must build more resilient operations that adapt to changing market conditions, supply chain disruptions, and technological advances. This will require investments in digital tools, flexible production systems, and agile decision-making processes. In one organisation, we implemented a digital twin, a virtual replica of our production system, to simulate different scenarios and optimise our production strategies in real time. This improved our ability to respond to changes in demand, supply chain disruptions, and other challenges, ensuring we could meet customer expectations even in uncertain conditions.

In conclusion, preparing for the future of manufacturing requires a proactive approach to emerging trends and technologies. By staying ahead of digitalisation, automation, sustainability, and AI developments, COOs can position their organisations to thrive in a rapidly changing landscape. Investing in technology, upskilling the workforce, and building resilience in operations will be essential for staying competitive in the future.

Chapter 7

Building a Resilient Organisation

> "The heart of a COO beats with process, precision, and progress."
> **Robert N. Jacobs**

This chapter focuses on building organisational resilience, a key strategy for ensuring long-term success in an increasingly volatile business environment. It emphasises the importance of preparing for, adapting to, and recovering from disruptions in ways that safeguard operations and strengthen competitive advantage. Key elements such as risk management, crisis preparedness, business continuity planning, and fostering employee resilience are discussed in detail. These strategies equip organisations to weather challenges effectively while seizing opportunities for growth and innovation.

7.1 - Understanding Organisational Resilience

Organisational resilience is the capacity of a business to anticipate, prepare for, respond to, and recover from disruptions while continuing to operate effectively. In the manufacturing sector, resilience is especially crucial due to the industry's dependence on complex supply chains, skilled labour, and technology-driven processes. Over my three decades as a COO, I've seen how building resilience into the core of an organisation not only helps it survive crises but thrive in the long term. In today's volatile business environment, resilience is more than just a buzzword; it's a strategic imperative.

At its core, organisational resilience is built on three key principles: preparedness, adaptability, and recovery. Preparedness involves anticipating potential risks and disruptions and implementing plans to mitigate them. Adaptability is about being flexible enough to respond to unforeseen changes quickly and effectively. Recovery refers to the organisation's ability to bounce back from disruptions, learning from the experience to improve future performance.

One of the key benefits of resilience is that it allows an organisation to maintain *continuity of operations* during times of crisis. Whether it's a global pandemic, a natural disaster, or a major supply chain disruption, resilient organisations have systems and processes that allow them to continue serving their customers, even under challenging conditions. During a major supply chain breakdown, I've worked with businesses that could continue delivering products by quickly switching to alternative suppliers and adjusting production schedules. This ability to continue operating preserved revenue and strengthened customer relationships when competitors struggled to meet demand.

Another benefit of resilience is that it builds *trust with stakeholders*. Employees, customers, suppliers, and investors all want to know that an organisation can weather storms. By demonstrating resilience, companies can build stronger relationships with these stakeholders, showing they are reliable partners even in times of uncertainty. In one of the organisations I led, we had a strong business continuity plan in place, which enabled us to keep our operations running during a regional power outage. Our ability to deliver on our promises during that disruption earned us long-term loyalty from several key customers who appreciated our reliability.

Resilient organisations are also better positioned to *seize opportunities* that arise during disruption. While some businesses may be paralysed by crisis, resilient companies can often identify and act on new market opportunities. In one instance, during an economic downturn, we shifted our focus to developing lower-cost alternatives for our products, recognising that many of our customers were under pressure to reduce spending. This proactive approach helped us maintain sales during a challenging period and opened up new markets we had not previously targeted.

Moreover, resilience helps organisations *reduce the impact of disruptions* on their workforce. Employees are often the most affected during a crisis, and organisations that have built resilience into their culture can support their teams more effectively. In one company, we invested in employee well-being initiatives and flexible working arrangements during a crisis, which helped our team stay productive and improved morale. A resilient workforce is more engaged and motivated to contribute to the organisation's success, even in difficult times.

Long-term competitiveness is another major benefit of organisational resilience. In today's global marketplace, disruptions are inevitable, whether from technological advancements, regulatory changes, or shifts in consumer demand. Resilient companies can better adapt to these changes and remain competitive over the long term. In one case, we could pivot quickly to adopt new technologies that reduced production costs, while some of our competitors were slower to react and ultimately lost market share.

In conclusion, organisational resilience is more than surviving crises; it's about thriving in a complex, ever-changing business environment. By focusing on preparedness, adaptability, and recovery, organisations can ensure continuity of operations, build trust with stakeholders, seize new opportunities, and maintain long-term competitiveness. In an increasingly volatile world, resilience is no longer a luxury; it's a necessity.

7.2 - Risk Assessment and Management

Risk assessment and management are foundational components of building a resilient organisation. In the manufacturing sector, risks can come from multiple directions, including supply chain disruptions, equipment failures, regulatory changes, and market volatility. Over my career, I've found that proactively identifying, assessing, and managing risks is key to maintaining operational stability and safeguarding the business from potentially catastrophic disruptions.

The first step in risk management is *identifying risks* across the organisation. This involves thoroughly reviewing all aspects of the business to determine where vulnerabilities lie. One tool I've often used is a risk matrix, which categorises risks by their likelihood and potential impact. For example, a supply chain issue with a key supplier might be deemed highly likely and impactful. At the same time, the failure of a specific machine might be considered low likelihood but still high impact. By mapping risks, you can prioritise which ones to address first. In one company I worked with, we used this approach to identify that our dependence on a single supplier for a critical component was a major risk. This led us to diversify our supplier base, reducing the likelihood of a major production disruption.

Once risks are identified, the next step is *assessing their potential impact*. Not all risks are created equal, and it's important to understand how each could affect the business regarding financial loss, operational disruption, or reputational damage. In one instance, we faced the risk of a key supplier quitting the business. By conducting a financial impact analysis, we determined that if the supplier failed, we could lose millions in delayed production and lost sales. This analysis allowed us to make the case for investing in alternative suppliers and building up safety stock, ultimately mitigating the risk when the supplier did go under.

Mitigating risks involves putting strategies in place to reduce the likelihood of the risk occurring or to lessen its impact if it does. Operational risks, such as equipment failure, might involve implementing preventive maintenance schedules and investing in newer, more reliable machinery. In one organisation, we had a history of frequent breakdowns on a key production line, which caused significant downtime. By investing in predictive maintenance technology, we identified potential issues before they led to failures, reducing downtime by 30% and saving the company millions in lost production.

Risk diversification is another critical element of risk management. In the manufacturing sector, supply chain risks are particularly acute, and relying too heavily on one supplier, region, or material can leave a company vulnerable. In one instance, we faced significant supply chain risks due to our reliance on a single supplier in a politically unstable region. To mitigate this risk, we diversified our supply chain by identifying secondary suppliers in different regions and increasing our inventory of critical materials. This diversification strategy paid off when political unrest led to delays from our primary supplier, but we could maintain production by shifting to our alternative suppliers.

Another aspect of risk management is *monitoring risks continuously*. Risks are dynamic and can change over time, so it's essential to have systems in place for regularly reviewing and updating risk assessments. In one company, we implemented a quarterly risk review process, where key risks were re-evaluated, and new risks were added as needed. This ongoing review allowed us to stay ahead of emerging risks, such as regulatory changes or shifts in customer demand, and adjust our strategies accordingly.

Cultural risk management is often overlooked but equally important. Employees at all levels of the organisation should be empowered to identify and report risks. In one company, we introduced a "speak-up" culture where employees were encouraged to raise concerns about potential risks related to safety, quality, or operational inefficiencies. This proactive approach helped us catch small issues before they became major problems and reinforced a culture of accountability and responsibility.

Risk transfer through insurance and contractual agreements can also be an effective strategy. In one organisation, we mitigated the financial risks associated with product recalls by investing in comprehensive product liability insurance. Similarly, we ensured that our contracts with suppliers included clauses that protected us from liability for delivery failures or quality issues. While insurance and contracts don't eliminate risks, they can significantly reduce certain events' financial impact.

Finally, risk management should be integrated into the organisation's strategic planning. In one company, we made risk assessment a key component of our annual strategic planning process. Each department was required to identify its top risks and develop mitigation plans, which were reviewed and approved by senior leadership. This ensured that risk management wasn't treated as a one-time exercise but an ongoing part of the business strategy.

In conclusion, risk assessment and management are essential for building a resilient organisation. By proactively identifying, assessing, and mitigating risks, manufacturing companies can reduce the likelihood of disruptions, minimise their impact, and ensure long-term stability. A robust risk management process protects the organisation and enhances its ability to adapt to changes and seize new opportunities in a rapidly evolving business environment.

7.3 - Crisis Management Planning

Crisis management planning is vital to building a resilient organisation, especially in the manufacturing sector, where disruptions can affect production, supply chains, and customer relationships. Over my three decades as a COO, I've learned that having a robust crisis management strategy is not just about reacting to problems as they arise but about being proactive, prepared, and organised. When a crisis hits, the companies that recover fastest have planned for the unexpected.

An effective crisis management plan begins with *identifying the crises that could impact the organisation.* These can range from natural disasters, such as floods or earthquakes, to operational crises, such as equipment failures, cybersecurity breaches, or supply chain disruptions. In one company I worked with, we began our crisis management planning by conducting a "crisis audit," where we identified potential scenarios that could disrupt our operations. These included everything from a fire in the plant to a critical supplier going out of business. By mapping out these possible crises, we could start planning how to address each one.

Once potential crises are identified, the next step is to develop *response plans* for each scenario. This includes outlining the immediate actions that need to be taken, who is responsible for each action, and how communication will be handled internally and externally. In one instance, we developed a crisis response plan for a scenario where our main production facility was rendered inoperable due to a natural disaster. The plan detailed how we would shift production to another facility, communicate with customers about potential delays, and manage the logistics of moving raw materials and finished products. This plan allowed us to respond quickly when we faced an actual crisis, minimising downtime and maintaining customer confidence.

Communication is at the heart of any effective crisis management plan. During a crisis, there's often a great deal of uncertainty and confusion, so it's crucial to have clear communication channels and protocols in place. In one company, we implemented a crisis communication framework that included a chain of command for decision-making, predefined communication templates, and designated spokespeople for internal and external communications. This ensured that information was disseminated quickly, consistently, and accurately, reducing the risk of misunderstandings or panic. We also developed a system for regular updates, ensuring that all stakeholders, from employees to customers, were informed as the situation evolved.

A key element of crisis management is *assigning clear roles and responsibilities*. Decisions must be made quickly during a crisis, and there's no time for confusion about who is responsible for what. In one organisation, we created a "crisis response team," which included operations, HR, IT, finance, and communications leaders. Each team member had specific roles and responsibilities depending on the nature of the crisis. For example, the head of IT was responsible for managing cybersecurity breaches, while the operations leader handled any disruptions to production. With this dedicated team in place, we coordinated our response more effectively and ensured that nothing fell through the cracks.

Testing and practising crisis management plans are essential to ensure they work when needed. One mistake I've seen companies make is creating crisis plans but never testing them in real-world scenarios. We ran regular crisis simulation exercises in one company to test our response plans. These exercises were designed to mimic real-life crises, such as a major equipment failure or a cyberattack, and involved everyone from senior leadership to front-line employees. The simulations allowed us to identify gaps in our plans, refine our procedures, and ensure that our team was prepared to respond quickly and effectively during a crisis.

Flexibility is another key component of a good crisis management plan. No two crises are exactly alike, and even the best-laid plans must be adaptable. In one instance, we had a crisis plan for a potential supply chain disruption. Still, when an unexpected transportation strike occurred, the crisis took a different form than anticipated. Because our team had been trained to think on their feet and adjust the plan as needed, we could find alternative shipping methods and avoid major delays in delivering our products. This flexibility allowed us to maintain our operations and keep our customers satisfied despite the unexpected nature of the disruption.

Another critical aspect of crisis management planning is ensuring that *key systems and data are backed up and protected*. During a crisis, especially one involving cyberattacks or natural disasters, the loss of data or the inability to access critical systems can cripple an organisation. In one company, we invested in cloud-based backups for our most important data and implemented redundancy systems for our key production equipment. This meant we could quickly recover our data and resume operations without significant downtime, even if a major disruption occurred. This level of preparedness is essential in today's digital world, where the risk of cyberattacks and data loss is ever-present.

Post-crisis evaluation and learning are important, often overlooked, parts of crisis management. After a crisis, it's essential to thoroughly review the organisation's response to identify what worked well and what could be improved. In one instance, after navigating a major supply chain disruption, we conducted a "lessons learned" session with our crisis response team. We identified several areas where communication could have been clearer, and our contingency plans could have been more robust. These insights strengthened our crisis management plan and prepared us better for future disruptions.

In conclusion, crisis management planning is about being proactive, organised, and flexible. By identifying potential crises, developing detailed response plans, ensuring clear communication, and regularly testing and refining those plans, organisations can respond to disruptions more effectively and minimise their impact. In today's unpredictable business environment, having a robust crisis management strategy is essential for maintaining operational stability, protecting the organisation's reputation, and ensuring long-term success.

7.4 - Business Continuity Planning

Business continuity planning (BCP) is crucial to building resilience in any manufacturing organisation. While crisis management focuses on responding to immediate disruptions, BCP ensures that core operations can continue, even during a crisis. Over my 30 years as a COO, I've seen how effective BCP can mean the difference between a temporary setback and a catastrophic failure. A well-structured BCP enables organisations to minimise downtime, protect revenue streams, and maintain customer trust during even the most severe disruptions.

The first step in developing a business continuity plan is identifying *critical functions*. Not all aspects of an organisation need to continue during a disruption; the goal is to ensure that the most essential operations remain intact. In one company, we began our BCP process by conducting a business impact analysis to identify which functions were most critical to our day-to-day operations. For a manufacturing company, these typically include production, supply chain management, logistics, and customer service. Once we identified these core functions, we developed plans to ensure they could continue, even if other business areas were temporarily halted.

Establishing backup systems and redundancy is essential for business continuity. Production equipment or supply chain disruptions in manufacturing can have immediate and costly consequences. We invested in backup machinery for one organisation's most critical production lines. If a key piece of equipment failed, we could quickly switch to a backup without halting production entirely. We also ensured that our supply chain was redundant, with multiple suppliers for key components and alternative shipping methods in place. This level of redundancy allowed us to keep operations running smoothly, even when unexpected disruptions occurred.

Another important element of BCP is *remote access to essential systems and data.* In today's digital world, many business functions depend on

IT systems, such as order processing, customer communication, and inventory management. Ensuring that these systems can be accessed remotely is critical for business continuity, especially in a disaster or a situation like the COVID-19 pandemic, where physical access to the workplace is restricted. In one company, we implemented cloud-based systems that allowed our key staff to access essential business applications from anywhere. This enabled us to maintain administrative functions, such as billing and customer support, even during a major natural disaster that affected our main office.

Workforce flexibility is also crucial for business continuity. A workforce that can adapt to new roles or responsibilities is invaluable during a disruption. In one instance, we faced a labour shortage due to a regional crisis, and many of our front-line employees could not come to work. Because we had cross-trained employees in multiple roles, we were able to reassign staff to cover essential functions, ensuring that production continued. Cross-training and flexible workforce planning are key strategies for ensuring that an organisation can maintain operations even when parts of the workforce are unavailable.

Supply chain continuity is another critical aspect of BCP. Many manufacturing companies rely on just-in-time inventory systems, which can be vulnerable to disruptions. In one company, we developed a business continuity strategy that included increasing our safety stock levels for critical components and identifying secondary suppliers in different regions. If our primary suppliers could not deliver due to a disruption, we could still maintain production. Additionally, we worked closely with our logistics partners to ensure that we had alternative shipping routes and methods available in case of transportation disruptions.

Regularly testing the business continuity plan is essential to ensure it works when needed. In one organisation, we conducted annual business continuity drills, simulating disruptions, such as a major IT outage or a supply chain breakdown, and testing our response. These drills helped us identify weaknesses in our plan and allowed us to refine our strategies. For example, during one drill, we discovered that our backup systems for critical data were not being updated frequently enough, which could have led to significant data loss during a real disaster. After identifying this gap, we implemented more frequent data backups, ensuring that we were better prepared for a potential crisis.

Maintaining clear communication during a disruption is another critical part of BCP. Employees, customers, and suppliers must know what is happening and how the organisation responds to the crisis. In one company, we developed a business continuity communication plan that included regular updates to all stakeholders, both internally and externally. This helped keep everyone informed, reduced uncertainty and ensured that customers trusted us even during difficult times. In particular, we ensured that our key customers were kept in the loop regarding any potential delays or disruptions to their orders, which helped maintain their confidence in our ability to deliver.

Finally, *regularly reviewing and updating the business continuity plan* is crucial for keeping it relevant. Business conditions, technologies, and risks evolve, and a BCP effective last year might not be sufficient today. In one organisation, we conducted a comprehensive review of our BCP every two years, updating it to reflect changes in our operations, supply chain, and external environment. This proactive approach ensured we were always prepared for new and emerging risks.

In conclusion, business continuity planning ensures that core operations can continue, even in the face of significant disruptions. Manufacturing organisations can minimise downtime, protect revenue, and maintain customer trust during crises by identifying critical functions, building redundancy into systems and supply chains, ensuring remote access to essential data, and maintaining workforce flexibility. Regular testing, clear communication, and continuous updates to the plan are essential for ensuring its effectiveness and adaptability to future challenges.

7.5 - Adaptability and Flexibility

Adaptability and flexibility are two of the most important characteristics a manufacturing organisation can develop to survive and thrive in today's rapidly changing business environment. Over the years, I've seen countless examples of businesses that flourished because they could pivot quickly in response to market shifts, technological advancements, and unexpected disruptions. The ability to adapt doesn't just help a company survive crises; it can also open new opportunities, foster innovation, and drive long-term success.

Adaptability refers to an organisation's ability to adjust its strategies, processes, and operations in response to internal or external changes. Flexibility, on the other hand, is about making these adjustments quickly and effectively. Together, they enable a business to not only react to changes but also anticipate them and turn challenges into opportunities.

The foundation of adaptability in an organisation is *having a flexible mindset at all levels*, from the leadership team to the shop floor. In one organisation I worked with, we made it a point to foster a culture of continuous learning and openness to change. This meant encouraging employees to embrace new technologies, experiment with new processes, and look for ways to improve the status quo. We reinforced this mindset by regularly holding innovation workshops and providing opportunities for cross-training, which allowed employees to gain new skills and move into different roles as needed. This flexible workforce became one of our greatest assets, enabling us to quickly adapt to shifts in customer demand or changes in our production environment.

Another key to building adaptability is *decentralised decision-making*. In fast-paced environments, organisations can't afford to wait for decisions to be made solely by top management. By empowering employees at different levels of the organisation to make decisions, companies can respond to changes more quickly and effectively. In one instance, we faced a sudden shortage of critical raw material, threatening to halt production. Rather than waiting for senior leadership to devise a solution, our production managers were empowered to source alternative materials from local suppliers. This autonomy allowed us to continue production with minimal disruption and fostered a sense of ownership and responsibility among the management team.

Agile operational systems are another important element of organisational flexibility. In one organisation, we implemented a modular production system to reconfigure our production lines quickly based on changing customer needs. This system enabled us to introduce new products to the market faster and adjust production volumes based on demand without extensive downtime or costly retooling. By building this flexibility into our operations, we could stay competitive in a constantly evolving industry.

Leveraging technology is also essential for building flexibility in an organisation. Advanced technologies, such as automation, artificial intelligence (AI), and the Industrial Internet of Things (IIoT), provide manufacturers with the tools to adapt quickly to changes. In one company, we invested in AI-driven predictive analytics systems that monitored our production lines in real-time. This technology allowed us to identify potential issues before they caused major disruptions, enabling us to adjust quickly and reduce downtime. Using cloud-based inventory and supply chain management systems, we responded to supply chain disruptions by quickly rerouting shipments or sourcing materials from alternative suppliers. These technologies made us more adaptable and improved overall operational efficiency.

Organisational structure can also play a role in fostering adaptability. Rigid hierarchies and silos often slow down decision-making and stifle innovation. We flattened our organisational structure into one, breaking down traditional departmental barriers and encouraging cross-functional collaboration. This allowed us to respond more quickly to changes in the market, as teams from production, sales, R&D, and finance were able to work together to solve problems and capitalise on new opportunities. For example, when customer preferences began shifting toward more sustainable products, our cross-functional teams were able to develop a new line of eco-friendly packaging in record time, helping us capture a growing market segment.

Scenario planning and forecasting are also essential tools for building adaptability. In one company, we conducted regular scenario planning exercises to prepare for potential disruptions or changes in the market. These exercises helped us identify potential risks and opportunities and develop contingency plans that could be activated quickly. For example, we ran a scenario where a key supplier went out of business, which allowed us to identify alternative suppliers and establish relationships with them in advance. When a real supply chain disruption occurred, we could pivot seamlessly, ensuring minimal impact on production.

Employee engagement and empowerment play a crucial role in adaptability. In one instance, we faced a significant challenge when a major customer suddenly changed their order specifications. Rather than relying solely on the leadership team to devise a solution, we empowered our front-line employees to propose adjustments to the production process. By giving them the authority to make decisions and experiment with new ideas, we could implement changes quickly and meet the customer's new requirements. This saved the contract and created a more engaged and motivated workforce, as employees saw the direct impact of their contributions.

Learning from past experiences is another critical factor in building adaptability. After each major disruption or change, conducting a thorough review is important to identify what worked, what didn't, and how the organisation can improve. In one company, we adopted a practice of conducting "post-mortem" reviews after every major project or crisis. These reviews allowed us to capture lessons learned, which were then integrated into our operational procedures and training programmes. This continuous learning process helped us become more adaptable as we constantly refined our strategies and processes based on real-world experiences.

In conclusion, building an adaptable and flexible organisation requires a combination of cultural, structural, and technological elements. By fostering a mindset of openness to change, decentralising decision-making, leveraging technology, and investing in agile operational systems, companies can respond quickly to disruptions and seize new opportunities. Adaptability and flexibility are essential for long-term success in today's fast-paced and uncertain business environment.

7.6 - Employee Resilience

An organisation's resilience is only as strong as the resilience of its people. Employees who can navigate stress, adapt to change, and recover from setbacks are essential to building a resilient organisation.

As a COO with decades of experience, I've seen firsthand how investing in employee resilience can significantly impact an organisation's ability to weather crises and maintain high performance during difficult times. Developing resilient employees requires training, support systems, and a workplace culture that values well-being and adaptability.

Resilient employees can maintain their productivity and mental well-being even in the face of uncertainty or pressure. One of the first steps to developing resilience in employees is to provide them with the *skills and tools* they need to manage stress and adapt to change. In one organisation, we implemented a resilience training programme that included workshops on stress management, emotional intelligence, and effective problem-solving. These workshops were designed to help employees build coping mechanisms for dealing with high-pressure situations, such as tight deadlines, unexpected disruptions, or personal challenges. Equipping our team with these skills improved overall morale and decreased stress-related absenteeism.

Open communication and transparency are also critical for fostering resilience in employees. When people are left in the dark about what's happening in the organisation, their anxiety levels rise, making it harder for them to remain focused and productive. In one instance, we faced financial uncertainty due to market volatility. Rather than withholding information, we held regular all-hands meetings to share the challenges and steps we were taking to address them. This transparency helped reduce rumours and speculation, and employees appreciated the honesty, which helped them stay focused and motivated.

Creating a supportive work environment is another key to building employee resilience. In one organisation, we introduced a well-being initiative providing employees access to mental health resources, including counselling services and wellness programmes. This initiative was designed to help employees manage the emotional and psychological stress that can come with workplace challenges. Additionally, we encouraged flexible working arrangements, such as remote work or adjusted hours, to accommodate employees' personal needs. By supporting the well-being of our team, we not only helped them become more resilient and saw an increase in productivity and job satisfaction.

Empowering employees to take ownership of their work is another effective strategy for building resilience. When people feel they have control over their tasks and responsibilities, they can better handle the pressures that come with them. In one organisation, we decentralised decision-making and gave front-line employees more autonomy to make decisions related to their work. This empowerment increased their sense of ownership and accountability and helped them develop problem-solving skills, contributing to their resilience. For example, employees were encouraged to brainstorm solutions and implement changes without waiting for managerial approval when a production issue arose. This level of autonomy gave them the confidence to handle future challenges more effectively.

Fostering a culture of continuous learning is another important aspect of developing resilient employees. When employees are encouraged to learn new skills, adapt to new technologies, and take on new challenges, they become more adaptable and better equipped to handle change. In one company, we implemented a cross-training programme where employees rotated between different departments to better understand the organisation's operations. This made our workforce more versatile and instilled confidence in our employees, making them feel more prepared to navigate new challenges. When the company later faced a sudden surge in demand for a new product, our cross-trained employees could step into new roles seamlessly, reassuring us that they were well-equipped to handle change and helping us meet the increased demand without significant disruptions.

Recognition and reward systems also play a crucial role in building resilience. Employees who feel valued and appreciated are likelier to remain engaged and committed, even during difficult times. In one organisation, we introduced an employee recognition programme where individuals and teams were acknowledged for their contributions, particularly during times of crisis or intense pressure. This recognition boosted morale and reinforced that the organisation valued resilience and adaptability. Employees who felt supported and recognised for their efforts were more likely to go above and beyond when future challenges arose.

Encouraging collaboration and teamwork can also help build resilience among employees. In one instance, we faced a significant operational challenge when a key supplier failed to deliver critical components on time. Rather than relying solely on leadership to solve the problem, we fostered a culture of collaboration by bringing together teams from procurement, production, and logistics to brainstorm solutions. This collaborative approach helped resolve the issue and strengthened the team's camaraderie and resilience. Employees who had worked together to overcome a shared challenge were more confident handling future disruptions.

Finally, it's important to *lead by example* regarding resilience. As a leader, demonstrating calmness, focus, and positivity in the face of adversity sets the tone for the entire organisation. In one organisation, during a particularly challenging period of restructuring, I made it a point to remain visible and approachable, addressing employees' concerns and maintaining a positive outlook. This leadership by example helped foster a sense of stability and resilience among the team, even as we navigated significant changes.

In conclusion, developing resilient employees is critical for building a resilient organisation. By providing employees with the tools and support they need to manage stress, encouraging open communication, fostering a culture of continuous learning, and recognising their efforts, organisations can help their workforce remain engaged and productive, even in the face of challenges. A resilient workforce is better equipped to handle crises and plays a key role in driving the long-term success and adaptability of the organisation.

7.7 - Maintaining Operational Stability

Operational stability during a crisis is key to an organisation's resilience. A manufacturing business, in particular, relies on a consistent production flow, supply chain management, and timely deliveries. In my experience as a COO, I've seen how crises, ranging from equipment breakdowns to large-scale external shocks like the

COVID-19 pandemic, can threaten this flow. However, organisations can maintain stability and minimise disruptions by employing the right strategies, even under the most challenging conditions.

The first step in maintaining operational stability is *identifying the most critical business functions and ensuring redundancy*. Every manufacturing operation has processes essential to keeping the business running, whether it's production lines, supply chain logistics, or IT infrastructure. We conducted a business impact analysis in one company to identify these critical functions. This helped us focus on protecting and supporting the operations that would have the most significant impact if disrupted. For example, in a power outage, we ensured backup generators were in place for key production lines, allowing us to continue manufacturing even if the grid went down.

Building redundancy into production systems is another critical technique. We invested in backup machinery for our most critical operations in one organisation. If a key piece of equipment failed, we could quickly switch to the backup without halting production. We also implemented redundant systems in our supply chain by sourcing materials from multiple suppliers. During one crisis, where our primary supplier was affected by a natural disaster, this redundancy allowed us to continue production using materials from alternative suppliers. Without this level of preparedness, our operations would have been severely disrupted, leading to missed deadlines and potential loss of customers.

Another technique to ensure stability is *implementing robust preventive maintenance schedules* for all critical equipment. Downtime due to unexpected equipment failure can be disastrous, particularly during a crisis when supply chains and production schedules are strained. In one company, we adopted predictive maintenance technologies that monitored the performance of our equipment in real-time. By identifying potential issues before they caused breakdowns, we reduced unplanned downtime by 40%. This proactive approach helped us maintain operational stability during normal times and proved invaluable during crises when the ability to keep production lines running without interruption was even more critical.

Cross-training employees is another effective way to maintain stability during a crisis. In many manufacturing environments, specific employees are trained to operate machinery or manage certain processes. However, it's not uncommon for key employees to be unavailable during a crisis, such as a labour shortage or an illness outbreak. We mitigated this risk in one organisation by cross-training employees to perform multiple roles. Someone else could keep operations running smoothly if a critical team member was absent. For example, when a wave of illness swept through our workforce, we could continue production without a significant drop in output because we had trained a backup team to manage the critical tasks. This flexibility within the workforce was essential to maintaining stability.

Strengthening supplier relationships is another technique that can ensure operational stability during a crisis. Manufacturing companies often rely on just-in-time supply chains, which can be particularly vulnerable to disruptions. In one instance, when a major supplier was at risk of going out of business, we took proactive steps to build stronger relationships with alternative suppliers. We also worked with our existing supplier to develop a contingency plan, which included ramping up production and storing additional inventory in anticipation of a potential disruption. This collaborative approach helped us avoid significant delays when the supplier eventually failed. Organisations can reduce the risk of supply chain disruptions by maintaining open lines of communication with suppliers and working closely with them during a crisis.

Establishing a crisis response team is another vital technique for ensuring operational stability. In one organisation, we created a dedicated crisis management team composed of leaders from key departments, including production, IT, logistics, and human resources. This team coordinated the organisation's response to any crisis, ensuring that decisions were made quickly and everyone was aligned on priorities. The crisis management team regularly conducted simulations and drills to prepare for disruptions like natural disasters, equipment failures, and supply chain issues. When a real crisis occurred, a flood that affected one of our production facilities, this team was able to respond swiftly and minimise the impact on our operations. By having a dedicated team, we could keep production going with minimal downtime despite the external challenges.

Effective communication is also critical to maintaining operational stability during a crisis. Employees, suppliers, and customers must know what is happening and how the organisation responds. In one company, we implemented a communication protocol that included regular updates to all stakeholders during a crisis. This ensured that employees knew what to expect and what was required of them, while customers were kept informed about any potential delays or changes to delivery schedules. Clear, consistent communication helped reduce uncertainty and allowed us to manage expectations more effectively. It also ensured that everyone worked from the same playbook, which helped prevent confusion and missteps during the crisis.

Leveraging technology can further enhance operational stability. In one instance, we adopted a cloud-based enterprise resource planning (ERP) system that allowed us to monitor and manage operations in real-time, even when team members were working remotely. This proved invaluable during a crisis where access to our physical facilities was restricted. Having our critical data and systems accessible in the cloud, we could continue managing production, supply chain, and customer orders without interruption. Additionally, real-time data allowed us to make quick, informed decisions about resource allocation, ensuring we could keep operations running smoothly.

Lastly, *establishing clear priorities* during a crisis is essential for maintaining operational stability. Not all business functions are equally critical, and during a crisis, it's important to focus resources on the areas that matter most. In one organisation, when faced with a significant disruption to our supply chain, we prioritised production for our most important customers and products. This allowed us to allocate our limited resources effectively, ensuring that we could meet the needs of our key customers, even if other areas of the business had to be temporarily scaled back. By setting clear priorities and communicating them across the organisation, we maintained stability in the areas that mattered most.

In conclusion, maintaining operational stability during a crisis requires proactive planning, flexibility, and strong leadership. By building redundancy into systems, cross-training employees, strengthening supplier relationships, and leveraging technology, organisations can minimise disruptions and continue operating effectively. Clear communication, well-defined priorities, and a dedicated crisis management team ensure the organisation can navigate crises with minimal impact on its operations.

7.8 - Case Study: Resilient Organisations Navigating Crises

Resilient organisations are distinguished by their ability to navigate crises with agility, efficiency, and a forward-thinking mindset. In this case study, I'll share two examples of manufacturing organisations that successfully navigated significant crises, demonstrating how resilience, rooted in strong leadership, preparation, and adaptability, can make the difference between survival and failure.

Case Study 1: Navigating a Global Supply Chain Disruption

One of the organisations I worked with was a global manufacturer of industrial components that relied heavily on just-in-time supply chains. In the wake of a major geopolitical conflict, the organisation faced severe disruption as one of its regional key suppliers could not deliver critical materials. This threatened to halt production entirely, which would have resulted in significant revenue losses and damaged customer relationships.

This organisation's proactive approach to risk management and supplier diversification made it resilient. Several years earlier, the company had conducted a thorough risk assessment of its supply chain and had identified this region as a potential risk. To mitigate this, we developed relationships with secondary suppliers in different regions and established contracts with them that allowed for rapid ramp-up in the event of a disruption.

When the supply chain disruption occurred, we immediately activated our contingency plan. Our procurement team contacted the alternative suppliers, who could step in and provide the necessary materials within a matter of days. Additionally, because we had a robust communication strategy, we could inform our customers about the situation and reassure them that there would be minimal impact on their orders. As a result, we maintained production with only a minor delay, avoided major financial losses, and strengthened our reputation as a reliable supplier.

The key lesson from this case is that *preparation and foresight* are essential to resilience. The organisation navigated a major disruption with minimal impact by identifying potential risks in advance and establishing alternative options.

Case Study 2: Adapting to a Sudden Shift in Market Demand

In another instance, I worked with a company that manufactured consumer electronics. The company had long been a leader in its field, but it was caught off guard by a sudden and dramatic shift in market demand as customers moved toward more sustainable and eco-friendly products. The company's existing product line was not designed with sustainability in mind, and sales began to decline as competitors launched more environmentally conscious alternatives.

What set this organisation apart was its ability to *adapt quickly* to the changing market. Recognising the situation's urgency, the leadership team convened a cross-functional task force to address the issue. This team, which included members from R&D, marketing, production, and supply chain, was mandated to develop a new line of sustainable products in record time.

By leveraging the company's existing capabilities and forming strategic partnerships with suppliers of eco-friendly materials, the task force was able to design and launch a new product line in just six months. This rapid response helped the company recover from its initial sales decline and positioned it as a leader in the growing market for sustainable electronics. As a result, the company saw a significant increase in sales and captured a new customer base that valued sustainability.

The key lesson from this case is that *organisational agility and cross-functional collaboration* are critical to resilience. By breaking down silos and empowering a dedicated team to respond to the market shift, the company was able to adapt quickly and turn a potential crisis into an opportunity for growth.

These case studies illustrate the importance of preparation, adaptability, and collaboration in building organisational resilience. Whether navigating supply chain disruptions or responding to changing market demands, resilient organisations anticipate risks, foster cross-functional collaboration, and move quickly to seize opportunities.

7.9 - Recovery and Learning

One of the most significant attributes of a resilient organisation is its ability to recover from crises and learn from them. Recovery is about getting the business back as quickly as possible. At the same time, learning involves analysing the crisis response to ensure the organisation is better prepared for future disruptions. Over my 30 years as a COO, I have seen how effective recovery and post-crisis learning can transform an organisation, enabling it to emerge stronger, more adaptable, and more capable of navigating future challenges.

The *first stage of recovery* is getting core operations back to normal as quickly and efficiently as possible. This requires a *well-coordinated recovery plan* that includes clear priorities for what needs to be restored first. In one organisation I worked with, we faced a major production outage due to a natural disaster that affected our primary manufacturing facility. Our recovery plan prioritised restoring power and water to the facility and restarting key production lines to meet our critical customer orders. Thanks to this structured approach, we could resume partial production within 48 hours and full operations within a week.

Effective communication is also essential during the recovery phase. Employees need to know what's expected of them, customers need updates on how the crisis will impact their orders, and suppliers need to understand what adjustments may be required. In one company, we established a recovery communication plan with regular updates to all stakeholders. This transparency helped reduce uncertainty and reassured employees and customers that we were on track to restore normal operations.

While *restoring operations is the immediate goal*, learning from the crisis sets resilient organisations apart. Once the crisis is under control and the organisation stabilises, conducting a thorough post-crisis analysis is time. This involves reviewing every aspect of the crisis response to understand what worked well and what didn't. After navigating a major cybersecurity breach in one organisation, we conducted a series of post-mortem meetings with teams across IT, operations, and leadership. We looked at how the breach occurred, how we responded, and what gaps existed in our security protocols. This review led to a complete overhaul of our cybersecurity policies, including additional employee training and stricter controls on access to sensitive data.

One of the most important outcomes of post-crisis analysis is the opportunity to *improve future responses*. In the manufacturing sector, this often involves updating crisis management plans, refining business continuity strategies, and making operational changes to prevent similar disruptions from occurring again. In one company, after facing repeated disruptions due to equipment failures, our post-crisis analysis led us to invest in more advanced predictive maintenance technologies. These tools allowed us to identify potential issues before they caused breakdowns, significantly reducing downtime and improving overall equipment reliability.

Engaging employees in the learning process is also critical. Employees directly involved in the crisis response often have valuable insights into what could have been done better. In one instance, we invited front-line workers to share their experiences during a production line failure. Their feedback highlighted several communication breakdowns between departments, which we addressed by introducing new protocols for cross-functional coordination during future crises. This improved our crisis response and empowered employees to feel more involved in shaping the organisation's resilience strategy.

Another key aspect of post-crisis learning is *reviewing external partnerships*. Crises often reveal the strengths and weaknesses of an organisation's relationships with suppliers, logistics providers, and other partners. In one case, a key supplier could not meet their commitments during a supply chain disruption, leading to significant delays in our production. As part of our recovery process, we conducted a detailed review of our supplier network and decided to diversify our supplier base. This strategic shift helped mitigate the risk of future disruptions and ensured we had more reliable backup options.

Continuous improvement should be embedded in the organisation's culture as part of the recovery and learning process. In one company, we created a formal "lessons learned" framework that was applied after every major project or disruption. This framework required teams to document what went wrong, what went right, and what changes were needed moving forward. These insights were then shared across the organisation, ensuring that all departments could benefit from the lessons learned, not just those directly involved in the crisis. Over time, this approach helped foster a culture of continuous improvement, where employees at all levels were encouraged to reflect on their experiences and propose solutions for making the organisation more resilient.

Investing in training and development is another outcome of effective post-crisis learning. Crises often expose organisational skill gaps, particularly in crisis management, leadership, and technical expertise. After navigating a significant IT outage in one organisation, we recognised that many of our employees lacked the necessary skills to manage the technology involved in our business continuity plan. We implemented a comprehensive training programme to address this, including technical skills and crisis management leadership development. This investment improved our ability to handle future disruptions and contributed to employee development and engagement.

Scenario planning is another valuable tool for improving future responses to crises. In one company, we used the insights from a previous crisis to develop a series of scenario-based drills that tested our readiness for future disruptions. These drills included simulations of everything from equipment failures to supply chain breakdowns. By running these exercises, we could identify weaknesses in our response strategies and improve them in real-time. Scenario planning helped us build muscle memory for responding to crises, ensuring we were ready to act quickly and effectively when a real disruption occurred.

Finally, one of the most important aspects of recovery and learning is celebrating the successes during the crisis. While it's essential to focus on what can be improved, it's equally important to acknowledge the team's efforts and recognise the wins, whether successfully restoring operations, meeting customer commitments despite challenges, or innovating new solutions under pressure. In one instance, after navigating a major crisis, we held a company-wide meeting where we celebrated the resilience and dedication of our team. This boosted morale and reinforced the importance of resilience as a core value of the organisation.

In conclusion, recovery and learning are fundamental to building a resilient organisation. Effective recovery involves clear priorities, strong communication, and a well-coordinated response to restore operations. Learning from crises, on the other hand, ensures that the organisation continuously improves and becomes more resilient over time. By engaging employees, improving systems, investing in training, and conducting scenario planning, organisations can turn crises into opportunities for growth and long-term success.

7.10 - Building a Resilient Culture

Building a resilient organisation starts with creating a culture that values and prioritises resilience. A resilient culture is one where employees at all levels are empowered to take ownership of challenges, adapt to changes, and continuously look for ways to improve. Over my years as a COO, I've seen that the organisations most successful at weathering crises are those where resilience is deeply embedded in the company's values, practices, and mindset. Developing such a culture requires deliberate effort and leadership, but the rewards are significant: a more engaged workforce, greater operational stability, and a stronger ability to navigate future disruptions.

One of the first steps in fostering a resilient culture is to *embed resilience into the organisation's values and mission*. Employees need to understand that resilience is not just a buzzword but a core part of how the organisation operates and succeeds. In one organisation, we made resilience one of our official company values, alongside other principles such as integrity and customer focus. This communicated that we expected every employee to contribute to building a resilient organisation by being adaptable, proactive, and solution-oriented. We reinforced this value in our performance reviews, where we evaluated employees on their technical skills and ability to respond to challenges and bounce back from setbacks.

Leadership plays a crucial role in shaping a resilient culture. Leaders must model the behaviours they want to see in their teams, particularly during times of crisis or change. In one instance, when we faced a major supply chain disruption, I made it a point to stay visible and engaged with employees throughout the crisis. I communicated openly about our challenges, shared updates on our progress, and encouraged the team to remain focused and adaptable. This level of transparency and leadership helped foster a sense of calm and stability among employees, even as we navigated the disruption.

Empowering employees to make decisions is another key aspect of building a resilient culture. In many organisations, decision-making is overly centralised, which can slow down responses during a crisis. To foster resilience, employees need to feel confident that they can take initiative and make decisions within their areas of responsibility. In one company, we decentralised decision-making by creating cross-functional teams empowered to solve problems and implement changes without senior leadership approval. This approach sped up our response times during crises and created a sense of ownership and accountability among employees, a critical component of resilience.

Continuous learning and improvement are also essential for building a resilient culture. A resilient organisation is constantly looking for ways to improve, both in times of crisis and during normal operations. In one company, we implemented a "lessons learned" framework where employees were encouraged to reflect on successes and challenges after completing major projects or navigating disruptions. These lessons were shared across the organisation, creating a culture of knowledge-sharing and continuous improvement. Over time, this focus on learning helped us become more agile and better prepared for future challenges.

Recognition and reward systems can further reinforce a resilient culture. Employees who demonstrate resilience, whether by finding creative solutions to problems, going above and beyond during a crisis, or showing adaptability in the face of change, should be recognised and rewarded for their efforts. We introduced a resilience award in one organisation as part of our employee recognition programme. This award was given to individuals or teams who exemplified resilience in their work, particularly during challenging times. By recognising these contributions, we reinforced the importance of resilience as a core organisational value and encouraged others to adopt similar behaviours.

Creating a safe environment for experimentation and risk-taking is another important factor in fostering a resilient culture. Employees need to feel they can take calculated risks and experiment with new ideas without fear of failure or punishment. In one organisation, we introduced an innovation lab where employees could test new ideas, processes, or technologies in a low-risk environment. This not only encouraged creativity but also helped employees build resilience by learning from both their successes and their failures. Over time, this approach helped create a culture where employees were more comfortable with change and better equipped to adapt to new challenges.

Open communication and transparency are also vital to building a resilient culture. In resilient organisations, employees at all levels are encouraged to speak up, share their concerns, and offer suggestions for improvement. In one instance, we faced a major operational challenge requiring significant production process changes. Rather than imposing changes from the top down, we held open forums where employees could voice their opinions and contribute ideas for addressing the issue. This inclusive approach helped us find better solutions and fostered a culture of collaboration and resilience, where employees felt empowered to contribute to the organisation's success.

Employee well-being and support are also crucial components of a resilient culture. Organisations that invest in their employees' physical, emotional, and mental well-being are better able to maintain resilience during stress or disruption. In one company, we introduced a well-being programme that included access to mental health resources, flexible work arrangements, and regular check-ins with employees to assess their stress levels. By prioritising employee well-being, we created a more engaged and resilient workforce where people were better equipped to handle challenges and maintain their productivity during difficult times.

Finally, *celebrating resilience* is an important way to embed it into the culture. After successfully navigating a significant crisis in one organisation, we held a company-wide event to celebrate the team's resilience and recognise the efforts of individuals who had gone above and beyond. This celebration boosted morale and reinforced the message that resilience was a core part of who we were as an organisation. It sent a clear signal that we valued perseverance, adaptability, and teamwork and that these qualities would continue to be critical to our success in the future.

In conclusion, building a resilient culture requires deliberate effort from leadership, a focus on empowerment and continuous improvement, and a commitment to employee well-being. By embedding resilience into the organisation's values, creating opportunities for learning and risk-taking, and recognising and celebrating resilient behaviours, organisations can foster a culture where employees are equipped to handle challenges and adapt to change. A resilient culture helps organisations navigate crises more effectively and contributes to long-term success and innovation.

Chapter 8

Strategic Partnerships and Collaboration

> "Great COOs don't just manage complexity; they simplify it."
>
> **Robert N. Jacobs**

This chapter examines the pivotal role of strategic partnerships and collaboration in enhancing business performance and competitiveness. The chapter underscores how partnerships can unlock opportunities for cost savings, innovation, and access to new markets. Illustrating real-life examples from the manufacturing sector highlights the importance of leveraging complementary strengths and working closely with partners to achieve mutual success. It further explores how to evaluate and select the right partners, maintain strong relationships, and navigate the complexities of global and cross-industry collaborations, positioning partnerships as a key tool for long-term growth and operational excellence.

8.1 - The Importance of Strategic Partnerships

Strategic partnerships are the backbone of modern manufacturing operations. No company can succeed in isolation in an increasingly interconnected and globalised world. Partnerships allow organisations to leverage the strengths of others, access new markets, reduce costs, and foster innovation. Having spent 30 years as a COO in the manufacturing sector, I've seen how strategic partnerships can transform businesses, enabling them to achieve far more than they could on their own.

At the core of any strategic partnership is the idea of *synergy*. When two or more companies collaborate, their combined capabilities can exceed the sum of their efforts. In one company I worked with, we entered a strategic partnership with a specialised materials supplier.

Our organisation had the production capacity and market reach, but we lacked the in-house expertise to develop a key component for a new product. Through this partnership, we combined our strengths: the supplier provided cutting-edge materials while we integrated their product into our manufacturing process. The result was a product superior to what we could have developed alone and brought to market faster, allowing us to outpace competitors. Strategic partnerships offer significant *cost-saving opportunities*. By pooling resources, companies can share the financial burden of research and development (R&D), production, and logistics. In another instance, we partnered with a logistics firm to optimise our supply chain. Instead of managing transportation in-house, which required significant capital investment and expertise, we outsourced this function to a partner whose core competency was logistics management. The partnership allowed us to focus on our manufacturing strengths while benefiting from the partner's economies of scale and advanced logistics technology. This decision reduced our transportation costs by 15% and improved delivery times, ultimately enhancing customer satisfaction.

Partnerships can also open doors to *new markets* and customer segments. In the manufacturing sector, especially when expanding globally, partnerships with local firms can provide critical insights into market dynamics, consumer preferences, and regulatory environments. In one company, we entered a joint venture with an Asian firm to penetrate that market. The local partner had a deep knowledge of the regulatory landscape and established relationships with suppliers and customers, significantly reducing our learning curve and mitigating the risks of entering a new market. This strategic partnership accelerated our expansion and allowed us to capture market share that would have taken years to build independently.

In addition to operational and market expansion benefits, strategic partnerships foster *innovation*. The pace of technological change in the manufacturing sector is rapid, and staying competitive often requires access to cutting-edge technologies or processes. Partnerships can provide access to these innovations without heavy in-house R&D investment. In one company, we collaborated with a technology startup that specialised in robotics and automation. By integrating their robotics solutions into our production lines, we improved our manufacturing efficiency by 20%. The partnership allowed us to adopt new technologies more quickly and at a lower cost than if we had developed them internally.

Risk sharing is another important benefit of strategic partnerships. Large capital investments in new technologies, production lines, or market expansions in manufacturing carry inherent risks. By partnering with other companies, these risks can be distributed, making bold moves more feasible. For example, in a previous role, we collaborated with a raw material supplier to develop a new product line. Both parties invested in the project, but by sharing the development and market entry costs, we significantly reduced the financial risk to each company. This risk-sharing approach made it possible to pursue an opportunity that might have been too risky for either company to tackle alone.

Moreover, strategic partnerships enhance a company's *agility* in responding to market changes. Whether it's fluctuating demand, supply chain disruptions, or shifting consumer preferences, partnerships can help organisations pivot quickly. In one case, we faced a sudden shortage of a critical raw material due to geopolitical tensions. Because we had established a strong partnership with a diversified supplier network, we could source the material from alternative locations, preventing a production halt. Without these partnerships, we would have faced weeks of downtime, resulting in missed orders and financial losses.

In conclusion, strategic partnerships offer many benefits, including cost savings, access to new markets, innovation, risk-sharing, and enhanced agility. These partnerships are not just about immediate gains; they create long-term value by fostering deeper collaboration, shared growth, and the ability to navigate complex business environments together. Strategic partnerships are not just an option for manufacturing businesses looking to stay competitive in a fast-evolving world; they are essential.

8.2 - Identifying Key Partners

Identifying the right strategic partners is a critical first step in forming successful collaborations. Not every company is a good fit, and choosing the wrong partner can lead to wasted resources, missed opportunities, and even damaged reputations. Based on my experience in the manufacturing sector, finding and evaluating potential partners requires a systematic approach that balances strategic alignment with practical considerations.

The first step in identifying potential partners is to *define the strategic objectives* of the partnership. Before even approaching a potential collaborator, it's essential to understand what your organisation hopes to achieve. Are you looking to reduce costs, enter new markets, develop new technologies, or enhance operational efficiency? In one organisation I led, we sought a partner to help us develop a new sustainable product line. Our objective was clear: we needed a partner with expertise in eco-friendly materials. This clarity helped us narrow our search to companies that aligned with our sustainability goals and could contribute specific expertise that we lacked in-house.

Once you have defined the objectives, the next step is to *evaluate the partner's capabilities*. A good partner should bring complementary technological, market reach, or operational efficiency strengths. In one instance, we sought a logistics partner to help streamline our distribution network. After evaluating several companies, we chose a partner that not only had an extensive logistics network but also had invested in advanced data analytics for supply chain optimisation. This alignment of capabilities allowed us to improve delivery times and reduce transportation costs by leveraging our partner's expertise in data-driven logistics.

In addition to capabilities, *cultural fit* is an often overlooked but critical factor in partnership success. Organisational cultural alignment ensures smoother collaboration, better communication, and a shared understanding of goals. In one partnership I managed, we collaborated with a company with a very different corporate culture, emphasising short-term gains over long-term value creation. While their capabilities were impressive, the cultural mismatch led to tensions in decision-making and disagreements on key strategic initiatives. After this experience, I learned to prioritise cultural fit as much as technical capabilities. When we partnered with another organisation in a subsequent project, we ensured that both companies shared a commitment to long-term growth and a collaborative approach to problem-solving, leading to a far more successful outcome.

Reputation and track record are also crucial when evaluating potential partners. A partner's performance history can provide valuable insights into how they will collaborate and whether they will meet expectations. Before entering into a partnership, conducting due diligence on the company's past projects, financial stability, and industry reputation is important. In one case, we were considering a joint venture with a company with strong capabilities in a niche manufacturing process. However, after conducting a background check, we discovered they had a history of supply chain disruptions and had previously failed to meet contract obligations with other partners. This red flag led us to reconsider the partnership, and we eventually chose a more reliable partner.

Shared values and vision for the future are also important when identifying potential partners. A successful partnership is built on a foundation of trust and shared goals. In one organisation, we entered a strategic alliance with a company that shared our commitment to sustainability and innovation. This alignment in values meant that both companies were equally invested in the partnership's long-term success, and we could collaborate more effectively because we were working toward the same vision. The partnership flourished, and together, we developed a range of sustainable products that became a key differentiator in the market.

Geographical considerations can also play a role in identifying the right partner. Sometimes, a local partner with expertise in a specific region can help overcome regulatory barriers, cultural differences, or logistical challenges. For example, when expanding into a new international market, partnering with a local company that understands the regulatory environment, consumer behaviour, and supply chain logistics can significantly reduce the risks associated with market entry. In one company, we partnered with a local manufacturer in South America to distribute our products in the region. Their knowledge of local regulations and relationships with key distributors allowed us to enter the market quickly and efficiently while avoiding many of the pitfalls that foreign companies often face when navigating new markets.

Finally, *flexibility and scalability* are important considerations when evaluating potential partners. The best partnerships can evolve and adapt to changing circumstances. In one case, we partnered with a technology firm to develop a new automation system for our production lines. The project's initial scope was limited to a single production line, but as the partnership progressed and proved successful, we expanded it to include multiple facilities. The partner's flexibility to scale their solution across our entire organisation was key to the partnership's long-term success.

In conclusion, identifying the right partners requires carefully evaluating strategic alignment, capabilities, cultural fit, and reputation. It's important to define clear objectives from the outset, conduct thorough due diligence, and ensure that both organisations share a common vision for the future. By following this structured approach, organisations can find partners to contribute to their success and help them achieve their strategic goals.

8.3 - Building Strong Partnerships

Building strong partnerships is more than just forming agreements; it fosters long-term, mutually beneficial relationships. Over my years as a COO, I've learned that the most successful partnerships are nurtured and actively managed. These relationships require trust, clear communication, alignment of goals, and a willingness to adapt to changing circumstances. Strong partnerships can unlock tremendous value for manufacturing organisations, enabling innovation, growth, and operational efficiency.

The first step in building strong partnerships is establishing *clear, mutual goals*. Both parties must have a shared understanding of what they aim to achieve through the partnership. In one of the organisations I worked with, we partnered with a supplier to co-develop a new product. We held joint planning sessions to define the product specifications, timeline, and financial expectations from the start. This early alignment ensured that both parties worked toward the same objectives, minimising misunderstandings and setting the stage for a successful collaboration.

One of the key elements of a successful partnership is *building trust*. Trust is earned over time through consistency, transparency, and reliability. In my experience, regular and open communication is essential to fostering trust between partners. In one company, we had a strategic partnership with a key supplier who provided critical components for our manufacturing process. To build trust, we implemented regular touchpoints with the supplier, including quarterly business reviews and monthly operational check-ins. These meetings allowed us to review performance metrics, discuss potential issues, and ensure that both sides were aligned on upcoming priorities. By maintaining an open dialogue, we could address small issues before they become major problems and build a solid foundation of trust.

Transparency and honesty are vital to any strong partnership. When challenges arise, it's important to communicate openly about the issues and work together to find solutions. In one partnership, we faced a major disruption when our logistics partner could not meet delivery deadlines due to unforeseen challenges in their operations. Rather than pointing fingers, we took a collaborative approach, openly discussing the root causes of the delays and brainstorming ways to improve the situation. This open, problem-solving mindset resolved the immediate issue and strengthened the relationship by demonstrating our commitment to mutual success. By being transparent, both sides felt comfortable bringing issues to the table, which improved overall collaboration.

Flexibility and adaptability are also key components of strong partnerships. Business environments are dynamic, and partnerships must evolve in response to changing circumstances. In one instance, we had a long-term partnership with a technology provider developing custom automation solutions for our production lines. As our business grew, we needed to scale the automation solutions across multiple facilities. Our partner demonstrated great flexibility by adjusting their approach and resources to accommodate our expanding needs. This adaptability was a critical factor in the long-term success of the partnership, allowing both parties to grow together and continue delivering value as the business evolved.

Mutual investment in the partnership is another important factor. Both parties must feel that they have "skin in the game." This investment can come in many forms, financial, operational, or even in terms of intellectual capital. In one company, we entered a joint development agreement with a supplier to create a new, high-tech component for our products. Both parties agreed to share the development costs and intellectual property. This mutual investment ensured that both companies were fully committed to the project's success, fostering deeper collaboration. The project ultimately resulted in a breakthrough product that gave us a competitive edge in the market, and the partnership flourished.

Shared risk and reward is another important element of building strong partnerships. In one instance, we partnered with a distribution company to expand our products into new markets. Instead of structuring the agreement as a simple transaction, we developed a profit-sharing model where both companies shared the financial risks and rewards of entering the new market. This shared commitment to success created a deeper bond between the companies, as both sides had a vested interest in making the venture work. The result was a successful expansion that benefitted both companies and solidified the partnership for years.

Another technique for developing strong partnerships is to foster collaboration and innovation actively. In one company, we worked closely with a partner to develop a new manufacturing process to reduce waste and improve efficiency. We encouraged cross-functional collaboration between our teams, setting up joint working groups that included engineers, production managers, and R&D specialists from both companies. By working together and sharing ideas, we were able to develop a process that was far more innovative than anything we could have achieved on our own. This collaborative approach improved the product and strengthened the relationship between the companies, as we shared in the project's success.

Regular performance reviews are essential for maintaining strong partnerships. In my experience, even the best partnerships need ongoing management to stay healthy and productive. In one case, we implemented a quarterly performance review process with a key supplier. We assessed key performance indicators (KPIs) such as delivery times, product quality, and cost targets during these reviews. These reviews helped us identify areas where performance could be improved and ensured that both sides remained accountable to the partnership's goals. By continually monitoring and adjusting our approach, we were able to keep the partnership on track and ensure long-term success.

Finally, *celebrating successes together* is an important way to reinforce the strength of a partnership. In one organisation, after completing a major project ahead of schedule, we hosted a joint celebration with our partner to recognise the hard work and collaboration that went into the achievement. This event boosted morale and reinforced the idea that we worked together toward shared success. Recognising and celebrating milestones is a powerful way to build goodwill and ensure both parties remain committed to the partnership's long-term objectives.

In conclusion, building strong partnerships requires trust, transparency, flexibility, and mutual investment. Organisations can develop deep, lasting relationships with their partners by aligning goals, fostering collaboration, and maintaining regular communication. These strong partnerships drive operational success and create opportunities for innovation, growth, and long-term value creation.

8.4 - Collaborative Strategies

Collaboration is at the heart of successful partnerships. Effective collaboration can distinguish between success and failure in the manufacturing sector, where complex supply chains, evolving technologies, and fast-changing markets are the norm. Over my years as a COO, I've seen firsthand how structured, thoughtful approaches to collaboration can transform relationships and drive better outcomes for all parties involved.

The first step in any successful collaboration is to *define clear roles and responsibilities*. When two or more organisations come together, it's crucial to establish who is responsible for what. Without clear delineation of roles, collaboration can quickly become chaotic, with duplication of effort, miscommunication, or tasks falling through the cracks. We collaborated with a technology partner in one company to implement a new automation system across our production lines. Early on, we established a detailed project plan that clearly outlined each party's responsibilities, from system design and implementation to testing and troubleshooting. This clear division of roles ensured the project ran smoothly, with both teams working harmoniously toward a common goal.

Open communication is another cornerstone of effective collaboration. In one partnership, we implemented a structured communication framework that included weekly progress meetings, shared project management software, and regular updates to senior leadership on both sides. By maintaining open lines of communication, we could address issues in real-time and ensure that both parties were aligned on the project's direction. This proactive approach to communication also helped prevent small misunderstandings from escalating into larger problems, keeping the collaboration on track and ensuring that both sides felt heard and valued.

Joint problem-solving is another powerful collaborative strategy. Rather than viewing problems as one party's responsibility to fix, successful collaborations treat challenges as opportunities for both sides to work together on solutions. In one instance, we faced a major supply chain disruption due to a raw material shortage. Instead of expecting our supplier to solve the problem independently, we collaborated, bringing our procurement and production teams together with their logistics and operations teams. By working together, we could find alternative materials, adjust our production schedules, and minimise the impact of the disruption. This joint problem-solving resolved the immediate issue and strengthened the partnership by demonstrating our commitment to mutual success.

Leveraging complementary strengths is another effective approach to collaboration. In one partnership, we worked with a firm that specialised in advanced data analytics. While we had deep expertise in manufacturing, we could not analyse large datasets to optimise production. By collaborating closely with their team of data scientists, we were able to leverage their analytical tools to identify inefficiencies in our production lines and implement improvements. This complementary approach allowed both sides to focus on what they did best, resulting in a more productive and innovative collaboration.

Co-creation of value is a key principle in successful collaborations. Rather than simply viewing the partnership as transactional, the most effective collaborations are those where both parties actively work together to create value. In one instance, we entered a joint venture with a supplier to develop a new product. Rather than simply purchasing their materials, we co-developed the product, sharing research, development, and production insights. This co-creation accelerated the development process and ensured that the final product met the needs of both companies and the market. By working together from the early stages, we were able to create a more innovative and successful product.

Shared technology platforms can facilitate better collaboration by providing a common framework within which both parties can work. In one collaboration, we implemented a shared project management platform that allowed our and our partner's teams to track progress, assign tasks, and share real-time updates. This transparency reduced the risk of miscommunication and ensured that both sides had full visibility into the project's status. Using shared technology platforms is particularly important in complex collaborations involving multiple teams, as it helps keep everyone aligned and accountable.

Establishing a culture of collaboration within the organisation is also important. In one company, we prioritised creating a collaborative environment where employees felt encouraged to work across teams and with external partners. We invested in training programmes focused on collaborative leadership, communication skills, and conflict resolution. This cultural shift made it easier for our teams to work effectively with partners, as they were equipped with the skills and mindset needed for successful collaboration. By fostering a collaborative culture internally, we were better positioned to build strong external partnerships.

Conflict resolution mechanisms are critical to the success of any collaboration. No matter how well-aligned the goals are, disagreements and conflicts are inevitable in any partnership. What distinguishes successful collaborations is how these conflicts are handled. In one collaboration, we disagreed over the scope of a joint project. Rather than allowing the conflict to escalate, we established a conflict resolution process from the outset of the partnership. This process included a clear escalation path involving senior leaders from both companies to mediate the discussion and find a solution that worked for both sides. By having this process in place, we could resolve the conflict quickly and maintain the strength of the partnership.

In conclusion, effective collaboration requires clear communication, defined roles, joint problem-solving, and a focus on creating value together. By leveraging complementary strengths, using shared technology platforms, fostering a culture of collaboration, and having mechanisms to resolve conflicts, organisations can build strong, successful partnerships that drive innovation and growth. Collaboration is not just about working together; it's about actively creating value and driving mutual success.

8.5 - Negotiation Skills

Negotiation is a critical skill in forming and maintaining strategic partnerships. A successful negotiation is not just about getting the best deal for your organisation; it's about finding a mutually beneficial outcome that lays the foundation for a strong, long-term relationship. Over my 30 years in the manufacturing sector, I've learned that the key to effective negotiation is preparation, understanding the interests of both parties and building trust. When done right, negotiation strengthens partnerships and fosters collaboration that benefits both sides.

The first step in a successful negotiation is thorough *preparation*. Going into a negotiation without a clear understanding of your goals and those of the other party is a recipe for failure. In one instance, we negotiated a supply agreement with a key materials provider. Before entering discussions, our team spent weeks analysing our cost structure, production forecasts, and potential alternative suppliers. We also researched the supplier's business model, market conditions, and competitive landscape. This preparation gave us a clear understanding of what we needed from the deal and where we had leverage. It also allowed us to anticipate the supplier's needs and craft proposals aligned with both parties' interests. Proper preparation ensured we were negotiating from a position of strength and understanding, which helped us secure favourable terms without compromising the long-term relationship.

Understanding the interests of both parties is essential in any negotiation. While focusing on your goals is easy, successful negotiators consider what others want. In one case, we negotiated a joint venture with a technology company to co-develop a new automation system. Rather than focusing solely on our needs, we spent time understanding the technology company's long-term vision, market challenges, and growth strategy. By framing our proposals to address their goals, such as giving them access to our customer base and helping them scale their technology, we created a deal that worked for both sides. Understanding their interests allowed us to negotiate from a collaborative mindset, making it easier to find common ground.

Building *rapport and trust* during the negotiation process is another crucial strategy. Trust is the foundation of any strong partnership, and the negotiation stage is the first opportunity to start building that trust. In one negotiation, we discussed a multi-year partnership with a logistics provider. From the outset, we made it a point to approach the discussions with transparency and a collaborative mindset. Rather than taking a hard-line approach, we framed the negotiation as discussing how both sides could win. This openness helped build trust between our teams, which made it easier to resolve contentious issues later in the negotiation. By fostering a relationship of trust from the start, we laid the groundwork for a strong partnership that lasted for years.

Creating a win-win situation is the goal of every negotiation. Too often, companies approach negotiations with a zero-sum mentality, where one party's gain is seen as the other's loss. However, in strategic partnerships, the most successful negotiations are those that create value for both sides. In one case, we negotiated a contract with a supplier to provide critical raw materials for our production lines. Rather than pushing for the lowest possible price, we explored ways to create additional value for both parties. This included agreeing to a longer-term contract that gave the supplier more financial security while locking in a favourable price for us over the long term. By focusing on creating value rather than simply cutting costs, we strengthened the partnership and secured better terms than we would have through a more adversarial approach.

Flexibility and creativity are essential in negotiation, especially when the parties have different starting positions. In one negotiation, we were far from our potential pricing partner. Rather than walking away, we sought creative solutions to bridge the gap. One idea was to adjust the payment structure to allow performance-based bonuses if certain milestones were met. This allowed us to reduce our upfront costs while allowing the partner to earn more if the project exceeded expectations. This creative approach helped us reach an agreement and incentivised both sides to perform at their best.

Active listening is another key to successful negotiation. In my experience, many negotiators focus too much on making their case and not enough on listening to the other side. In one negotiation, we were in discussions with a key distribution partner. Initially, the talks were tense, as both sides had conflicting views on pricing and market access. However, during one meeting, I decided to step back and focus entirely on listening to the partner's concerns. This shift in approach allowed me to understand better their priorities, which helped us find a compromise that worked for both sides. By actively listening, we were able to turn a contentious negotiation into a productive collaboration.

Managing emotions is also critical during negotiations. High-stakes discussions can sometimes lead to frustration or defensiveness, especially when the parties disagree on key terms. However, maintaining a calm, professional demeanour is essential for keeping the negotiations on track. In one instance, we were negotiating a long-term partnership, and tensions began to rise when we reached an impasse on a major issue. Rather than letting emotions dictate the conversation, we took a short break to allow both sides to cool down and reflect. When we resumed, we approached the issue with fresh perspectives, and we were able to reach a compromise. Managing emotions during negotiation helps prevent small disagreements from derailing the entire process.

Another important strategy is to *know when to walk away*. Not every negotiation will result in a deal; sometimes, the best decision is to step back and reassess. In one case, we were negotiating with a potential supplier unwilling to meet our quality standards at a reasonable price for our business. After several rounds of discussions, it became clear that the gap between our positions was too wide. Rather than compromising on quality or price, we chose to walk away from the deal and seek alternative suppliers. While walking away can be difficult, it's essential to recognise when a deal is not in your organisation's best interest and have the confidence to make that decision.

Finally, *clearly and comprehensively documenting agreements* is essential to avoid misunderstandings later. In one partnership negotiation, we worked with our legal team to document every agreement aspect thoroughly, including performance metrics, payment terms, and conflict resolution procedures. This detailed documentation provided clarity and avoided ambiguity, ensuring that both sides knew exactly what was expected. Clear documentation also made holding both parties accountable throughout the partnership easier.

In conclusion, successful negotiation in strategic partnerships is about preparation, understanding both parties' interests, building trust, and creating value for both sides. Organisations can secure favourable terms by approaching negotiations with a collaborative mindset, listening actively, managing emotions, and being flexible and creative while laying the foundation for a strong, long-term partnership. Negotiation is not about winning at the other party's expense but finding solutions that benefit everyone involved.

8.6 - Managing Partnerships

Managing partnerships effectively is just as important as establishing them. Once a partnership is formed, ongoing oversight and optimisation are required to ensure both parties continue to derive value. Over my career, I've managed countless partnerships, and I've found that the key to success lies in regular communication, performance monitoring, and a proactive approach to problem-solving. Strong partnerships evolve, and managing them well can turn them into long-term assets for the organisation.

One of the most important aspects of managing partnerships is *regular communication*. A partnership is like any other relationship; it requires attention and nurturing to thrive. In one organisation, we partnered with a technology provider responsible for implementing automation solutions across our production lines. We established regular touchpoints with their team to ensure the partnership progressed smoothly, including weekly project meetings, monthly operational reviews, and quarterly strategic planning sessions. These regular communications allowed us to track progress, address issues in real-time, and ensure that both sides remained aligned on goals. Without this consistent communication, small problems could have escalated into major issues, but by staying connected, we could maintain a strong working relationship.

Performance monitoring is another critical component of managing partnerships. Establishing clear metrics from the outset and regularly assessing how well the partnership is meeting those goals is important. In one case, we partnered with a logistics provider responsible for managing our supply chain. From the beginning, we defined key performance indicators (KPIs) such as on-time delivery rates, cost per shipment, and customer satisfaction. These KPIs were tracked and reviewed during our monthly meetings, and any deviations from targets were addressed immediately. By continuously monitoring performance, we ensured that the partnership delivered on its promises and remained beneficial for both parties.

Proactively addressing issues is essential for keeping partnerships on track. No matter how well-structured a partnership is, challenges will inevitably arise, whether it's a supply chain disruption, a disagreement over strategy, or a shift in market conditions. The key is to address these challenges proactively rather than letting them fester. In one partnership, we encountered a significant issue when our partner could not meet production targets due to a shortage of raw materials. Rather than waiting for the problem to escalate, we convened a joint task force to investigate the root cause and develop a solution. By tackling the issue head-on, we were able to resolve the problem quickly and maintain the integrity of the partnership.

Flexibility and adaptability are also crucial in managing long-term partnerships. Business environments change, and partnerships need to evolve to remain relevant. In one instance, we partnered with a supplier initially focused on providing a specific material for our production lines. As market demand shifted, we needed to develop new products that required different materials. Instead of ending the partnership, we worked with the supplier to expand their offerings and co-develop the new materials we needed. This flexibility allowed us to maintain the partnership while adapting to changing market conditions. Strong partnerships can evolve and grow over time rather than remain static.

Joint problem-solving is another important aspect of managing partnerships. When challenges arise, it's important to approach them as a team rather than as adversaries. In one case, we faced a quality issue with a component supplied by a partner. Rather than placing blame, we approached the issue collaboratively, bringing together our quality control team and the supplier's engineers to identify the root cause. We quickly resolved the issue by working together and improving the quality of the product. This collaborative approach solved the immediate problem and strengthened the partnership by demonstrating our commitment to mutual success.

Reviewing and renegotiating terms over time is another important aspect of managing partnerships. As circumstances change, it may be necessary to adjust the terms of the agreement to ensure that the partnership remains beneficial for both parties. In one instance, we had a long-term partnership with a distribution company that initially worked well. However, as our business grew, the original terms of the agreement no longer reflected the increased volume of orders we were processing. Rather than allowing this misalignment to strain the relationship, we proactively approached the partner to renegotiate the contract. We maintained a positive and productive relationship by adjusting the terms to reflect our business's new realities.

Finally, it's important to recognise and celebrate achievements in a partnership, as it's a powerful way to build goodwill and ensure commitment to long-term success. In one organisation, after completing a major project ahead of schedule, we held a joint celebration with our partner. This was not just a recognition of the hard work and collaboration that went into achieving the milestone but also a boost to morale and a reinforcement of the sense that we worked together toward shared success. Such celebrations are crucial in strengthening partnerships and reinforcing the collaborative spirit.

In conclusion, a partnership's success hinges on effective management, which involves regular communication, performance monitoring, flexibility, and a proactive approach to problem-solving. By addressing challenges collaboratively, being open to renegotiating terms, and celebrating successes, organisations can ensure that their partnerships remain strong and continue to deliver value over the long term. This kind of effective partnership management turns short-term collaborations into long-term strategic assets.

8.7 - Case Study: Successful Partnerships

A successful partnership in manufacturing can transform not just the organisations involved but also the industry landscape. Over the years, I've seen how strategic collaborations between manufacturers and suppliers, technology firms, and logistics providers have driven innovation, improved operational efficiency, and opened up new market opportunities. In this case study, I'll share two examples of partnerships I've been involved in, highlighting how strategic alignment, clear communication, and mutual investment created value for both sides.

Case Study 1: Co-developing a New Product Line with a Material Supplier

One of my most successful partnerships involved collaborating with our manufacturing company and a material supplier to co-develop a new, eco-friendly product line. The project began when we identified a growing demand in the market for sustainable packaging solutions. Our company had the production capabilities but lacked the expertise and access to the specialised materials needed to develop eco-friendly packaging.

We approached a well-regarded material supplier that specialised in recycled and biodegradable materials. From the outset, we knew this would be a complex partnership requiring deep collaboration and joint innovation. We aligned our goals with the supplier upfront to ensure the partnership's success. Both companies were committed to developing a product that met regulatory standards for sustainability and maintained the durability and quality our customers expected.

We took a *co-development approach* to the partnership, which meant that both teams, our engineers and the supplier's material scientists, worked closely together throughout the process. We formed cross-functional teams, including both companies' R&D, production, and procurement experts. These teams met regularly to share updates, troubleshoot problems, and adjust the development plan. This collaborative approach was essential because it allowed us to combine our manufacturing expertise with the supplier's knowledge of materials science, resulting in a superior product that neither company could have developed alone.

One of the keys to this partnership's success was *transparency*. Both sides shared detailed data on production capabilities, material properties, and cost structures. This openness fostered trust and allowed us to make informed decisions about product design, pricing, and production timelines. For example, when we encountered an issue with the durability of one of the biodegradable materials, the supplier was transparent about the challenges they faced in refining the material. This honesty allowed us to adjust our production timeline and provide our customers with realistic delivery expectations, which helped maintain trust throughout the process.

The partnership's results were outstanding. Within 12 months, we successfully launched a new line of sustainable packaging that met our customers' needs and positioned both companies as leaders in the growing market for eco-friendly products. The new product line quickly became one of our top sellers, driving significant revenue growth for both companies. Additionally, the partnership strengthened our relationship with the supplier, and we've since collaborated on several other projects, further cementing our mutual success.

The key takeaway from this case study is that *co-development and transparency* are critical to successful partnerships. By working closely together, sharing information openly, and aligning our goals from the beginning, we could innovate and bring a new product to market faster and more efficiently than we could have independently.

Case Study 2: Enhancing Operational Efficiency Through a Logistics Partnership

In another successful partnership, we worked with a logistics provider to streamline our supply chain and improve delivery performance. Our manufacturing company faced growing customer demand, but our existing logistics operations struggled to keep up. We needed a partner that could provide transportation services and supply chain optimisation expertise.

We partnered with a global logistics firm with extensive experience managing complex supply chains. Both parties agreed that the partnership aimed to improve delivery times, reduce transportation costs, and enhance overall supply chain visibility. We took a *data-driven approach* to the partnership, using real-time analytics to monitor our logistics operations and identify areas for improvement.

One of the most valuable aspects of this partnership was the *collaborative problem-solving* that occurred when we faced logistical challenges. For example, we experienced significant delays at one point due to a bottleneck at one of our key distribution centres. Rather than placing blame or expecting the logistics provider to fix the issue independently, we brought together our operations team and their logistics experts to work on a solution. Through a series of joint workshops, we identified the root cause of the delays and a mismatch between our inventory levels and shipping schedules. We implemented new processes to better align our production with our shipping needs.

The logistics provider also introduced us to new technologies significantly improving our supply chain efficiency. We gained full visibility into our logistics operations by implementing a transportation management system (TMS) that tracked real-time shipments. This allowed us to proactively address potential issues, such as weather-related delays or capacity shortages before they impacted our customers. As a result, we reduced our average delivery times by 15% and cut transportation costs by 10%.

What made this partnership so successful was the *mutual investment* in the relationship. Both companies invested time and resources into making the partnership work and were willing to adapt to changing circumstances. The logistics provider tailored their solutions to meet our specific needs, and we, in turn, adjusted our internal processes to align more closely with their recommendations. This flexibility allowed us to create a more efficient, cost-effective supply chain that benefited both companies.

The partnership also grew beyond its initial scope. After optimising our domestic logistics operations, we expanded our domestic logistics operations to include international shipping. The logistics provider helped us navigate complex customs regulations and introduced us to new international shipping routes that reduced transit times and costs. This expansion into global logistics further strengthened the partnership and contributed to our international growth.

The key takeaway from this case study is that *collaborative problem-solving and mutual investment* are essential to long-term partnership success. We created a more efficient, flexible, and scalable logistics operation by working together to address challenges and continuously seeking improvement.

8.8 - Leveraging Partnerships for Growth

Strategic partnerships are not just about operational efficiency; they can also be powerful drivers of business growth. When leveraged effectively, partnerships can help companies access new markets, develop new products, and create new revenue streams. In my experience, organisations that view partnerships as growth engines rather than transactional arrangements unlock far more value over the long term.

Expanding into new markets is one of the most effective ways to leverage partnerships for growth. In one of the organisations I worked with, we partnered with a local distributor in Asia to enter that market. We had a strong product offering but lacked the local market knowledge and distribution channels needed to succeed in the region. By partnering with a company that had deep expertise in the local market, we were able to scale our operations and establish a foothold quickly. The local distributor provided us access to their established retail networks, navigated regulatory hurdles on our behalf, and offered insights into consumer preferences that allowed us to tailor our product offerings to the market. This partnership enabled us to grow our international sales significantly quickly.

Joint ventures are another way to use partnerships to drive growth. In one case, we entered into a joint venture with a technology firm to develop a new automation solution for the manufacturing industry. Both companies brought complementary expertise to the table, we provided the manufacturing know-how, while the technology firm brought cutting-edge automation technology. Together, we developed a product that became a game-changer for the industry, and the joint venture allowed us to share in the profits. By combining our resources and expertise, we accelerated product development, brought the solution to market faster, and captured a larger share of the growing automation market.

Partnerships can also be leveraged for growth by *developing new products or services*. In one instance, we collaborated with a software company to create a new data analytics tool for manufacturing. Our manufacturing expertise gave us a deep understanding of the industry's pain points, while the software company had the technical capabilities to develop the solution. We created a product that addressed a major market need by working together, helping manufacturers optimise their production processes through data-driven insights. The partnership allowed us to enter the software market, which became a new revenue stream for our business. This collaboration also positioned us as a thought leader in the industry, further enhancing our brand and reputation.

Another way to leverage partnerships for growth is to *tap into new customer segments*. In one case, we partnered with a company in an adjacent industry to cross-sell our products to their customer base. We manufactured components used in the automotive industry, and our partner served the aerospace sector. By collaborating, we introduced our products to aerospace customers who had similar needs but were unaware of our offerings. This partnership opened up a new customer segment, leading to significant revenue growth. We could expand our reach without costly marketing campaigns or business development efforts by leveraging the partner's customer relationships.

Innovation partnerships can also drive growth by enabling companies to stay ahead of technological trends. We partnered with a research institution in one organisation to develop new product materials. This collaboration allowed us to access cutting-edge research and expertise that we didn't have in-house. The result was the development of a new material that improved the durability and performance of our products, which gave us a competitive advantage in the market. By leveraging the research institution's resources, we could innovate faster and at a lower cost than if we had pursued the development internally.

Finally, partnerships can be used to *scale operations more quickly*. In one instance, we formed a strategic alliance with a manufacturing firm with excess capacity in its production facilities. Rather than investing in building new production lines, we outsourced some of our production to this partner. This allowed us to scale our operations quickly to meet growing demand without the capital expenditure and time required to expand our facilities. The partnership provided both companies with growth opportunities; our partner was able to utilise their excess capacity more efficiently while we increased our production volume and met market demand.

In conclusion, leveraging partnerships for growth requires a strategic approach. Whether through market expansion, joint ventures, new product development, or tapping into new customer segments, partnerships can drive significant growth when both parties are aligned and committed to long-term success. Organisations that view partnerships as a way to innovate, expand, and create new value are better positioned to capitalise on growth opportunities and stay ahead of the competition.

8.9 - Addressing Partnership Challenges

No partnership is without its challenges. Even the strongest strategic alliances will encounter obstacles that must be addressed to maintain a productive and positive relationship. Over my 30 years of experience as a COO, I've faced numerous partnership challenges, ranging from misaligned objectives to cultural differences. I've learned that handling these challenges often determines whether the partnership thrives or deteriorates. Successful partnerships require proactive problem-solving, open communication, and, in some cases, compromise to ensure both parties remain committed to the long-term goals of the relationship.

One of the most common partnership challenges is *misaligned objectives*. At the outset of a partnership, both parties might appear to have shared goals, but differences in priorities can emerge as the collaboration progresses. For instance, one company may be focused on short-term cost savings, while the other is more interested in long-term market expansion. In one partnership I managed, we encountered this issue when our partner prioritised rapid market entry while we were focused on building a sustainable, long-term supply chain. To address this challenge, we convened strategy alignment meetings where both parties laid out their goals and timelines. We negotiated a compromise by openly discussing our objectives and recognising where they diverged, allowing for phased market entry and developing a more robust supply chain. Communication and flexibility were key to resolving this issue; both sides were willing to adjust their expectations to ensure the partnership's success.

Cultural differences can also pose significant partnership challenges, especially when working with international partners. Organisational culture differences, such as varying decision-making processes, communication styles, or attitudes toward risk, can lead to misunderstandings and frustration. In one partnership with a company based in a different country, we struggled with communication, as their corporate culture valued hierarchy and formal decision-making, while our organisation operated with a more decentralised, agile approach. To bridge this gap, we implemented cultural training for our teams, where we learned more about each other's business practices and communication preferences. Additionally, we agreed on a formal communication protocol that respected both parties' cultural norms, such as regular, structured meetings with clear agendas. By being sensitive to cultural differences and finding ways to accommodate them, we improved collaboration and prevented further misunderstandings.

Conflicting timelines can also create tension in partnerships. In one instance, we worked with a supplier to develop a new product component. While our team was pressured to launch the product by a specific date, the supplier faced delays in their production process that threatened to push back the timeline. Rather than escalating the situation, we approached the issue collaboratively, holding a series of meetings to understand the root cause of the delays and explore alternative solutions. Ultimately, we worked out a phased delivery plan, where the supplier delivered the components in batches, allowing us to begin production on schedule while they completed their work. The key lesson here is the importance of *collaborative problem-solving*; instead of focusing on the problem, we worked together to find a solution that met both parties' needs.

Another challenge in partnerships is *imbalanced contributions*. Sometimes, one party may feel they are contributing more resources, expertise, or effort than the other, leading to resentment. In one partnership I managed, our company felt we were shouldering a disproportionate amount of the R&D work for a joint product development project. After internal discussion, we decided to constructively raise the issue with our partner. During our conversation, it became clear that they were unaware of the extent of the imbalance and were more than willing to take on additional responsibilities. We restructured the project plan to distribute the workload more evenly, which restored balance and prevented further tension. The solution to this challenge was *open communication and recalibration*; we avoided long-term damage to the relationship by addressing the issue early and working together to adjust the project plan.

Disputes over intellectual property (IP) are another frequent source of conflict in partnerships, especially when the collaboration involves the co-development of new products or technologies. In one case, we entered into a joint development agreement with a technology partner, but as the project progressed, disagreements arose over ownership of the resulting IP. Both sides had invested significant resources in the development process, and both wanted to retain rights to the IP. To resolve this issue, we brought legal counsel to mediate the discussion and help draft a comprehensive IP agreement outlining ownership rights, licensing terms, and revenue-sharing arrangements. The key to resolving this challenge was *clarity and legal support*; by clearly defining the terms of IP ownership early on, we could protect both parties' interests and prevent future disputes.

Performance issues can also strain partnerships, particularly when one party is not meeting quality, delivery, or service expectations. In one partnership, we faced consistent delays from a supplier that were impacting our production schedules. Initially, we tried to work around the delays by adjusting our processes, but as the issue persisted, it became clear that a more direct approach was needed. We scheduled a performance review with the supplier, where we presented data on the delays and their impact on our operations. Together, we worked out a performance improvement plan that included specific targets, additional resources, and a timeline for improvement. By addressing the issue openly and collaboratively, we got the partnership back on track and ensured that both parties benefited from improved performance.

Financial disagreements can also challenge partnerships, particularly when one party feels they are not receiving a fair share of the revenue or cost savings. We worked with a distribution partner in one partnership to expand our products into new markets, but disagreements arose over profit-sharing terms. Our partner felt they were taking on more risk and deserved a larger share of the profits, while we believed our brand and product investment justified the existing split. To resolve this issue, we brought in a financial mediator to review the agreement and objectively analyse the contributions and risks on both sides. Based on their recommendations, we adjusted the profit-sharing terms to reflect the partnership's evolving nature, satisfying both parties. The solution here was *objective mediation and fairness*; bringing in an impartial third party allowed us to resolve the dispute without damaging the relationship.

Evolving business needs can also challenge long-standing partnerships. What worked at the beginning of the partnership may no longer be relevant as the business grows or market conditions change. In one case, we had a long-term partnership with a supplier, but as our company expanded into new markets, we needed the supplier to scale their operations and provide a wider range of products. However, the supplier could not meet our evolving needs, which created tension in the relationship. Rather than ending the partnership, we worked with the supplier to explore ways they could invest in new capabilities and expand their product offerings. In the interim, we sourced some materials from alternative suppliers but maintained the relationship with our long-term partner. The key to addressing this challenge was *adaptability and patience*; by working with the supplier to help them grow alongside us, we could preserve a valuable partnership while meeting our business needs.

In conclusion, addressing partnership challenges requires a proactive, collaborative approach. Whether the issue is misaligned goals, cultural differences, performance problems, or financial disputes, the key is to address the issue openly and work together to find solutions. Strong communication, flexibility, and a willingness to recalibrate when necessary are essential for overcoming challenges and ensuring that the partnership remains productive and beneficial for both sides. Every partnership will face challenges, but with the right approach, these challenges can be turned into opportunities for growth and improvement.

8.10 - The Future of Strategic Partnerships

Strategic partnerships are evolving as the business landscape continues to change. In the manufacturing sector, partnerships are increasingly critical for driving innovation, addressing global challenges, and accessing new markets. As the world becomes more interconnected and industries face greater pressure to innovate and operate sustainably, several key trends and emerging opportunities will shape the future of strategic partnerships. Based on my three decades of experience, I believe the following trends will define the future of partnerships in the manufacturing sector.

The first major trend is the growing importance of *technology partnerships*. As digital transformation accelerates, manufacturers increasingly partner with technology firms to integrate advanced technologies like artificial intelligence (AI), machine learning, and the Internet of Things (IoT) into their operations. These technologies can revolutionise manufacturing by improving efficiency, reducing waste, and enabling more predictive decision-making. In the future, partnerships between traditional manufacturers and tech companies will become even more common as manufacturers seek to harness the power of data analytics, automation, and AI to remain competitive. For example, in one organisation I worked with, we partnered with a tech startup to implement an AI-driven predictive maintenance system that reduced machine downtime and improved production efficiency.

These types of partnerships will only grow in importance as manufacturers look to stay ahead of the curve in an increasingly digital world.

Sustainability-focused partnerships will also play a critical role in the future of manufacturing. As consumers, governments, and investors emphasise sustainability, manufacturers must find ways to reduce their environmental impact and develop more sustainable products. This will lead to more partnerships focused on sustainability initiatives, such as reducing carbon emissions, developing eco-friendly materials, and implementing circular economy practices. In one case, we partnered with a recycling company to develop a closed-loop system for our packaging materials, allowing us to reuse materials and reduce waste. These sustainability-focused partnerships address environmental concerns and create new business opportunities by appealing to eco-conscious consumers and meeting regulatory requirements.

Another emerging trend is the rise of *cross-industry partnerships*. As industries converge and the lines between sectors blur, manufacturers will increasingly collaborate with companies outside their traditional industry boundaries. For example, automotive manufacturers are now partnering with technology firms to develop autonomous vehicles, while consumer goods companies collaborate with healthcare providers to create wearable health devices. These cross-industry partnerships allow manufacturers to tap into new expertise, explore innovative business models, and create products that meet the changing needs of consumers. In one organisation, we partnered with a healthcare company to develop specialised components for medical devices, allowing us to enter a new market and expand our product portfolio. This type of cross-industry collaboration will become more common as manufacturers look for new ways to diversify and innovate.

Global partnerships will also continue to grow in importance as manufacturers expand into new markets and navigate increasingly complex global supply chains. Many manufacturers previously relied on local or regional partnerships, but today's globalised economy requires companies to form partnerships that span multiple countries and regions. These global partnerships allow manufacturers to access new markets, source materials more efficiently, and build resilient supply chains. However, they also come with challenges, such as navigating different regulatory environments, managing cross-cultural differences, and dealing with geopolitical risks. In one case, we partnered with a logistics provider with expertise in international shipping and customs regulations, allowing us to expand our operations into new markets with minimal disruption. As globalisation continues to reshape the business landscape, these types of partnerships will be essential for manufacturers looking to grow internationally.

Agile and flexible partnerships will also become more prevalent as manufacturers face increasing uncertainty and volatility in the market. In the past, many partnerships were long-term and rigid, but today's fast-paced business environment requires partnerships that can adapt quickly to changing circumstances. This means that future partnerships must be more flexible, with terms that allow for rapid adjustments in response to market shifts, technological advancements, or supply chain disruptions. For example, in one partnership, we built a clause that allowed us to adjust production volumes based on changing demand, which provided both parties with the flexibility needed to respond to fluctuations in the market. These agile partnerships will be crucial for manufacturers that need to stay agile and responsive in an unpredictable world.

Finally, the future of strategic partnerships will be shaped by *collaborative innovation*. As industries become more complex and competitive, companies will increasingly look to their partners for co-innovation opportunities. Rather than developing new products or processes in isolation, manufacturers will collaborate with their partners to co-create solutions that drive value for both parties. This could involve joint research and development, shared innovation labs, or co-investment in new technologies. In one case, we co-developed a new automation solution with a technology partner, allowing us to bring a more advanced product to market faster than we could have. This type of collaborative innovation will become more common as companies realise the benefits of pooling resources and expertise to accelerate innovation and stay ahead of competitors.

In conclusion, the future of strategic partnerships in manufacturing will be defined by technology integration, sustainability, cross-industry collaboration, globalisation, agility, and collaborative innovation. Manufacturers that embrace these trends and leverage partnerships to drive growth, innovation, and operational efficiency will be better positioned to succeed in an increasingly complex and competitive business environment. Strategic partnerships will continue to be a powerful tool for manufacturers to navigate the challenges and opportunities of the future.

Chapter 9

Technology and Digital Transformation

> "Excellence in operations is the art of getting ahead by staying two steps behind the problem."
>
> **Robert N. Jacobs**

This chapter focuses on the pivotal role of technology and digital transformation in modern manufacturing. The chapter explores how advancements such as Industry 4.0, automation, artificial intelligence (AI), and the Industrial Internet of Things (IIoT) revolutionise production processes. It highlights the transformative potential of these technologies in improving efficiency, enhancing product quality, and meeting the increasing demands of a competitive global marketplace.

By providing real-world examples, the chapter emphasises the importance of leveraging digital tools strategically to drive operational success. Furthermore, it addresses the challenges of implementing new technologies, underscoring the need for a clear digital strategy, strong leadership, and change management to ensure long-term sustainability and innovation.

9.1 - The Role of Technology in Manufacturing

Technology has always been a catalyst for change in the manufacturing sector. From the first industrial revolution to today's digital age, technological innovations have continually reshaped how products are designed, produced, and delivered. As a COO with three decades of experience, I've witnessed how technological advancements have opened new doors for manufacturers, making operations more efficient, improving product quality, and enabling companies to meet ever-increasing market demands. Today, the most transformative technologies in manufacturing fall under the umbrella of *Industry 4.0*, which marks the fourth industrial revolution. These include automation, artificial intelligence (AI), the Industrial Internet of Things (IIoT), big data analytics, and cloud computing. Each of these technologies plays a distinct role in reshaping manufacturing processes, and understanding how they work together is essential for any organisation looking to stay competitive. *Automation* is perhaps the most well-known and widespread technology in the manufacturing sector. Using robotics and automated systems to perform repetitive, complex, or hazardous tasks has significantly increased productivity, reduced human error, and lowered production costs. In one of the organisations I led, we implemented robotic systems on our assembly lines, which allowed us to increase production throughput by 25% while maintaining consistent product quality. Automation doesn't replace human workers entirely, but it complements their skills, freeing them up to focus on more value-added tasks, such as quality control and process optimisation.

Artificial Intelligence (AI) and machine learning have become game-changers in manufacturing, particularly in optimising processes and predictive maintenance. AI algorithms can analyse vast amounts of data in real-time, identifying inefficiencies and recommending adjustments to improve operational performance. In one case, we used AI to optimise our production scheduling. Previously, our scheduling was done manually, often resulting in delays or bottlenecks. Implementing an AI-driven system reduced scheduling errors and optimised machine usage, leading to a 15% improvement in overall efficiency. AI also plays a crucial role in predictive maintenance by identifying patterns in equipment performance and predicting when a machine is likely to fail, allowing us to perform maintenance before breakdowns occur.

The *Industrial Internet of Things (IIoT)* is another critical technology transforming manufacturing. IIoT refers to the network of interconnected devices, sensors, and machines that collect and share data in real-time. These connected devices provide manufacturers with unprecedented visibility into their operations. In one organisation, we implemented IIoT sensors on our production equipment to monitor real-time performance metrics, such as temperature, pressure, and vibration. This data allowed us to adjust our processes immediately, reducing downtime and improving product quality. Additionally, IIoT-enabled systems can communicate with each other, enabling greater automation and more efficient use of resources.

Big data and analytics are also essential technologies in the modern manufacturing landscape. Manufacturers generate massive amounts of data from their operations, but the ability to analyse this data effectively provides a competitive advantage. Data analytics can optimise supply chains, forecast demand, and improve decision-making. In one company, we used advanced analytics to gain insights into our supply chain performance. Analysing data on supplier lead times, transportation routes, and inventory levels, we identified bottlenecks and inefficiencies costing us time and money. We improved our on-time delivery rate by 20% by addressing these issues.

Cloud computing has also revolutionised the way manufacturers manage their operations. Cloud-based systems allow companies to store and access data remotely, enabling greater collaboration, scalability, and flexibility. In one instance, we implemented a cloud-based enterprise resource planning (ERP) system that integrated our operations into a single platform, from production and inventory management to finance and customer service. This allowed us to access real-time data from anywhere, streamline department communication, and make more informed decisions. Cloud computing also provides the infrastructure to support other Industry 4.0 technologies, such as AI and IIoT.

Additive manufacturing (3D printing) is another key technology recently gaining traction. While traditionally used for prototyping, additive manufacturing is now used to produce end-use parts in the aerospace, automotive, and healthcare industries. In one project, we used 3D printing to create custom parts for a product that required small production runs. This technology allowed us to reduce lead times and lower production costs compared to traditional manufacturing methods. Additive manufacturing also enables greater design flexibility, allowing engineers to create complex geometries that would be impossible or cost-prohibitive with conventional methods.

Finally, *augmented reality (AR) and virtual reality (VR)* are emerging technologies beginning to find applications in manufacturing, particularly in training, maintenance, and product design. In one organisation, we used AR to assist technicians with equipment maintenance. AR provided step-by-step repair instructions by overlaying digital information onto the physical world, reducing downtime and improving accuracy. Conversely, VR is used for product design and simulation, allowing engineers to test and refine designs in a virtual environment before moving to production.

In conclusion, the role of technology in manufacturing cannot be overstated. From automation and AI to IoT and cloud computing, these technologies drive operational efficiency, reduce costs, and enable manufacturers to innovate faster. The key to success is understanding how these technologies work together and implementing them to align with the organisation's strategic goals. As technology evolves, manufacturers that embrace these advancements will be well-positioned to thrive in the competitive global marketplace.

9.2 - Digital Transformation Strategies

Digital transformation is no longer a luxury for manufacturers; staying competitive in today's fast-paced, data-driven world is necessary. As a COO, I've seen the transformative power of digitalisation firsthand, having led several organisations through the process of integrating digital technologies into their operations. Digital transformation is about more than just implementing new technologies; it's about rethinking business models, processes, and culture to leverage the full potential of digital tools.

One of the most important aspects of a successful digital transformation is to *define a clear strategy* from the outset. Digitalisation should not be approached as a series of isolated technology projects. Instead, it should be driven by a comprehensive strategy that aligns with the organisation's long-term goals. In one organisation I worked with, we embarked on a digital transformation initiative to improve operational efficiency and reduce costs. We started by thoroughly assessing our current processes and identifying areas where digital technologies could add the most value, such as production scheduling, inventory management, and supply chain optimisation. By having a clear strategy, we could focus our efforts on the areas that would deliver the greatest impact rather than adopting technology for technology's sake.

Another critical factor in digital transformation is *executive buy-in and leadership*. In my experience, digital initiatives that are not fully supported by top leadership often fail to gain traction. When I led a digital transformation initiative at a large manufacturing company, one of the first steps was to secure the support of the CEO and other senior executives. We held workshops and presentations to demonstrate the potential benefits of digitalisation, using data from early pilot projects to build the business case. Once we had executive buy-in, we mobilised the entire organisation around the digital agenda, ensuring that everyone, from top management to front-line workers, understood the importance of the transformation and how it would benefit the company.

Starting small and scaling is another effective approach to digital transformation. Rather than trying to digitalise the entire organisation simultaneously, I've found that beginning with a few key pilot projects is often more successful. In one company, we started by implementing a digital production planning system in a single facility. This allowed us to test the technology, refine our processes, and measure the results before rolling it out across all our sites. The success of this pilot project not only provided us with valuable insights and helped build momentum for the broader digital transformation. Once we demonstrated the tangible benefits, such as improved production efficiency and reduced downtime, we could scale the initiative across the entire organisation.

Change management is another critical component of digital transformation. Introducing new technologies often requires significant changes in how people work, and without proper support, employees can resist these changes. In one instance, we implemented an advanced data analytics platform to optimise our supply chain operations. Initially, some employees hesitated to adopt the new system, as it required them to learn new skills and change their routines. We developed a comprehensive change management programme to address this, including training, communication, and support. We provided employees with hands-on training sessions, set up a help desk to answer questions, and regularly communicated the new system's benefits. This approach eased the transition and ensured that employees were fully engaged with the digital tools, ultimately leading to a smoother implementation.

Data governance and security are also crucial considerations in digital transformation. As organisations collect and store more data, it's important to have robust data governance policies to ensure that data is accurate, accessible, and secure. In one digital transformation project, we faced challenges with data silos; different departments were using separate systems that didn't communicate with each other, leading to inconsistencies and inefficiencies. To address this, we implemented a centralised data management platform that integrated data from across the organisation. We also established clear data governance protocols, including data ownership, access controls, and regular audits, to ensure that our data remained secure and compliant with regulations.

Collaboration and partnerships are also key to successful digital transformation. In many cases, manufacturers may not have all the in-house expertise needed to implement advanced digital technologies. We partnered with a leading technology firm in one organisation to develop and implement an AI-driven predictive maintenance system. This partnership allowed us to leverage their technical expertise while focusing on our core manufacturing strengths. By collaborating with external partners, we accelerated our digital transformation while mitigating risks associated with implementing new technologies. Partnerships like this can provide access to cutting-edge tools and innovations that may be out of reach for a company to develop while offering expert guidance on best practices.

Another important aspect of digital transformation is *fostering a culture of innovation and continuous improvement*. Digital transformation is not a one-time project; it's an ongoing process that requires continuous adaptation to new technologies and market demands. In one company I worked with, we introduced an innovation lab where employees could experiment with new digital tools, test ideas, and develop new processes in a low-risk environment. This lab became a hub for cross-functional collaboration, where employees from different departments could work together to solve problems and innovate. By creating a culture that encouraged experimentation and learning, we were able to foster an environment where digital tools were embraced, and employees felt empowered to drive the transformation forward.

Measuring success and ROI is crucial in any digital transformation initiative. While it's easy to get caught up in the excitement of implementing new technologies, it's essential to track progress and measure the impact of these initiatives on the business. We implemented a real-time data analytics platform to optimise inventory management in one project. By carefully tracking key performance indicators (KPIs) such as inventory turnover, order fulfilment rates, and carrying costs, we could quantify the system's benefits and demonstrate a clear return on investment (ROI). These metrics justified the initial investment and helped us refine our approach and identify additional areas for improvement.

Agility and adaptability are also critical for sustaining a digital transformation. As technological change continues to accelerate, organisations must remain agile and be willing to adjust their strategies. In one case, we began our digital transformation by focusing on automation. Still, as AI and machine learning tools became more sophisticated, we shifted our focus to predictive analytics and data-driven decision-making. By staying flexible and continuously evaluating emerging technologies, we were able to pivot and take advantage of new opportunities that aligned with our overall business objectives.

In conclusion, digital transformation is essential for any manufacturing organisation looking to remain competitive in the modern economy. The key to success lies in having a clear strategy, securing executive buy-in, starting small and scaling, managing change effectively, and fostering a culture of innovation. Collaboration, data governance, and continuous measurement of success are critical components that ensure the digital transformation is successful and sustainable over the long term. Manufacturers can unlock new efficiency, innovation, and growth levels by approaching digitalisation strategically and proactively.

9.3 - Data Analytics and Insights

Data is an organisation's most valuable asset in today's manufacturing environment. Collecting, analysing, and acting on data is a competitive advantage that can drive operational efficiency, improve decision-making, and fuel innovation. Over my 30 years as a COO, I've seen how data analytics has transformed how businesses operate, enabling them to make more informed decisions and optimise every aspect of their operations.

The first step in leveraging data for decision-making is to *collect the right data*. In many organisations, data is collected from multiple sources, production lines, supply chains, customer interactions, and financial systems, but it's often fragmented or siloed. One of the biggest challenges I encountered early in my career was integrating disparate data sources. In one organisation, we had multiple systems that didn't communicate with each other, making it difficult to get a comprehensive view of our operations. To solve this, we implemented an enterprise resource planning (ERP) system that integrated data from across the company, giving us real-time visibility into everything from inventory levels to production schedules. This integration was key to making data-driven decisions because it allowed us to access all the information we needed in one place.

Once the right data is collected, the next step is to *analyse that data effectively*. Data analytics tools can help manufacturers identify patterns, trends, and inefficiencies in their operations. In one case, we used data analytics to optimise our production processes by analysing machine data. We could pinpoint areas where inefficiencies occurred and implement targeted improvements by looking at factors such as machine downtime, production rates, and quality defects. For example, we discovered that a particular machine was prone to breakdowns during certain shifts, which led us to adjust our maintenance schedule and improve operator training. These data-driven insights helped us reduce downtime and improve production efficiency by 12%.

Predictive analytics is another powerful tool manufacturers can use to anticipate and address issues before they become problems. In one company, we implemented a predictive maintenance system that used data from sensors on our production equipment to predict when a machine would fail. The system could predict when maintenance was needed by analysing data such as temperature, vibration, and usage patterns, allowing us to perform repairs before a breakdown occurred. This reduced downtime and extended our equipment's lifespan, resulting in significant cost savings. Predictive analytics can also be applied to other manufacturing areas, such as demand forecasting and supply chain management, helping organisations make more informed decisions and reduce risk.

Data visualisation is another key component of leveraging data for decision-making. Even with the most advanced analytics tools, data can be overwhelming if not presented in a way that's easy to understand and act upon. In one organisation, we implemented a dashboard system that provided real-time visualisations of key performance indicators (KPIs). This dashboard was accessible to managers and front-line employees, giving everyone visibility into how the business performed. The visualisations made it easy to spot trends, identify areas for improvement, and track progress toward our goals. For example, by monitoring KPIs such as on-time delivery rates and production output in real-time, we could quickly adjust our operations, ensuring that we stayed on track to meet customer demands.

Using data for continuous improvement is another key aspect of data-driven decision-making. Data analytics can often reveal opportunities for process improvements that might not be immediately obvious. In one instance, we used data from our supply chain to identify bottlenecks in our distribution network. By analysing transportation routes, warehouse operations, and lead times, we discovered that certain routes were consistently causing delays. Armed with this information, we were able to renegotiate contracts with our logistics providers and optimise our shipping routes, resulting in faster deliveries and lower transportation costs. This continuous improvement approach, driven by data, helped us remain agile and responsive to changes in the market.

Collaboration between departments is also essential for maximising the value of data analytics. In many organisations, different departments have their data but rarely share it. In one company, we broke down these silos by creating cross-functional teams that included members from production, finance, marketing, and supply chain. These teams used data from across the organisation to tackle specific challenges, such as reducing production costs or improving customer satisfaction. By bringing together insights from different parts of the business, we were able to develop more comprehensive solutions and make better decisions.

Security and data integrity are critical considerations when leveraging data for decision-making. As organisations collect more data, they become more vulnerable to cyber threats and breaches. In one case, we faced a security breach that compromised some of our sensitive operational data. This experience reinforced the importance of strong cybersecurity measures, including encryption, access controls, and regular audits. Protecting data is essential for compliance and risk management and ensuring that the data used for decision-making is accurate and reliable.

In conclusion, data analytics has the power to transform manufacturing operations by providing insights that drive better decision-making and continuous improvement. Manufacturers can optimise operations, reduce costs, and improve customer satisfaction by collecting the right data, using advanced analytics tools, and fostering collaboration across departments. Data is a powerful asset, but the ability to analyse and act on that data truly creates value. As technology evolves, organisations that embrace data-driven decision-making will be better positioned to succeed in an increasingly competitive market.

9.4 - Cybersecurity

As manufacturing becomes more interconnected through digital technologies, cybersecurity has emerged as one of the industry's most critical issues. The rise of smart manufacturing, connected devices, and cloud-based systems has created new vulnerabilities that cybercriminals can exploit. A single breach can disrupt production and result in significant financial losses, data theft, and reputational damage. Over my years as a COO, I've seen firsthand how vital it is to implement strong cybersecurity measures to protect manufacturing operations from these growing threats.

The first step in developing an effective cybersecurity strategy is identifying *the organisation's critical assets and vulnerabilities.* In manufacturing, these often include production systems, intellectual property, customer data, and supply chain networks. In one organisation I worked with, we conducted a comprehensive risk assessment to identify our most vulnerable areas. Our production systems, increasingly connected through the Industrial Internet of Things (IIoT), were highly susceptible to cyberattacks. This led us to implement a series of security protocols, including network segmentation, to isolate critical systems from other parts of the business and reduce the potential impact of a breach.

One of the biggest challenges in cybersecurity is the *growing complexity of cyber threats.* Cyberattacks have become more sophisticated, targeting IT systems and operational technology (OT) environments that control physical processes on the factory floor. In one case, we experienced an attempted attack on our manufacturing execution system (MES), which controls production scheduling and quality management. The attackers sought to disrupt our operations by manipulating production data. Fortunately, our cybersecurity team detected the intrusion early, thanks to real-time monitoring systems that flagged unusual activity. This incident underscored the importance of continuous monitoring and real-time threat detection to catch potential breaches before they cause significant damage.

Network segmentation is one of the most effective strategies for protecting critical manufacturing systems. By dividing a network into separate segments, organisations can limit the spread of an attack if a breach occurs in one part of the system. In one manufacturing plant I managed, we implemented network segmentation to isolate our production systems from corporate IT systems. This separation ensured attackers couldn't access or disrupt our production processes even if our IT network was compromised. This approach, combined with strong access controls, created multiple layers of security that made it much harder for cybercriminals to reach our most valuable assets.

Employee training and awareness are also critical components of a robust cybersecurity strategy. One of the most common ways cyberattacks occur is through phishing emails or other social engineering techniques that exploit human vulnerabilities. In one organisation, we introduced a cybersecurity training programme that educated employees on recognising phishing attempts, avoiding suspicious links, and reporting potential threats. We also conducted regular phishing simulations to test their awareness and ensure they followed best practices. By making cybersecurity part of the company culture, we significantly reduced the likelihood of an attack succeeding due to human error.

Multi-factor authentication (MFA) is another essential security measure that should be implemented in any manufacturing organisation. MFA adds an extra layer of security by requiring users to provide two or more verification factors to access sensitive systems. In one instance, we implemented MFA for all employees who accessed our production management systems, ensuring that even if an attacker obtained a password, they would still need an additional verification method, such as a security token or mobile app authentication, to gain access. This simple but effective security measure helped protect our critical systems from unauthorised access.

As manufacturing relies more heavily on cloud-based systems, *cloud security* has become a top priority. Cloud platforms offer scalability and flexibility but introduce new risks if not properly secured. In one organisation, we moved much of our data storage and software applications to the cloud as part of our digital transformation. To protect this data, we worked closely with our cloud provider to implement strong encryption protocols, access controls, and regular security audits. We also ensured that our cloud provider adhered to industry-specific compliance standards, such as ISO 27001 and the General Data Protection Regulation (GDPR), to protect our data and ensure regulatory compliance.

Another critical component of cybersecurity in manufacturing is *third-party risk management*. Many manufacturers rely on suppliers, contractors, and other third parties to access their systems or data, creating potential vulnerabilities. In one case, we experienced a security incident caused by a third-party contractor accessing our production systems. The contractor's system was compromised, and attackers used their credentials to attempt to infiltrate our network. After this incident, we tightened our third-party risk management protocols by conducting more rigorous security assessments of all our partners and limiting their access to only the systems they needed. We also required all third parties to adhere to our security standards and regularly audited their compliance.

Incident response planning is another critical element of cybersecurity. No matter how strong an organisation's defences are, there is always a chance that a breach will occur. A well-defined incident response plan ensures the organisation can respond quickly and effectively to contain the breach, minimise damage, and recover from the attack. In one organisation, we developed a detailed incident response plan that outlined the steps to be taken in the event of a cyberattack. This plan included identifying key response teams, notifying affected stakeholders, and restoring affected systems. We also conducted regular drills to ensure that everyone in the organisation knew their roles and responsibilities in the event of an attack. This preparedness allowed us to respond quickly and minimise the impact of an actual cyberattack that occurred later.

Finally, *regulatory compliance* plays a significant role in cybersecurity for manufacturing. Many industries have specific regulations governing data protection and cybersecurity, such as GDPR in Europe or the NIST Cybersecurity Framework in the United States. We implemented a cybersecurity programme aligned with one organisation's industry standards and regulatory requirements. This protected our operations and ensured we complied with legal and contractual obligations. Failing to meet regulatory requirements can result in heavy fines, legal consequences, and damage to a company's reputation, so staying current on evolving regulations and ensuring that cybersecurity programmes meet the necessary standards is essential.

In conclusion, cybersecurity is a critical concern for modern manufacturing operations. As the sector becomes increasingly connected and reliant on digital technologies, manufacturers must implement strong cybersecurity measures to protect their operations from cyber threats. Key strategies include network segmentation, continuous monitoring, employee training, multi-factor authentication, cloud security, third-party risk management, incident response planning, and regulatory compliance. By taking a proactive approach to cybersecurity, manufacturers can safeguard their operations, protect their intellectual property, and maintain the trust of their customers and partners.

9.5 - smart manufacturing

Smart manufacturing, the cornerstone of the Industry 4.0 revolution, is a powerful force that integrates advanced technologies such as artificial intelligence (AI), robotics, the Industrial Internet of Things (IIoT), big data analytics, and cloud computing into manufacturing processes. As a COO who has overseen multiple smart manufacturing initiatives, I've seen how these technologies can transform traditional production systems, making them more efficient, flexible, and responsive to market demands. This transformation reassures us of the potential and confidence in the future of manufacturing.

At the heart of smart manufacturing is the concept of *interconnectivity*. Smart factories use sensors, connected devices, and data analytics to gather real-time information about every aspect of the production process, from raw materials and machine performance to inventory levels and product quality. This interconnected system allows manufacturers to make more informed decisions, optimise production, and improve efficiency. In one organisation, we implemented IIoT sensors across our production lines to monitor machine performance in real-time. This allowed us to detect potential issues early, such as equipment operating outside its optimal parameters, and perform maintenance before a breakdown occurred. The result was a 20% reduction in machine downtime and improved production efficiency.

Automation and robotics are key components of smart manufacturing. While traditional automation has been a part of manufacturing for decades, smart manufacturing takes automation to the next level by integrating AI and machine learning. In one organisation, we deployed AI-powered robots that could adjust their real-time behaviour based on data inputs. Our assembly lines used these robots to handle repetitive tasks, such as welding and material handling. What made these robots "smart" was their ability to learn from their environment and optimise their actions based on feedback. For example, if a robot detected a deviation in product specifications, it would automatically adjust its settings to correct the issue, improving quality control and reducing waste.

Predictive maintenance is another powerful application of smart manufacturing technologies. Traditional maintenance strategies, such as preventive maintenance, rely on scheduled servicing based on time intervals. However, smart manufacturing leverages IIoT sensors and AI to predict when equipment is likely to fail based on real-time data. In one manufacturing plant I managed, we implemented a predictive maintenance system that used sensor data to monitor machine health. By analysing factors such as temperature, vibration, and operating hours, the system predicted when a machine was likely to experience a failure and scheduled maintenance accordingly. This predictive approach reduced unplanned downtime and extended our equipment's lifespan, resulting in significant cost savings.

Data-driven decision-making is central to the success of smart manufacturing. The vast amounts of data generated by connected devices and sensors provide manufacturers with insights that can be used to optimise every aspect of the production process. In one case, we used data analytics to improve our inventory management system. By analysing sales trends, production rates, and supplier lead times, we could better forecast demand and adjust our inventory levels accordingly. This reduced the amount of capital in excess inventory while ensuring we had the right materials to meet customer orders. Making data-driven decisions in real-time is one of the most significant advantages of smart manufacturing.

Customisation and flexibility are also key benefits of smart manufacturing. Traditional manufacturing processes are often rigid and optimised for mass production. However, smart manufacturing enables greater flexibility, allowing manufacturers to produce smaller batches of customised products without sacrificing efficiency. In one project, we implemented a flexible production system that used AI and robotics to reconfigure production lines based on customer orders quickly. This allowed us to offer a range of customised products with minimal lead times, giving us a competitive edge in a market where customer preferences were constantly changing.

Digital twins are another innovative technology in the smart manufacturing ecosystem. A digital twin is a virtual model of a physical asset, such as a machine, production line, or even an entire factory. These digital models use real-time data from sensors to simulate how the physical asset will perform under different conditions. In one organisation, we used digital twin technology to simulate the impact of various production scenarios on our factory's output and efficiency. This allowed us to test different strategies, such as adjusting production schedules or reconfiguring machine layouts, without disrupting production. The insights gained from these simulations helped us optimise our processes and make more informed decisions, ultimately improving our overall performance.

Supply chain optimisation is another area where smart manufacturing technologies can significantly impact. Manufacturers can gain better visibility into their supply chains using real-time data and AI-driven analytics and make more informed sourcing, production, and distribution decisions. We implemented an integrated supply chain management system in one company that connected our suppliers, production facilities, and distribution centres through a single platform. This system used real-time data to track inventory levels, monitor supplier performance, and predict demand fluctuations. As a result, we reduced lead times, minimised stockouts, and improved overall supply chain efficiency.

Smart manufacturing technologies also enhance energy efficiency and sustainability. We used IIoT sensors in one project to monitor energy consumption across our production lines. By analysing the data, we identified several inefficiencies in our energy usage and adjusted to reduce waste. This lowered operating costs and helped us meet our sustainability goals by reducing our carbon footprint. Smart manufacturing technologies enable manufacturers to monitor and optimise energy usage in real-time, leading to more sustainable operations.

In conclusion, smart manufacturing represents the future of the manufacturing industry. By integrating advanced technologies such as AI, IIoT, robotics, and data analytics, manufacturers can optimise their operations, improve quality control, reduce costs, and increase flexibility. The key to success lies in understanding how these technologies work together and implementing them to align with the organisation's strategic goals. As the manufacturing sector evolves, companies embracing smart manufacturing will be better positioned to compete in an increasingly digital and data-driven world.

9.6 - IoT and Connectivity

The Internet of Things (IoT) has revolutionised manufacturing by enabling seamless connectivity between machines, devices, and systems. The Industrial Internet of Things (IIoT) specifically refers to integrating IoT technologies into industrial processes, bringing unprecedented visibility and control over operations. In my 30 years as a COO in manufacturing, I've seen how IIoT has transformed factory floors, supply chains, and maintenance processes, making operations more efficient, agile, and data-driven.

At its core, *IIoT involves using sensors, actuators, and networked devices* to collect and exchange data in real-time. This connected ecosystem enables manufacturers to monitor equipment performance, track inventory, optimise production schedules, and improve efficiency. In one organisation I worked with, we implemented IIoT sensors on all our key machinery, including production lines, conveyors, and packaging equipment. These sensors provided us with real-time data on machine performance, such as temperature, vibration, and operational status. This level of connectivity allowed us to detect issues early, such as machines operating outside their optimal parameters so that we could perform preventive maintenance before a breakdown occurred.

Real-time monitoring and predictive maintenance are two of the most powerful applications of IIoT. By continuously collecting data from connected devices, manufacturers can gain real-time insights into the health of their equipment and predict when maintenance is required. In one plant, we used IIoT sensors to monitor the wear and tear on critical components of our production equipment. The system analysed pressure, heat, and operational hours data to predict when a part was likely to fail. This allowed us to schedule maintenance during planned downtime, reducing unplanned outages and extending the lifespan of our equipment. Predictive maintenance, driven by IIoT, saved us 15% in maintenance costs and improved machine uptime by 20%.

Connectivity between systems is another significant benefit of IIoT. In traditional manufacturing environments, different systems, such as production, inventory management, and quality control, often operate in silos, leading to inefficiencies and communication gaps. However, with IIoT, these systems can be integrated and communicate seamlessly. We implemented an integrated IoT platform in one organisation that connected our production lines with our enterprise resource planning (ERP) system. This allowed us to synchronise production schedules with inventory levels in real-time. For example, if an unexpected delay occurred on the production line, the system automatically adjusted inventory and shipping schedules to minimise disruptions to our supply chain. This level of connectivity improved operational efficiency and enhanced our ability to respond quickly to changes in demand or supply chain challenges.

Improved supply chain visibility is another key advantage of IIoT. Manufacturers can gain insights into inventory levels, supplier performance, and transportation logistics by using connected devices to track the movement of goods and materials throughout the supply chain. In one company, we equipped our warehouses and distribution centres with IoT-enabled tracking devices that monitored the location and status of inventory in real-time. This allowed us to optimise stock levels, reduce the risk of stockouts, and ensure timely deliveries to our customers. Additionally, we used IoT sensors to monitor the condition of temperature-sensitive materials during transit, ensuring that our products met quality standards upon delivery.

Energy management is another area where IIoT can drive significant improvements. Manufacturers can identify inefficiencies and reduce energy waste by using IoT sensors to monitor energy consumption across different parts of the production process. In one project, we implemented an IIoT-based energy management system that tracked energy usage across our production lines, lighting, and heating systems. By analysing the data, we identified several areas where we used more energy than necessary, such as running equipment at full capacity during non-peak hours. Based on these insights, we adjusted our energy usage patterns. We reduced our overall energy consumption by 10%, lowering operating costs and contributing to our sustainability goals.

Another benefit of IoT connectivity is enhanced quality control. By integrating sensors directly into production lines, manufacturers can monitor product quality in real-time and detect defects early in the process. In one case, we used IoT-enabled cameras and sensors to inspect products as they moved down the assembly line. These sensors detected size, shape, or colour anomalies, alerting operators to potential quality issues. This system allowed us to catch defects before they reached the final stages of production, reducing rework and improving overall product quality.

The *scalability of IIoT solutions* is also a critical factor in their success. As production demands increase or new technologies are introduced, IIoT systems can be expanded and adapted to meet changing needs. We started with a pilot IIoT implementation on a single production line in one company. After seeing the benefits, such as improved machine uptime and better quality control, we scaled the system to other parts of the factory, eventually expanding it to include our warehouses and supply chain partners. This scalability allowed us to realise incremental benefits while keeping costs and risks manageable during the early stages of implementation.

Remote monitoring and control capabilities are also greatly enhanced by IIoT. With connected devices, manufacturers can monitor and manage operations from anywhere worldwide. In one organisation, we implemented a cloud-based IIoT platform that allowed us to monitor the performance of our production equipment remotely. This was particularly useful for our operations in multiple locations, where managers could access real-time data on machine performance, inventory levels, and production schedules from a centralised dashboard. This remote capability improved operational efficiency and enabled us to respond quickly to issues, even at geographically distant facilities.

Security considerations are paramount when implementing IIoT technologies. As more devices and systems become connected, the risk of cyberattacks increases. In one company, we experienced an attempted cyberattack on our IoT-enabled systems. Fortunately, we had implemented strong security measures, such as network segmentation, encryption, and regular security audits, which helped prevent the attackers from accessing our critical systems. Securing IoT devices and networks requires technology, policies, and continuous monitoring to identify and address vulnerabilities before they can be exploited.

In conclusion, IoT and IoT technologies are revolutionising manufacturing by enabling real-time monitoring, predictive maintenance, improved supply chain visibility, and enhanced quality control. The connectivity provided by IIoT allows manufacturers to integrate their operations more closely, optimise production processes, and respond quickly to changing conditions. While the benefits are significant, it's important to approach IoT implementations with careful planning, strong cybersecurity measures, and a focus on scalability to ensure long-term success. As the manufacturing sector embraces IoT, those that leverage its full potential will gain a competitive edge in efficiency, flexibility, and innovation.

9.7 - Case Study: Successful Digital Transformations

Digital transformation in manufacturing is a journey that requires careful planning, investment, and commitment from leadership. In my experience, successful digital transformations improve operational efficiency and enable organisations to innovate, adapt to market changes, and achieve long-term growth. In this section, I will share two examples of digital transformations that I led, illustrating the strategies, challenges, and outcomes that resulted from embracing digitalisation in manufacturing.

Case Study 1: Leveraging Data Analytics for Supply Chain Optimisation

One organisation faced significant challenges in managing its global supply chain. The company operated multiple production facilities in different regions, and our supply chain was complex, involving a network of suppliers, logistics providers, and distribution centres. We frequently encountered delayed shipments, inconsistent inventory levels, and rising transportation costs. To address these challenges, we embarked on a digital transformation initiative using data analytics to optimise our supply chain operations.

The first step in this transformation was to implement a centralised data platform that integrated data from our suppliers, production facilities, warehouses, and logistics partners. This platform gave us real-time visibility into every aspect of our supply chain, allowing us to track the movement of goods, monitor inventory levels, and analyse supplier performance. With this data, we used advanced analytics tools to identify patterns and trends contributing to inefficiencies. For example, we discovered that certain suppliers consistently missed delivery deadlines, causing delays in our production schedules. With this insight, we renegotiated contracts with underperforming suppliers and diversified our supplier base to reduce risk.

We also used predictive analytics to improve our demand forecasting and inventory management. By analysing historical sales data, market trends, and external factors such as weather and geopolitical events, we could forecast demand more accurately and adjust our inventory levels accordingly. This helped us reduce stockouts and excess inventory, resulting in a 15% reduction in carrying costs and a 20% improvement in on-time deliveries.

The results of this digital transformation were substantial. Our supply chain became more agile, resilient, and cost-effective. We reduced lead times, improved supplier performance, and achieved greater visibility into our operations, allowing us to make data-driven decisions that enhanced efficiency and customer satisfaction. This transformation improved our operational performance and positioned the company for future growth by enabling us to respond more quickly to market changes.

Case Study 2: Implementing Smart Manufacturing for Improved Productivity

In another organisation, we faced operational inefficiencies and inconsistent product quality challenges. Our production lines relied heavily on manual processes, leading to output variability and frequent downtime. To address these issues, we launched a digital transformation initiative focused on implementing smart manufacturing technologies, including automation, IIoT, and data analytics.

We installed IIoT sensors across our production lines to monitor real-time machine performance. These sensors provided data on factors such as machine speed, temperature, and vibration, which we used to detect potential issues before they caused downtime. We also implemented predictive maintenance systems that used AI to analyse sensor data and predict when maintenance was needed. This allowed us to schedule maintenance during planned downtime, reducing unplanned outages and improving machine uptime by 25%.

In addition to predictive maintenance, we implemented automated quality control systems that used IoT-enabled cameras and sensors to inspect products as they moved through the production line. These systems detected defects in real time, alerting operators to issues and allowing us to make adjustments before defective products reached the end of the line. This automated quality control system reduced the number of defective products by 30% and improved overall product consistency.

To further improve productivity, we introduced AI-driven robots to handle repetitive tasks such as material handling and assembly. These robots worked alongside our human operators, performing tasks with greater precision and speed. Automating these processes reduced cycle times and increased production throughput by 20%.

The results of this digital transformation were dramatic. We significantly improved productivity, product quality, and machine uptime, lowering operating costs and higher customer satisfaction. This transformation also empowered our workforce by giving them access to real-time data and advanced tools that enhanced their ability to perform their jobs. As a result, the company became more competitive in the market and better positioned to meet the growing demand for high-quality products.

In conclusion, these case studies demonstrate the transformative power of digitalisation in manufacturing. Whether focused on supply chain optimisation or smart manufacturing, digital transformation initiatives can substantially improve efficiency, quality, and agility. The key to success is a clear strategy, a commitment to leveraging data and technology, and the willingness to invest in the people and systems needed to drive change. By embracing digital transformation, manufacturers can unlock new performance levels and set themselves up for long-term success in an increasingly competitive market.

9.8 - Managing Technological Change

Integrating new technologies into a manufacturing operation is a complex task that requires more than just purchasing and installing new equipment. It demands a strategic approach considering the impact on people, processes, and the overall business. Over my years as a COO, I've witnessed successful and unsuccessful attempts to introduce new technologies. The difference often lies in how well the technological change is managed, from initial planning and communication to implementation and post-launch optimisation.

The first step in successfully managing technological change is to *align technology integration with business goals*. Too often, companies adopt new technologies without clearly understanding how they will support their strategic objectives. In one organisation I worked with, we considered adopting a new automation system for our assembly line. While the technology was impressive, it became clear during the planning phase that the system would not align with our primary goal of increasing customer customisation. Instead, it was optimised for high-volume, standardised production, which would have been counterproductive for our business model. By aligning technology adoption with our strategic goals, we avoided investing in a solution that wouldn't deliver the desired outcomes.

Engaging key stakeholders early is another critical factor for success. When introducing new technologies, involving employees, managers, and other stakeholders from the beginning is essential. In one instance, we integrated a new enterprise resource planning (ERP) system across multiple departments. To ensure a smooth transition, we involved representatives from every department in the planning and decision-making. This helped us identify potential issues early on, such as how the new system would impact workflows and also helped build buy-in among employees. We created a sense of ownership and commitment to making the technology work by giving stakeholders a voice.

Effective communication is key throughout the entire process of integrating new technologies. Employees may resist change if they don't understand why it's necessary or how it will benefit them. In one company, we implemented a change management communication plan that involved regular employee updates about the upcoming technology rollout. We explained the reasons for the change, how it aligned with the company's goals, and what benefits it would bring, such as improved efficiency and reduced manual work. We reduced resistance and ensured a smoother transition by addressing employee concerns and providing clear, transparent communication.

Training and support are also essential to the successful adoption of new technologies. Employees often need to develop new skills to use the new systems effectively. In one manufacturing plant I managed, we introduced an advanced automation system that required operators to shift from manual tasks to more technology-driven roles. We developed a comprehensive training programme to support this transition, including hands-on workshops, online courses, and on-the-job training. We also designated "super users" within each department who received advanced training and could act as internal resources to support their colleagues. This approach helped employees feel more comfortable with the new technology and ensured they could use it to its full potential.

Pilot testing is not just a step; it's a crucial phase in successfully implementing new technology. By starting with a smaller-scale implementation, companies can identify potential challenges, gather feedback, and make adjustments before deploying the technology on a larger scale. In one instance, we introduced a new data analytics platform to improve decision-making in our supply chain. Rather than implementing it across the entire company, we began with a pilot project in one region. This allowed us to test the system, refine the data inputs, and ensure it delivered the expected benefits. The lessons learned during the pilot phase were instrumental in helping us optimise the platform and ensuring a smoother rollout across the rest of the organisation.

Managing cultural change is another important consideration when introducing new technologies. Technology integration often requires changes in how people work, which can be met with resistance if not handled carefully. In one organisation, we faced significant pushback when introducing a new digital production management system that replaced many manual processes. To address this, we held workshops and open forums where employees could ask questions, express concerns, and share their thoughts about the new system. We also made a point to highlight how the system would make their jobs easier, such as reducing paperwork and improving workflow efficiency. We reduced resistance by addressing the cultural aspects of change, making employees feel involved, and ensuring a successful implementation.

Ongoing monitoring and optimisation are critical after the initial rollout of new technology. A system rarely works perfectly right out of the gate, so continuous monitoring is essential to identify any issues and opportunities for improvement. After implementing a new automated inventory management system in one organisation, we set up a feedback loop with the operations team to track the system's performance. We identified several areas where the system wasn't functioning as expected, such as inaccuracies in stock levels, and worked with the technology provider to fine-tune the software. This ongoing optimisation ensured that the technology delivered its full value and met the needs of the business.

Balancing short-term disruptions with long-term benefits is a key challenge in managing technological change. Introducing new systems often causes temporary disruptions to established workflows, and it's important to manage these short-term challenges while keeping the long-term benefits in mind. In one project, we implemented a new manufacturing execution system (MES) that required a temporary slowdown in production while employees were trained on the new system. While this caused some initial frustration, we clarified that the short-term disruption would lead to long-term efficiency, quality, and output improvements. Within a few months of implementation, the benefits became clear, and the initial disruption was well worth the investment.

Collaboration with technology providers is also an important part of managing technological change. Many new technologies require close collaboration between the manufacturer and the technology provider to ensure a successful implementation. In one case, we worked closely with our automation technology provider to customise the system to meet our needs. This involved regular meetings, feedback sessions, and adjustments to the software to ensure that it integrated seamlessly with our existing processes. This collaborative approach allowed us to avoid common pitfalls when introducing new technologies and ensured the system was tailored to our unique requirements.

In conclusion, successfully managing technological change requires a strategic, people-focused approach. Aligning technology integration with business goals, engaging stakeholders early, providing clear communication and training, and conducting pilot tests are critical to a smooth transition. Ongoing monitoring, cultural management, and collaboration with technology providers are also essential for optimising the new system and achieving long-term success. When managed effectively, technological change can unlock new levels of efficiency, innovation, and competitive advantage for manufacturing organisations.

9.9 - Balancing Technology and Human Factors

As manufacturing operations become more automated and data-driven, it's essential to balance technology and human expertise. Technology can enhance efficiency, improve accuracy, and reduce costs, but it should not replace the critical human skills necessary for innovation, problem-solving, and decision-making. As a COO, I've witnessed the benefits of integrating technology into manufacturing. Still, I've also seen the risks of over-reliance on machines at the expense of human judgment.

One of the key challenges in balancing technology and human factors is *ensuring that technology is used to augment, rather than replace, human capabilities*. Automation, robotics, and AI are powerful tools, but they are most effective when combined with human oversight and expertise. In one organisation, we introduced AI-driven quality control systems that used machine learning algorithms to detect defects in our products. While the AI system was highly accurate, it worked best when paired with human operators who could verify the results and make final decisions. This human-technology collaboration reduced the number of false positives and ensured that the quality control process remained efficient and accurate.

Upskilling the workforce is another critical component of balancing technology and human factors. As new technologies are introduced, employees must have the skills and knowledge to work alongside these tools. In one company, we implemented advanced automation systems in our assembly lines, which required operators to shift from manual tasks to more technology-driven roles. To support this transition, we developed a training programme to upskill our employees in data analysis, machine programming, and system troubleshooting. This investment in upskilling ensured that our employees could use the new technology effectively and empowered them to take on more advanced roles, leading to higher job satisfaction and retention.

Human judgement and decision-making remain essential, even in highly automated environments. While AI and data analytics can provide valuable insights and recommendations, many situations still require human judgment to interpret the data and make decisions. In one project, we used AI to optimise our production scheduling. Still, there were times when external factors, such as unexpected changes in customer demand or supply chain disruptions, required human intervention to adjust the schedule. By combining AI-driven insights with human expertise, we could make more informed decisions that accounted for data and context.

Fostering a culture of innovation is also important for ensuring that human skills remain at the forefront of the organisation. Technology can automate routine tasks and improve operational efficiency, but human creativity and problem-solving drive innovation. In one organisation, we created an innovation lab where employees could experiment with new technologies, test ideas, and develop new processes. This lab became a hub for cross-functional collaboration, where employees from different departments worked together to solve problems and explore new opportunities. By fostering a culture of innovation, we ensured that technology was used to enhance, rather than stifle, the creativity and expertise of our workforce.

Empowering employees to take ownership of technology is another way to strike the right balance. In one company, we implemented a digital production management system that provided real-time data on machine performance and production schedules. Rather than relying solely on managers to make decisions based on this data, we empowered front-line operators to use the system to identify issues and make adjustments. This approach improved operational efficiency and gave employees a sense of ownership over the technology, making them more engaged and proactive in their roles.

In conclusion, balancing technology and human factors is about using technology to complement and enhance human skills, not replace them. Manufacturers can create a more collaborative and efficient working environment by investing in upskilling, fostering innovation, and empowering employees to take ownership of technology. The key is to recognise that while technology can automate and optimise many processes, human judgement, creativity, and expertise remain essential for driving innovation and achieving long-term success.

9.10 - Future Technological Trends

As we look to the future, technological advancements will continue to reshape the manufacturing landscape at an accelerated pace. Staying ahead of these changes is critical for companies that want to remain competitive and drive operational excellence. In my three decades as a COO, I've seen how quickly technology can evolve, and the organisations that successfully anticipate and prepare for emerging trends are the ones that thrive in the long term. The key is adopting new technologies and building an organisational culture and infrastructure that allows continuous adaptation and innovation.

One of the most significant future trends is the continued rise of *artificial intelligence (AI) and machine learning (ML)*. While AI is already making strides in predictive maintenance and quality control, the next wave of AI will be even more advanced, enabling greater autonomy in decision-making and process optimisation. AI-driven systems will move beyond their current roles to perform more complex tasks such as dynamic production scheduling, supply chain optimisation, and product design. In one organisation, we experimented with an AI system that could autonomously adjust production schedules based on real-time demand fluctuations and inventory levels. While still in its early stages, the system demonstrated enormous potential to reduce lead times and improve resource allocation. In the future, AI systems like this will become more sophisticated, allowing manufacturers to operate with greater agility and precision.

5G technology is another emerging trend that will have a transformative impact on manufacturing. The advent of 5G will enable faster, more reliable communication between machines, devices, and systems, facilitating real-time data exchange on an unprecedented scale. This will enhance the capabilities of the Industrial Internet of Things (IIoT) by providing the low-latency, high-bandwidth connectivity needed for advanced applications such as autonomous robots, augmented reality (AR) in maintenance, and real-time video analytics for quality control. In one project I oversaw, we tested 5G-enabled robotic systems that could communicate and coordinate with each other in real-time, allowing for greater precision and flexibility in our assembly lines. As 5G becomes more widespread, it will unlock new possibilities for smart manufacturing and connected operations.

Another critical trend is the *increased integration of digital twins*. Digital twins, virtual replicas of physical assets, processes, or systems, are already used in advanced manufacturing environments to simulate and optimise operations. Digital twins will become more pervasive, enabling manufacturers to model entire factories or supply chains in real time. This will allow for more accurate forecasting, scenario planning, and risk management. For example, a digital twin of a production facility could simulate how different configurations, machine settings, or staffing levels would impact output and quality before making changes in the real world. This type of predictive simulation can save time, reduce costs, and minimise the risks associated with operational changes. In one case, we used a digital twin to model the impact of adding a new production line to our facility. The simulation helped us identify potential bottlenecks and inefficiencies, allowing us to optimise the layout before making any physical changes.

Additive manufacturing (3D printing) will evolve significantly in the coming years. While it has primarily been used for prototyping and small production runs, advancements in materials science and printing technologies enable additive manufacturing for large-scale production and more complex products. In one organisation I worked with, we used 3D printing to produce custom parts for aerospace components. The technology allowed us to produce lightweight, complex geometries that would have been impossible to create using traditional manufacturing methods. As additive manufacturing technology continues to mature, it will open up possibilities for mass customisation, reducing lead times and creating more sustainable production methods by minimising material waste.

The *rise of quantum computing* is another trend that, while still in its early stages, holds great promise for the manufacturing industry. Quantum computing has the potential to solve complex optimisation problems that are beyond the capabilities of classical computers. This could revolutionise supply chain management, materials discovery, and process optimisation. For example, quantum algorithms could be used to simulate the properties of new materials or chemicals, accelerating the development of innovative products. While practical applications of quantum computing in manufacturing are still a few years away, companies that begin exploring the possibilities now will be better positioned to take advantage of this powerful technology when it becomes commercially viable.

Sustainability and the circular economy will also drive future technological trends in manufacturing. As consumers, regulators, and investors pressure companies to reduce their environmental impact, manufacturers must adopt new technologies that support more sustainable practices. This includes using renewable energy, implementing energy-efficient production processes, and adopting circular economy principles such as recycling and reusing materials. IoT and AI will enable manufacturers to monitor and optimise their energy usage, reduce waste, and minimise emissions. In one organisation, we implemented an IoT-based energy management system that reduced our energy consumption by 15% by identifying inefficiencies in our production processes. Future advancements in sustainability-focused technologies will help manufacturers meet stricter regulatory requirements and improve their environmental footprint.

Human-machine collaboration will continue to evolve as robotics and AI become more integrated into manufacturing environments. Rather than replacing human workers, the next generation of collaborative robots (cobots) will work alongside humans, augmenting their capabilities and enhancing productivity. In one factory, we introduced cobots to assist with repetitive tasks such as material handling and assembly. These cobots were designed to work safely alongside human operators, allowing them to take on more complex, value-added tasks while the robots handled the more mundane aspects of production. As cobots become more advanced, their role in manufacturing will expand, enabling greater flexibility and efficiency on the factory floor.

Blockchain technology is another trend that will play a growing role in manufacturing, particularly in areas such as supply chain transparency, traceability, and quality assurance. Blockchain provides a secure, immutable ledger that can track the movement of goods and materials throughout the supply chain, ensuring that data is accurate and trustworthy. In one pilot project, we used blockchain to track the provenance of raw materials from our suppliers to ensure that they met our sustainability standards. This not only improved transparency but also provided our customers with greater confidence in the integrity of our products. As supply chains become more global and complex, blockchain technology will be increasingly important for ensuring compliance, reducing fraud, and improving overall supply chain visibility.

Finally, the future of manufacturing will be shaped by *augmented reality (AR) and virtual reality (VR)* technologies. AR and VR are already used for training, product design, and maintenance, but their applications will expand as the technologies become more advanced. AR can provide real-time guidance to workers on the factory floor, overlaying digital instructions onto physical machines to assist with tasks such as assembly, repair, or quality control. Conversely, VR allows engineers and designers to create and test virtual prototypes before physical production begins. In one organisation, we used AR to provide technicians real-time instructions for maintaining complex machinery. This reduced errors and downtime while also improving safety. As AR and VR technologies become more accessible and user-friendly, their use in manufacturing will continue to grow, enabling more immersive, efficient, and accurate processes.

In conclusion, various emerging technologies will define the future of manufacturing, from AI and 5G to quantum computing and blockchain. Manufacturers that stay ahead of these trends by investing in the right technologies, upskilling their workforce, and fostering a culture of innovation will be well-positioned to succeed in an increasingly competitive and digitalised world. While the pace of technological change can be daunting, the opportunities for growth, efficiency, and sustainability are immense.

Chapter 10

Measuring and Sustaining Excellence

> "Operations success isn't measured by what goes right, but by how quickly you fix what goes wrong."
>
> **Robert N. Jacobs**

This final chapter emphasises the critical importance of defining, measuring, and continuously improving operational excellence within an organisation. The chapter outlines how operational excellence is not merely about efficiency but creating a cohesive environment where leadership, strategy, and processes align towards long-term success. It explores key components such as leadership, employee engagement, standardising processes, and a relentless focus on customer value.

The chapter also highlights the significance of implementing robust measurement frameworks, driving continuous improvement through Lean and Six Sigma methodologies, and using real-time data systems to foster accountability and ownership at all levels. It concludes by advocating for organisations to embrace innovation, sustain improvements through regular performance reviews, and foster a culture that continuously strives for operational excellence.

10.1 - Defining Operational Excellence

Operational excellence is more than just efficiency; it's about creating a culture and a system where every part of the organisation works together toward continuous improvement and long-term success. Over my 30 years as a COO, I've seen that true operational excellence requires a holistic approach encompassing leadership, strategy, performance, and accountability. It's not just about doing things right; it's about doing the right things consistently across every level of the organisation. Each individual's role is crucial in this holistic approach, and understanding this importance can lead to a more effective and efficient operation.

At its core, operational excellence means optimising processes, reducing waste, and delivering consistent customer value. However, it goes deeper than that. To achieve operational excellence, an organisation must align its operations with its broader strategic goals. This requires a clear understanding of what excellence looks like in your industry and a commitment to building a culture that encourages continuous improvement. In one of the companies I led, operational excellence was defined as meeting and exceeding our production targets while maintaining the highest quality standards. This involved a relentless focus on eliminating inefficiencies, improving cycle times, and reducing costs, all while ensuring that customer satisfaction remained our top priority.

Leadership plays a crucial role in defining excellence. In my experience, operational excellence starts at the top. Leaders must set the tone by establishing clear goals, providing the necessary resources, and fostering a culture of accountability. One of the most impactful things I've done as a COO is regularly communicating the company's vision for excellence to the entire organisation. This included holding town hall meetings, providing transparent updates on performance metrics, and recognising employees who embodied the principles of operational excellence. By doing this, we created a shared understanding of success and ensured that every employee, from the factory floor to the executive suite, understood their role in achieving it.

Process standardisation is another key element of operational excellence. Standardising processes ensures that tasks are completed consistently, efficiently, and with minimal variation. In one of the manufacturing plants I managed, we implemented standard operating procedures (SOPs) for every critical task, from production to quality control. These SOPs were not just written documents; they were living guidelines regularly reviewed, updated, and improved based on employee feedback and performance data. This level of process discipline allowed us to minimise errors, reduce waste, and ensure that our operations ran efficiently.

Employee engagement is also critical to achieving excellence. The people closest to the processes, those on the front lines, often have the best insights into how to improve operations. In one organisation, we implemented a programme encouraging employees to submit ideas for process improvements. Every suggestion was reviewed, and those that were implemented were rewarded. This empowered employees and created a culture of continuous improvement where everyone felt responsible for driving the company toward operational excellence. One of the most memorable examples came from an assembly line worker who suggested a small adjustment to the layout of the workstations. This simple change reduced bottlenecks, increased throughput, and saved the company thousands of pounds annually.

Finally, *customer focus* is at the heart of operational excellence. Delivering value to customers consistently is the ultimate measure of success. In one instance, we developed a real-time system for gathering and analysing customer feedback. This allowed us to quickly identify areas where we fell short and make adjustments before small issues became big problems. Keeping the customer at the centre of everything we did ensured that our operations aligned with their expectations and needs.

In conclusion, operational excellence is more than optimising processes; it's about creating a system that aligns people, processes, and strategy to achieve long-term success. Organisations can achieve operational excellence by fostering strong leadership, standardising processes, engaging employees, and maintaining a relentless focus on the customer. It's not a one-time achievement but an ongoing journey of improvement, where the pursuit of perfection is built into the company's DNA.

10.2 - Developing a Measurement Framework

One of the most critical elements in achieving and sustaining operational excellence is having a robust measurement framework. You cannot manage what you cannot measure, and without clear, actionable data, it's impossible to know whether your organisation is on track to meet its goals. In my experience as a COO, setting up systems to measure success is more than just tracking metrics; it's about developing a comprehensive approach that provides insights into every aspect of the business, from production to customer satisfaction.

The first step in developing a measurement framework is identifying *key performance indicators (KPIs)* that align with your organisation's strategic objectives. KPIs should be relevant, measurable, and tied to short-term and long-term goals. In one of the organisations I led, we identified several core KPIs essential to achieving our vision of operational excellence, including cycle time, defect rates, on-time delivery, and employee engagement. Each of these KPIs was carefully chosen because it reflected an area that directly impacted our ability to deliver value to our customers and drive operational efficiency.

Balanced scorecards can be an effective tool for developing a measurement framework. In one instance, we implemented a balanced scorecard approach that focused on four key areas: financial performance, customer satisfaction, internal processes, and learning and growth. This approach allowed us to track a range of metrics that provided a holistic view of our performance, ensuring that we weren't overly focused on one area at the expense of another. For example, while tracking traditional financial metrics such as profit margins and return on assets, we also measured operational metrics like production efficiency, quality, and customer feedback. This balance ensured that we were sustainably driving performance across all business areas.

It's also important to ensure that your measurement systems provide *real-time data* whenever possible. In today's fast-paced business environment, waiting until the month's or quarter's end to review performance data is often too late. In one of the companies I managed, we implemented a digital dashboard system that provided real-time visibility into key metrics such as machine uptime, production output, and order fulfilment rates. This system allowed managers to identify and address issues as they arose rather than waiting for a performance review. For example, if a machine was underperforming or experiencing frequent downtime, we could see that data in real-time and immediately dispatch maintenance teams to address the issue. The ability to make quick, data-driven decisions significantly improved our operational efficiency and reduced downtime.

Accountability and ownership are crucial for ensuring the measurement framework drives improvement. In one organisation, we assigned clear ownership for each KPI, ensuring that someone was responsible for monitoring the metrics, analysing the data, and driving improvements. This accountability created a sense of ownership and urgency, as employees knew they were directly responsible for the performance of their area. In one instance, we set a target for reducing cycle time in our production process, and the team leader responsible for this metric implemented a series of changes that reduced cycle time by 10% over six months.

Regular performance reviews are another essential component of a successful measurement framework. In my experience, it's not enough to track data; you need to review it regularly, analyse trends, and take action based on the insights. In one company, we held monthly performance review meetings to discuss each department's KPIs, identify areas where performance lags, and develop action plans to address any issues. These meetings provided a forum for cross-functional collaboration and ensured everyone aligned on the company's priorities.

Finally, ensuring that the data collected is meaningful and actionable is important. In one instance, we tracked many metrics, but many didn't provide actionable insights. We took a step back, evaluated which metrics were truly driving performance, and focused on a smaller set of KPIs that provided more valuable information. For example, we replaced some vanity metrics, such as total units produced, with more meaningful metrics, like first-pass yield, which gave us a clearer picture of our production efficiency and quality.

In conclusion, developing a measurement framework is about more than just tracking numbers; it's about creating a system that provides real-time, actionable insights into every aspect of the business. Organisations can ensure that their measurement systems drive continuous improvement and operational excellence by identifying the right KPIs, using balanced scorecards, implementing real-time data systems, and fostering accountability. The key is to measure what matters and use that data to make informed decisions that move the organisation closer to its strategic goals.

10.3 - Continuous Improvement

Continuous improvement is the backbone of operational excellence. It's the philosophy that no matter how well an organisation performs, there's always room for improvement. Throughout my career, I've found that fostering a continuous improvement culture requires the right tools, leadership, and mindset. It's about creating an environment where employees at every level feel empowered to identify inefficiencies, suggest improvements, and take ownership of making processes better every day.

One of the most effective techniques for driving continuous improvement is *Lean manufacturing*, which focuses on eliminating waste and maximising value for the customer. In one of the companies I managed, we implemented Lean principles across our entire operation, from production to supply chain management. This involved mapping out every process to identify non-value-added activities, such as excess inventory, unnecessary movement of materials, and rework. By eliminating these inefficiencies, we were able to reduce costs, improve cycle times, and increase customer satisfaction. For example, by reorganising the layout of our production floor and implementing just-in-time (JIT) inventory practices, we reduced lead times by 15% and improved on-time delivery rates.

Kaizen, the practice of continuous, incremental improvement, is another powerful tool for driving ongoing enhancement. Kaizen is about making small, everyday improvements that add significant gains over time. In one organisation, we implemented daily Kaizen meetings, where teams gathered at the start of each shift to discuss opportunities for improvement. These meetings were focused on small, actionable changes that could be implemented quickly. For example, one of our assembly line teams identified ways to streamline switching out tools, saving several minutes on each shift. While this might seem like a small improvement, over a year, it added hundreds of hours of saved time and significantly boosted productivity. The beauty of the Kaizen approach is that it fosters a culture where employees feel empowered to make a difference, even in the smallest ways.

Six Sigma is another well-established method for driving continuous improvement, particularly regarding reducing defects and improving quality. Six Sigma uses data-driven analysis and statistical tools to identify the root causes of process variability and eliminate defects. In one manufacturing organisation I led, we trained several team members to become Six Sigma Green Belts, responsible for leading improvement projects throughout the company. One of the most successful projects involved reducing the defect rate in our welding process, causing delays and increasing rework. Using Six Sigma methodologies such as the DMAIC (Define, Measure, Analyse, Improve, Control) framework, the team could identify the defects' causes and implement changes that reduced the defect rate by 25%.

Gemba walks are another valuable technique for driving continuous improvement. Gemba, a term from Lean manufacturing, refers to the "real place" where work is done. A Gemba walk involves managers and leaders going to the shop floor to observe processes firsthand, talk to employees, and identify areas for improvement. In one organisation, I made it a point to conduct Gemba walks regularly with my leadership team. These walks allowed us to see what was happening on the ground and allowed employees to share their insights and ideas directly with us. Many of the most impactful improvements came from our feedback during these Gemba walks, such as adjusting machine placement to reduce unnecessary movement and reconfiguring workflows to minimise bottlenecks.

Employee engagement is critical to the success of any continuous improvement initiative. The people closest to the work often have the best ideas for improving it, and it's important to create a culture where employees feel comfortable suggesting changes. In one company, we implemented an idea submission system where employees could submit their suggestions for process improvements. Every suggestion was reviewed, and those that were implemented were recognised and rewarded. This approach encouraged a culture of continuous improvement and made employees feel valued and involved in the organisation's success. One particularly impactful idea came from a production worker who suggested a minor adjustment to how materials were loaded into our machines. This change reduced material waste by 10%, saving the company thousands of pounds annually.

Cross-functional collaboration is another important element of continuous improvement. Improving one process can often have ripple effects across the entire organisation. In one company, we created cross-functional improvement teams that included members from different departments, such as production, quality control, and supply chain. These teams worked together to identify areas where processes intersected and how improvements in one area could benefit the entire organisation. One of the most successful projects involved streamlining our product development process by improving communication between our design and production teams. By aligning these departments more closely, we reduced the time it took to bring new products to market by 20%.

Technology and data analytics also play an increasingly important role in continuous improvement. In one organisation, we implemented a real-time data analytics platform that provided insights into every aspect of our production process, from machine performance to quality control. This allowed us to monitor key performance indicators (KPIs) in real-time and quickly identify areas where improvements could be made. For example, we identified a machine underperforming due to frequent maintenance issues by analysing machine uptime and downtime data. This insight allowed us to focus our improvement efforts on that machine, ultimately increasing its uptime by 15%.

Finally, *leadership support and commitment* are essential for sustaining continuous improvement. In my experience, continuous improvement initiatives often fail when seen as short-term projects rather than long-term ones. As a leader, it's important to demonstrate that continuous improvement is a core part of the organisation's culture, not just a temporary initiative. In one organisation, we established a formal continuous improvement programme that included regular training, leadership involvement, and clear metrics for success. This programme became a permanent part of our operations, and over time, it led to significant improvements in productivity, quality, and employee engagement.

In conclusion, continuous improvement is not just about using the right tools; it's about creating a culture where everyone is empowered to identify inefficiencies and make changes that drive long-term success. Whether through Lean, Kaizen, Six Sigma, Gemba walks, or cross-functional collaboration, the key is to approach improvement as an ongoing journey rather than a one-time effort. By engaging employees, using data to drive decisions, and providing strong leadership support, organisations can achieve lasting improvements that contribute to operational excellence.

10.4 - Benchmarking and Performance Reviews

Benchmarking and performance reviews are crucial for any organisation striving for operational excellence. They provide a structured way to evaluate performance, compare it to industry standards, and identify areas for improvement. Over my years as a COO, I've seen how benchmarking and regular performance reviews can transform an organisation by providing clear, actionable insights into its strengths and weaknesses. These tools help track progress and foster a culture of accountability and continuous improvement.

Benchmarking involves comparing your organisation's performance against industry standards or the best practices of leading companies. The goal is to identify where you stand and understand why top-performing companies excel and how you can adopt similar practices. In one organisation, we benchmarked our production efficiency against industry leaders. We identified several areas where we were falling behind by analysing their use of automation, lean manufacturing techniques, and supply chain management. One key insight was that our competitors had implemented more advanced production scheduling systems that allowed them to reduce lead times and optimise machine utilisation. Armed with this knowledge, we invested in new scheduling software and made changes to our production processes, resulting in a 12% improvement in overall efficiency.

Internal benchmarking is also valuable for identifying your organisation's best practices. We operated multiple manufacturing plants in one company, each with processes and performance metrics. By benchmarking the performance of our best-performing plant against the others, we identified specific practices, such as better inventory management and more effective use of automation, that could be implemented across all locations. This internal benchmarking process improved performance across the organisation and fostered a sense of healthy competition and collaboration between the plants.

Performance reviews are equally important for tracking progress and holding teams accountable. In my experience, regular reviews ensure that everyone is aligned with the company's goals and that any issues are addressed promptly. In one organisation, we held quarterly performance reviews where each department presented its KPIs, discussed any challenges, and outlined its improvement plans. These reviews were not just about reporting results; they were a forum for problem-solving and collaboration. For example, during one review, the supply chain team reported difficulties meeting on-time delivery targets due to delays from a key supplier. By involving other departments in the discussion, we identified a solution: adjusting production schedules to accommodate the supplier's lead times, ultimately improving our delivery performance.

Data transparency is critical to the success of both benchmarking and performance reviews. In one company, we implemented a digital dashboard system that provided real-time access to performance data for every department. This transparency ensured that everyone had access to the same information and could see their performance compared to others. It also made performance reviews more effective, as managers came to the table clearly understanding their team's performance and could engage in more productive discussions about how to improve. This system also allowed us to track performance trends over time, helping us identify long-term improvements and areas that required sustained attention.

One of the most important aspects of benchmarking and performance reviews is the focus on *continuous improvement*. It's not enough to measure performance; you must use that data to drive action. In one instance, we identified that our product defect rate was higher than the industry average. We traced the issue through performance reviews and benchmarking to a specific production line where operator training had been inconsistent. By implementing a more robust training programme and introducing regular skills assessments, we reduced the defect rate by 20% within six months. This improvement wouldn't have been possible without the insights from benchmarking and performance reviews.

Setting realistic stretch targets is also essential for getting the most out of these tools. In one organisation, we set ambitious but achievable targets based on the benchmarking data we gathered. For example, after benchmarking our on-time delivery rate against industry leaders, we set a target to improve our rate by 10% within one year. This target pushed us to make necessary improvements, such as streamlining our order processing system and improving supplier communication. By setting clear, measurable goals based on benchmarking data, we ensured that our teams were focused on continuous improvement and had a clear roadmap for achieving operational excellence.

In conclusion, benchmarking and performance reviews are indispensable tools for any organisation committed to operational excellence. By comparing performance against industry standards, identifying internal best practices, and holding regular performance reviews, organisations can gain valuable insights into their strengths and weaknesses. The key is to use these insights to drive continuous improvement, set ambitious but achievable targets, and foster a culture of accountability and collaboration. When done effectively, benchmarking and performance reviews provide a powerful mechanism for ensuring that the organisation stays on track and continually improves over time.

10.5 - Recognising and Rewarding Success

Recognising and rewarding success is critical to sustaining operational excellence. Over my 30 years as a COO, I've learned that people are the heartbeat of any organisation. How you motivate, recognise, and reward them can make all the difference in maintaining high performance. Employees who feel appreciated and valued for their contributions are likelier to stay engaged, continue improving, and commit to the organisation's goals.

Establishing clear recognition criteria is the first step in effectively recognising and rewarding success. Employees need to know what excellence looks like in the context of their work, and they need to understand the specific behaviours, outcomes, or achievements that will be rewarded. We developed a recognition programme in one organisation aligned with our key performance indicators (KPIs). We clarified that excellence wasn't just about hitting production targets or reducing costs but also about living our company values, such as collaboration, innovation, and customer focus. This holistic approach to recognition helped foster a culture where people understood that success was not just about individual performance but about contributing to the organisation's overall success.

Public recognition is a powerful motivator and doesn't always have to be linked to financial rewards. In one company, we held monthly all-hands meetings where we publicly recognised employees who contributed significantly to our continuous improvement efforts. Whether it was a team that reduced cycle time by implementing Lean principles or an individual who went above and beyond to solve a customer problem, we highlighted their efforts in front of their peers. Public recognition made those employees feel appreciated and inspired others to strive for similar performance levels. I've found that people are often more motivated by the opportunity to be recognised and respected by their colleagues than by financial rewards.

Monetary rewards are still important in recognising success but should be tied to meaningful achievements. In one organisation, we implemented a performance-based bonus system directly linked to individual and team performance metrics. By tying bonuses to clear, measurable outcomes, such as improving production efficiency, reducing waste, or achieving quality targets, we incentivised employees to focus on the areas that mattered most to the company's success. This performance-based system not only drove better results but also made the process of rewarding employees more transparent and fair.

Customising rewards to the preferences of individual employees or teams can also be effective. Not everyone is motivated by the same things; personalising rewards can make recognition more meaningful. In one case, we discovered that some employees valued additional time off more than financial bonuses, while others preferred professional development opportunities. We introduced a flexible rewards programme that allowed employees to choose from various options, such as extra vacation days, training programmes, or monetary bonuses. This approach made our recognition efforts more personal and showed employees that we understood and valued their needs.

Another important aspect of recognising success is celebrating *team achievements*, not just individual ones. In many organisations, success results from collaboration across departments and teams, and recognising this collective effort is essential. In one company, we implemented a "team of the month" programme where we recognised teams that had worked together to achieve significant improvements. For example, one cross-functional team successfully streamlined the product development process by improving communication between engineering and manufacturing. By recognising the entire team, we reinforced that success is often a collective effort and collaboration is a key driver of operational excellence.

Creating a culture of everyday recognition is just as important as formal recognition programmes. While bonuses and awards are great for significant achievements, it's the everyday recognition from managers and peers that keeps employees motivated on a day-to-day basis. In one organisation, we trained managers to regularly acknowledge the small wins, whether it was an employee who stayed late to finish a critical task or a team that devised a creative solution to a problem. These informal recognitions, whether as a quick "thank you" or a shout-out during a meeting, went a long way in building a positive, engaged workforce.

Peer recognition can also be a powerful tool for motivating teams. In one company, we introduced a peer-to-peer recognition programme where employees could nominate their colleagues for demonstrating company values or achieving excellence in their roles. This system allowed recognition to come not just from managers but from peers, creating a more inclusive and collaborative environment. The programme was well-received, as employees appreciated being recognised by their colleagues who understood the nuances and challenges of their day-to-day work.

Consistency in recognition is crucial. One of the most common pitfalls I've seen in organisations is the inconsistency in how recognition is applied. When recognition is sporadic or only focused on a select few employees, it can create feelings of resentment or disengagement among others. In one organisation, we prioritised recognising success at every company level, from the factory floor to the executive suite. Whether recognising a production worker for achieving a perfect attendance record or acknowledging a manager for leading a successful process improvement initiative, we ensured that everyone could be recognised for their contributions.

Lastly, *feedback loops* are essential in ensuring that recognition efforts are effective. We regularly sought employee feedback on our recognition and rewards programmes in one organisation. We asked whether they felt the recognition was meaningful, whether the reward criteria were clear, and how the system could be improved. This feedback allowed us to refine our programmes and ensure they remained relevant and motivating. For example, after receiving feedback that the recognition process felt too top-down, we expanded our peer recognition system and gave teams more autonomy in selecting their "team champions."

In conclusion, recognising and rewarding success is not just about handing out bonuses or awards, it's about creating a culture where employees feel valued, appreciated, and motivated to contribute to the organisation's success. Organisations can foster a culture of excellence that drives sustained performance by establishing clear criteria, making recognition public and meaningful, customising rewards, and celebrating individual and team achievements. Consistency, inclusivity, and feedback are key to ensuring that recognition efforts have a lasting impact on employee engagement and operational success.

10.6 - Sustainability and Corporate Responsibility

Incorporating sustainability and corporate responsibility into operations has become essential to achieving and sustaining operational excellence. In today's world, customers, investors, and regulators expect businesses to operate environmentally and socially responsibly. Over my career, I've seen companies embracing sustainability as a core part of their operations enhance their reputation, improve efficiency, reduce costs, and open new market opportunities. Achieving operational excellence increasingly means aligning your business practices with environmental, social, and governance (ESG) principles.

Sustainability begins with a commitment from leadership. It's not enough for sustainability to be a buzzword or a marketing tool, it must be embedded into the company's strategy and culture. In one organisation I led, we made sustainability a core pillar of our business strategy. We recognised that the company's long-term success depended on financial performance and our ability to reduce our environmental footprint and operate responsibly. To that end, we developed a comprehensive sustainability strategy that included goals for reducing carbon emissions, minimising waste, and improving energy efficiency. This commitment came from the top, with the CEO and executive team leading the charge and holding the entire organisation accountable for achieving these goals.

Measuring and tracking sustainability performance is critical for making meaningful progress. As with any other area of operational excellence, you need data to understand where you stand and measure improvement over time. In one company, we developed a sustainability scorecard that tracked key metrics such as energy consumption, water usage, waste generation, and carbon emissions. By setting specific, measurable goals, such as reducing energy consumption by 10% over five years, we were able to drive focused efforts across the organisation. For example, we identified several energy inefficiencies in our manufacturing process and invested in energy-efficient equipment that reduced our environmental impact and lowered our operating costs.

Integrating sustainability into supply chain management is another critical aspect of corporate responsibility. In one organisation, we worked closely with our suppliers to ensure they adhered to the same sustainability standards we aimed for. We developed a code of conduct that required our suppliers to reduce waste, minimise emissions, and ensure fair labour practices. By working collaboratively with our suppliers, we were able to make our entire supply chain more sustainable. In one instance, we partnered with a supplier to switch to biodegradable packaging materials, significantly reducing plastic waste generated by our products.

Circular economy principles are becoming increasingly important in sustainable manufacturing. The traditional linear model of "take, make, dispose" is being replaced by circular models focusing on reducing waste, reusing materials, and recycling products at the end of their life cycle. In one project, we introduced a closed-loop system for our production waste. We worked with a recycling partner to collect and reprocess scrap materials from our production lines, turning them back into usable raw materials. This reduced waste sent to landfills and lowered our material costs. Over time, the circular economy approach helped us build a more sustainable and cost-effective operation.

Energy efficiency is one of the easiest and most impactful ways to incorporate sustainability into operations. In one manufacturing plant I managed, we conducted an energy audit to identify areas where we could reduce our energy consumption. Based on the audit's recommendations, we installed energy-efficient lighting, upgraded our HVAC systems, and introduced a smart energy management system that optimised energy use across the plant. These improvements reduced our energy consumption by 15%, significantly lowering our operating costs and carbon footprint. We also invested in renewable energy sources, such as solar panels, which decreased our reliance on non-renewable energy.

Reducing waste and emissions is another key focus of sustainable operations. In one company, we implemented a waste minimisation programme that focused on reducing waste at every stage of the production process. This involved working with suppliers to reduce packaging waste, optimising our production processes to minimise scrap materials, and developing recycling programmes for both production and office waste. We also set ambitious targets for reducing carbon emissions, investing in cleaner production technologies and working with logistics providers to optimise our transportation routes and reduce fuel consumption. Over time, these efforts reduced our environmental impact and enhanced our reputation with customers and stakeholders who valued our commitment to sustainability.

Sustainability reporting is becoming an increasingly important part of corporate responsibility. Investors, customers, and regulators seek transparency in how companies address environmental and social issues. In one organisation, we developed an annual sustainability report that detailed our progress toward our ESG goals, including data on our carbon footprint, waste reduction efforts, and social responsibility initiatives. This report was shared publicly, helping build trust with our stakeholders and demonstrating our commitment to sustainability. It also provided a valuable tool for internal accountability, allowing us to track our performance and identify areas where we needed to improve.

Corporate social responsibility (CSR) goes beyond environmental sustainability, it also includes a focus on social issues such as fair labour practices, diversity and inclusion, and community engagement. In one organisation, we launched several CSR initiatives that focused on giving back to the communities where we operated. This included sponsoring local education programmes, supporting environmental conservation projects, and offering volunteer opportunities for our employees. These initiatives strengthened our relationship with the community and enhanced employee morale and engagement, as they felt proud to work for a company that was committed to making a positive impact.

In conclusion, sustainability and corporate responsibility are no longer optional for organisations seeking operational excellence. By embedding sustainability into every aspect of operations, from energy efficiency and waste reduction to responsible sourcing and community engagement, companies can reduce their environmental impact, improve efficiency, and build stronger relationships with customers, investors, and communities. The key is to treat sustainability as a long-term strategic priority, with clear goals, measurable outcomes, and a commitment from leadership. As the world becomes more focused on environmental and social responsibility, organisations that lead in sustainability will be well-positioned for long-term success.

10.7 - Case Study: Sustained Operational Success

Long-term excellence is achieved when an organisation goes beyond short-term gains and builds a system that ensures sustained high performance over the years. As a COO, I've had the privilege of leading several organisations through periods of long-term operational success. I've seen firsthand what it takes to maintain excellence over the long haul. It requires strong leadership, continuous improvement, and an unwavering commitment to the company's core values and objectives.

Case Study 1: Achieving Operational Excellence Through Continuous Improvement

In one manufacturing company, we embarked on a long-term journey of continuous improvement, adopting Lean manufacturing principles as the foundation of our strategy. The company had been struggling with inefficiencies in its production processes, leading to high costs, delayed shipments, and declining customer satisfaction. We aimed to turn things around and build a system to sustain operational excellence over the long term.

We began by conducting a detailed analysis of our operations, identifying key areas where waste could be eliminated and processes could be streamlined. One of the first initiatives we launched was a company-wide Kaizen programme, where cross-functional teams worked together to identify inefficiencies and propose solutions. These teams included employees from all levels of the organisation, which helped ensure that everyone was engaged in the improvement process.

One particularly impactful project was initiated to address a major bottleneck in the assembly line- the time it took to switch between different product lines. This changeover process was causing unnecessary downtime and reducing overall throughput. Implementing Lean tools such as SMED (Single-Minute Exchange of Dies) reduced changeover times by 40%, allowing us to increase production capacity without adding new equipment. Over several years, we applied this approach to other business areas, steadily improving our cycle times, reducing waste, and increasing overall efficiency.

The results were impressive. Within two years, we reduced our production lead times by 30%, lowered costs by 15%, and improved our on-time delivery rate from 85% to 98%. But more importantly, we had created a culture of continuous improvement that persisted long after the initial gains were made. Employees, inspired by the company's proactive approach to identifying opportunities for improvement, became more proactive. The company's leadership was fully committed to sustaining our gains and providing security despite changing market conditions. The company maintained its competitive edge by continuing to refine its processes and improve efficiency.

Case Study 2: Sustaining Excellence Through Strategic Leadership and Innovation

In another organisation, we faced a different set of challenges. The company had been highly successful for many years, but growth had plateaued, and operational performance was beginning to decline. Leadership was focused on maintaining profitability, but little emphasis was on innovation or adapting to changing market demands. Our challenge was reversing the decline and positioning the company for long-term growth and excellence.

The first step we took was to realign the company's leadership team around a shared vision of operational excellence. This involved revisiting the company's mission and values and ensuring everyone understood the importance of innovation, customer focus, and continuous improvement. We also introduced new performance metrics aligned with our long-term goals, emphasising customer satisfaction and making the audience feel integral to the company's success. We focused on product quality and operational efficiency, aiming to deliver the best possible service to our customers.

One of the key initiatives we launched was a product innovation programme to revitalise our product line and address new market opportunities. We created cross-functional teams that included members from R&D, marketing, production, and supply chain, all working together to develop new products to meet evolving customer needs. This collaborative approach ensured that innovation was not happening in silos but was integrated into every part of the business. Over time, we introduced several successful new products that reinvigorated the brand and increased market share.

At the same time, we focused on improving operational performance by adopting new technologies and optimising our supply chain. One of our most impactful changes was implementing a digital supply chain management system that provided real-time visibility into our inventory levels, supplier performance, and logistics operations. This allowed us to reduce lead times, improve supplier collaboration, and optimise our inventory management, resulting in a 20% reduction in inventory holding costs and a 10% improvement in on-time delivery.

Sustaining these gains required ongoing leadership support and a commitment to continuous improvement. We held regular performance reviews, tracking progress against our key performance indicators (KPIs) and identifying areas for improvement. Over several years, the company not only reversed its operational decline but also positioned itself as a leader in its industry, with a strong focus on innovation, customer satisfaction, and operational excellence.

Key Takeaways for Sustaining Operational Excellence

Both of these case studies highlight several key principles for sustaining operational excellence over the long term:

1. **Leadership Commitment:** Long-term excellence starts at the top. Leadership must be fully committed to operational excellence in words and actions. This means setting a clear vision, providing the necessary resources, and holding everyone accountable for achieving results. In both organisations I worked with, leadership was deeply involved in the improvement process, regularly reviewing performance and driving the continuous improvement agenda.
2. **Culture of Continuous Improvement:** Sustaining excellence requires a culture where employees are empowered to identify inefficiencies, suggest improvements, and take ownership of their work. In both case studies, we fostered a culture of continuous improvement through Kaizen initiatives, employee engagement programmes, and regular performance reviews. This culture ensured that improvements were not one-time events but part of the company's DNA.
3. **Data-Driven Decision Making:** Long-term success depends on having the right data to make informed decisions. In both organisations, we implemented systems that provided real-time visibility into our operations, allowing us to identify issues early and make data-driven decisions, whether using data to improve production efficiency or optimise the supply chain; having accurate and timely information was critical to sustaining excellence.
4. **Innovation and Adaptability:** One of the biggest risks to long-term operational success is complacency. In both case studies, we recognised the need to innovate and adapt to changing market conditions. Whether through product innovation or new technologies, we continuously look for ways to stay ahead of the competition and meet evolving customer needs.
5. **Employee Engagement:** Sustaining excellence over the long term requires the active involvement of employees at every level of the organisation. We engaged employees through training, recognition programmes, and empowerment initiatives. We built a more motivated and engaged workforce by giving employees a voice in the improvement process and recognising their contributions.

In conclusion, sustaining operational excellence over the long term requires strong leadership, a culture of continuous improvement, data-driven decision-making, innovation, and employee engagement.

Achieving excellence is a journey, not a destination, and companies that commit to these principles will be better positioned to maintain their competitive edge and achieve sustained success.

10.8 - Overcoming Plateaus

Operational plateaus are a common challenge in any organisation's journey toward excellence. After an initial phase of rapid improvement, many companies reach a point where progress slows, making it increasingly difficult to maintain momentum. Over my years as a COO, I've encountered this challenge several times. I've learned that overcoming plateaus requires a proactive approach, a willingness to challenge the status quo, and a renewed focus on innovation and continuous improvement.

One of the most effective strategies for overcoming plateaus is to *revisit and refine your goals*. In many cases, operational plateaus occur because the organisation has achieved its initial goals and has not set new, more ambitious targets. In one company, we had successfully reduced lead times and improved production efficiency, but after sustained growth, we found that progress had stalled. To reignite momentum, we took a step back and re-evaluated our goals. We realised that while we had achieved many of our initial objectives, there were new opportunities for improvement that we hadn't yet explored. We set more ambitious targets for product quality, customer satisfaction, and innovation, which gave the organisation a renewed sense of purpose and direction.

Innovation and technology adoption are also critical for breaking through operational plateaus. In one organisation, we had implemented Lean principles and significantly improved our production processes, but progress had slowed after a few years. To overcome this plateau, we introduced new technologies such as automation, data analytics, and predictive maintenance. By adopting these technologies, we could optimise our processes further, reduce downtime, and increase overall efficiency. This renewed focus on innovation helped us break through the plateau and achieve new levels of operational performance.

Cross-functional collaboration can also be a powerful tool for overcoming stagnation. In one case, we reached an operational plateau in our product development process, where new product launches were consistently delayed. To address this issue, we brought together cross-functional teams from R&D, production, marketing, and supply chain to identify bottlenecks and develop solutions. This collaborative approach helped us streamline product development and fostered greater communication and alignment across departments. As a result, we reduced the time-to-market for new products by 15%, overcoming the plateau and positioning the company for future growth.

Challenging the status quo is essential when progress stalls. In many cases, operational plateaus occur because people become comfortable with the status quo and resist change. In one organisation, we faced a plateau in our quality improvement efforts. Despite making initial gains, our defect rate had stopped improving, and we were struggling to identify new opportunities for improvement. We challenged our teams to think differently about the problem to break through this plateau. We introduced design thinking workshops and held brainstorming sessions encouraging employees to develop unconventional solutions. This fresh approach led to several innovative ideas, including redesigning our quality control process and reducing defects by 20%.

Leadership plays a crucial role in overcoming operational plateaus. Leaders must be vigilant about recognising when progress has stalled and proactively addressing it. In one company, we implemented a leadership training programme that focused on helping managers identify and overcome operational plateaus. This included teaching them how to set new stretch goals, foster a culture of continuous improvement, and encourage their teams to take calculated risks. By empowering our leaders to take ownership of the improvement process, we were able to reignite momentum and push through the plateau.

Employee engagement and empowerment are also critical for overcoming stagnation. In many cases, plateaus occur because employees feel disengaged or lack ownership of the improvement process. In one organisation, we reached a plateau in our employee productivity metrics. To address this, we introduced a programme encouraging employees to take ownership of their work and suggest improvements. We implemented a recognition system that rewarded employees for innovative ideas and improving their processes. This initiative helped us break through the productivity plateau and increased employee engagement and morale.

In conclusion, overcoming operational plateaus requires a proactive approach that focuses on setting new goals, embracing innovation, fostering cross-functional collaboration, and challenging the status quo. Leadership, employee engagement, and a willingness to take calculated risks are key to breaking through stagnation and maintaining momentum toward operational excellence. By adopting these strategies, organisations can continue progressing, even when it feels like they've hit a ceiling.

10.9 - Evolving with the Industry

One of the most significant challenges in sustaining operational excellence is evolving continuously with industry changes. Like many others, the manufacturing sector is subject to rapid technological advancements, shifting market demands, and evolving regulatory environments. Over my 30 years as a COO, I've seen how companies that successfully adapt to these changes maintain their competitive edge while those that fail to evolve fall behind. Ensuring your organisation stays agile and responsive to external changes is crucial for long-term success.

The first step in adapting to industry changes is to *stay informed and proactive about emerging trends*. In my experience, companies that consistently monitor industry developments are better positioned to take advantage of new opportunities and mitigate risks. In one organisation I worked with, we created a dedicated "innovation team" whose sole responsibility was to track trends in technology, market dynamics, and customer preferences. This team provided regular reports to senior leadership, highlighting emerging technologies such as AI, IoT, and robotics and shifting customer expectations around sustainability and product customisation. By staying informed, we were able to make strategic investments in new technologies that positioned us as industry leaders in smart manufacturing.

Technology adoption is one of the most critical areas manufacturers need to evolve. Technological innovation has accelerated significantly over the past decade, and manufacturers that embrace new technologies are more likely to achieve operational efficiency and agility. In one case, our company was slow to adopt automation, which resulted in higher labour costs and production inefficiencies. When we recognised this gap, we made a concerted effort to invest in automation technologies such as robotics and machine learning-driven production optimisation. This investment allowed us to reduce production cycle times, improve product quality, and lower operating costs. The key lesson here was that evolving with the industry requires a willingness to invest in new technologies, even if it means temporary disruptions during implementation.

Customer demands and expectations also evolve rapidly, and companies must be agile enough to respond. In one instance, we noticed a significant shift in customer preferences toward more customised, personalised products. Traditional manufacturing methods, which were geared toward mass production, were not well-suited to meet these demands. To address this challenge, we introduced flexible manufacturing systems that allowed us to produce smaller, customised batches without sacrificing efficiency. This move helped us meet customer expectations and gave us a competitive advantage in a market where customisation was becoming increasingly important. Adapting to evolving customer demands requires manufacturers to be flexible and open to new working methods.

Regulatory changes can also have a significant impact on operations. Over the years, I've seen many organisations struggle to keep up with new environmental, safety, and quality regulations, which can disrupt operations if not managed proactively. In one organisation, we faced new environmental sustainability regulations requiring us to reduce our carbon emissions significantly. Rather than viewing these regulations as a burden, we saw them as an opportunity to innovate. We invested in energy-efficient production technologies and renewable energy sources, which helped us meet regulatory requirements and reduced our long-term operating costs. Adapting to regulatory changes requires a proactive approach; companies must anticipate changes and take action before compliance becomes an issue.

Supply chain disruptions are another area where manufacturers need to be adaptable. Global supply chains have become increasingly complex, and disruptions, natural disasters, political instability, or pandemics can have ripple effects on production. In one case, we experienced significant supply chain disruptions due to a key supplier leaving the business. To mitigate the risk of future disruptions, we diversified our supplier base and implemented a more robust supplier risk management system. This approach allowed us to quickly pivot when another disruption occurred, ensuring our production lines were not impacted. The lesson is that manufacturers must build resilience into their supply chains, making them flexible and agile enough to respond to unexpected challenges.

Workforce skills are also evolving, and manufacturers must ensure their employees have the skills to operate in a more digital, automated environment. In one company, we recognised that many of our production workers did not have the skills to work with the new technologies we were implementing, such as advanced robotics and data analytics systems. To address this, we launched an upskilling programme that trained employees to operate and maintain these new technologies. This improved our operational performance and increased employee engagement and retention, as workers felt valued and supported in their professional development. Adapting to industry changes means recognising that your workforce is a key asset and ensuring they have the tools and skills to thrive in a changing environment.

Industry collaborations and partnerships can also help companies stay ahead of industry changes. In one case, we formed a strategic partnership with a technology firm that specialised in AI-driven predictive maintenance solutions. By collaborating with this partner, we were able to integrate cutting-edge AI technologies into our operations, improving our machine uptime and reducing maintenance costs. Collaborations like this allow companies to leverage external expertise and resources, accelerating their ability to adapt to industry trends. Rather than trying to develop every new technology in-house, manufacturers should be open to partnering with external experts who can help them innovate and evolve.

Agility and adaptability need to be embedded in the organisation's culture. In one organisation, we implemented several initiatives to foster a more agile mindset among employees. This included encouraging cross-functional collaboration, promoting a culture of experimentation, and rewarding employees for taking calculated risks. By fostering a culture of adaptability, we could respond more quickly to industry changes and stay ahead of the competition. The ability to evolve with the industry is not just about implementing new technologies or responding to external challenges; it's about building a mindset that embraces change and sees it as an opportunity for growth.

In conclusion, evolving with the industry is essential for maintaining long-term operational excellence. Companies that proactively monitor industry trends, adopt new technologies, respond to customer demands, adapt to regulatory changes, and build resilient supply chains are better positioned to succeed in an ever-changing environment. By fostering a culture of agility and innovation, manufacturers can stay ahead of industry changes and continue to deliver value to their customers. Adapting to change is not a one-time effort; it's an ongoing process that requires commitment, investment, and a willingness to challenge the status quo.

10.10 - Creating a Legacy of Excellence

Creating a legacy of excellence means going beyond short-term success and building an organisation that consistently delivers high performance, innovation, and value over the long term. It's about creating systems, processes, and a culture that will sustain excellence even as leadership changes, markets evolve, and new challenges emerge. Over my years as a COO, I've learned that building a lasting legacy requires visionary leadership, a strong organisational culture, and an unwavering commitment to continuous improvement.

Visionary leadership is at the heart of creating a legacy of operational excellence. Leaders focus on immediate results, and the organisation's long-term success is more likely to leave a lasting impact. In one organisation I led, the CEO envisioned creating a company known for its operational excellence and innovation. This vision was communicated clearly to every level of the organisation and shaped everything we did, from strategic planning to day-to-day operations. By consistently reinforcing this vision, the leadership team created a sense of purpose and direction that continued to drive the organisation long after the initial improvements were made. Leaders who create a legacy of excellence think beyond their tenure and focus on building a sustainable future for the company.

Building a strong organisational culture is another critical factor in creating a legacy of excellence. A company's culture is the foundation upon which long-term success is built. In one organisation, we prioritised creating a culture of accountability, collaboration, and continuous improvement. This culture was reinforced through every aspect of the business, from how we recruited and trained employees to how we measured performance and rewarded success. One of the most impactful things we did was to align our recognition and rewards programmes with our core values, ensuring that employees who embodied the company's commitment to excellence were recognised and celebrated. Over time, this culture became ingrained in the organisation, ensuring operational excellence was a goal and a way of life.

Institutionalising continuous improvement is essential for sustaining excellence over the long term. In one company, we implemented a continuous improvement programme built into the organisation's fabric. This programme included regular Kaizen events, cross-functional improvement teams, and a formal process for employees to submit improvement ideas. This programme was successful because it was not a one-time initiative but an ongoing process embedded in our operations. By institutionalising continuous improvement, we ensured that the company would continue to evolve and improve, even as market conditions changed and new challenges emerged.

Succession planning is another key element of building a legacy of excellence. Leadership transitions can be a critical point of vulnerability for any organisation, and companies that don't plan for these transitions risk losing the momentum they've built. In one organisation, we developed a robust succession planning process that identified and developed future leaders at every company level. This process included leadership development programmes, mentoring, and cross-functional assignments that helped prepare high-potential employees for leadership roles. Investing in the next generation of leaders ensured that the company would continue to thrive even after the current leadership team moved on.

Innovation and adaptability are also essential for building a legacy of excellence. In one case, the company had been highly successful for many years, but as the market evolved, it became clear that we needed to innovate to stay competitive. Rather than resting on our past successes, we launched a series of innovation initiatives to revitalise our product line and improve our operational efficiency. These initiatives included investing in new technologies, developing new products, and exploring new markets. By embracing innovation and staying adaptable, we were able to maintain our leadership position in the market and continue to deliver value to our customers.

Mentorship and knowledge transfer are crucial for ensuring that the principles of operational excellence are passed down through the organisation. We implemented a formal mentorship programme in one organisation where senior leaders were paired with high-potential employees. This programme helped develop future leaders but also ensured that the knowledge and experience of our most seasoned employees were passed down to the next generation. Mentorship is a powerful tool for creating a lasting legacy because it helps instil the values, skills, and behaviours essential for long-term success.

Measuring and celebrating success is another important part of building a legacy of excellence. In one company, we regularly tracked our progress toward operational goals and celebrated milestones. This reinforced the importance of operational excellence and kept employees motivated and engaged. Celebrating success is more than just recognising achievements; it reinforces the behaviours and practices that lead to long-term success.

In conclusion, creating a legacy of operational excellence requires visionary leadership, a strong organisational culture, continuous improvement, and a focus on innovation and adaptability. It's about building systems and processes to sustain excellence over the long term, even as the organisation evolves. Companies can build a lasting impact beyond individual leaders or short-term successes by developing future leaders, institutionalising continuous improvement, and fostering a culture of accountability and collaboration. A legacy of excellence is about creating a foundation to support the organisation's growth and success for years.

Conclusion

"The hallmark of a great COO? Making the difficult look seamless and the complex seem simple."

Robert N. Jacobs

Throughout *The COO's MBA: The COO's Blueprint to Operational Excellence*, we've explored the critical dimensions of operational excellence, from laying a solid foundation to adapting to the ever-changing manufacturing landscape. We began with understanding the evolving role of the COO in manufacturing, emphasising the importance of strategic vision and aligning operations with company goals. Key concepts such as Lean manufacturing, Six Sigma, and Kaizen were discussed as indispensable tools for mastering operational efficiency and driving continuous improvement.

We delved into the financial aspects of the COO role, exploring how to leverage key financial metrics, manage costs, and make sound investment decisions. Building high-performance teams emerged as a central theme, where we saw that leadership styles must adapt to the team's needs, and recognising success plays a pivotal role in sustaining motivation. Customer focus was another cornerstone of operational excellence, with lessons on building strong relationships, enhancing the customer experience, and aligning quality assurance with customer expectations.

Innovation, technology, and digital transformation were explored in detail, with examples of how emerging technologies like AI, IoT, and smart manufacturing transform the industry. We examined how to drive innovation while balancing risk and leveraging partnerships for long-term growth. Finally, we explored organisational and individual resilience, highlighting the importance of adaptability, risk management, and crisis planning to ensure business continuity.

Throughout each chapter, the recurring themes of leadership, continuous improvement, data-driven decision-making, and fostering a culture of excellence were reinforced as the key pillars upon which operational success is built.

The Path Forward

The journey toward operational excellence is not a destination but an ongoing learning, adapting, and improving process. As you move forward in your role as COO, it is essential to remain vigilant about the evolving challenges and opportunities within your organisation and the wider industry. Here are some next steps to guide you on this path:

1. **Stay Aligned with Strategic Goals:** Continuously ensure that your operational objectives are aligned with your organisation's broader strategic vision. Operations must support the company's long-term growth, innovation, and sustainability goals.
2. **Commit to Continuous Improvement:** Lean and Six Sigma are not one-off initiatives; they should become ingrained in the fabric of your organisation. Regularly revisit processes to find inefficiencies, empower your teams to suggest improvements, and focus relentlessly on eliminating waste and enhancing value.
3. **Invest in Technology and Innovation:** The digital transformation is far from over. COOs must keep pace with technological advancements such as AI, machine learning, robotics, and smart manufacturing. Evaluate how emerging technologies can improve efficiency, reduce costs, and drive growth in your context.
4. **Foster a High-Performance Culture:** Develop your leadership team, mentor rising leaders, and create a culture that values collaboration, accountability, and innovation. High-performance teams are built on trust, communication, and a shared commitment to excellence.
5. **Embrace Sustainability and Corporate Responsibility:** The future of manufacturing is sustainable, and COOs must play a leading role in ensuring their operations meet environmental, social, and governance (ESG) standards. Sustainability isn't just a regulatory requirement; it's a competitive advantage that drives efficiency and strengthens your brand.
6. **Measure and Sustain Excellence:** Develop robust measurement frameworks that provide real-time insights into

operational performance. Use data to guide decisions, identify areas for improvement, and celebrate successes. Long-term excellence depends on consistent tracking, analysis, and action.
7. **Prepare for the Unexpected:** Crises and disruptions are inevitable, whether from supply chain breakdowns, economic shifts, or natural disasters. Build resilience in your organisation by creating strong risk management systems, fostering adaptability, and developing comprehensive crisis management plans.

Final Words of Inspiration

Being a COO is one of any organisation's most challenging yet rewarding roles. You are the engine driving operational success, the bridge between strategy and execution, and the leader responsible for turning vision into reality. As you embark on or continue your journey toward operational excellence, remember that your impact extends far beyond the walls of your factory or office. The decisions you make, the teams you build, and the culture you foster have the power to transform your organisation and set it on a path of sustainable success.

Leadership in operations is not just about achieving financial targets or hitting production goals; it's about creating an environment where people can thrive, innovation is encouraged, and excellence becomes the norm. Your ability to navigate challenges, adapt to change, and inspire your teams will determine the legacy you leave behind.

As you face the pressures and complexities of the modern manufacturing world, stay focused on the core principles of operational excellence: continuous improvement, customer focus, strategic alignment, and resilience. These pillars will guide you through the uncertainties and help you build an agile, innovative, and equipped organisation for the future.

Remember that operational excellence is a journey that requires dedication, perseverance, and an unwavering commitment to progress. The road ahead may be demanding, but it is filled with opportunities to make a lasting impact. Embrace the challenges, confidently lead, and never stop striving for excellence. Your journey

Conclusion

as a COO is not just about managing operations; it's about creating a legacy of success that will inspire and empower future generations.

In the words of renowned business leader Peter Drucker, "The best way to predict the future is to create it." As COO, you have the power to shape your organisation's future. Seize that opportunity with courage, vision, and the drive to continuously improve.

Printed in Great Britain
by Amazon